Inside the
Wild Early Years of
MuchMusic

The Nation's
Music Station

muchmusic

IS THIS LIVE?

CHRISTOPHER WARD

 Random House Canada

For John, who wound us up and let us go.
And to Rachel, who loves John Hughes movies "for the music."

PUBLISHED BY RANDOM HOUSE CANADA

Copyright © 2016 Christopher Ward

www.penguinrandomhouse.ca

Random House Canada and colophon are registered trademarks.

Library and Archives Canada Cataloguing in Publication

Ward, Christopher, author
    Is this live? : inside the wild early years of MuchMusic : the nation's music station /
Christopher Ward.

Includes index.
Issued in print and electronic formats.

ISBN 978-0-345-81034-2
eBook ISBN 978-0-345-81035-9
        1. MuchMusic (Television station : Toronto, Ont.)—History. I. Title.

ML3534.6.C2W256 2016   782.42166   C2016-902556-X

Interior design by CS Richardson

Jacket images: (tv) istockphoto.com/paci77; others supplied courtesy of the author

Printed and bound in China

2 4 6 8 9 7 5 3 1

Penguin
Random House
RANDOM HOUSE CANADA

(Title pages) David Bowie meets his fans on Queen Street West, August 1987

Contents

Foreword

It's impossible to talk about the beginnings of MuchMusic without talking about Christopher Ward, because in many ways there is so much of Christopher Ward *in* MuchMusic.

I've had the privilege of knowing Christopher for thirty-four years.

In 1982 Christopher and I auditioned for the touring company of the famous Toronto comedy theatre known as the Second City. I was still in high school, living at home.

I was eighteen years old.

Christopher was thirty-two, already an accomplished songwriter and musician, and I knew of him because he had hosted an afterschool television show on the CBC called *Catch Up*. The Second City touring company auditions went on all day. It came down to Christopher and me . . . Christopher got the job.

He came over and said, "They picked me, but I saw your audition and I think they should have picked you." People say things like that and rarely mean it, but Christopher is a generous and special human being.

A few months later, now nineteen, on my last day of high school, I auditioned again, and this time I was hired by the Second City touring company, joining Christopher in the troupe playing every small town outside of Toronto. We spent countless hours in a crowded van through blistering heat, sideways rain, and the unforgiving Canadian winter. I was a punk rocker filled with piss and vinegar with no life skills whatsoever. Christopher, on the other hand, knew the rigours of the road. I came to describe him as an "entertainment survivalist." He knew it was a good idea to get a sandwich for the long post-show drive back to Toronto. He knew to keep a Tuborg beer on ice in the van. He knew to get a Walkman. He knew to make a good mixtape. I, however, was often hungry, thirsty and bored.

Knowing I would never get it together, he took mercy on me. Without judgment, he would buy an extra sandwich—for me; keep an extra Tuborg—for me; get a splitter for his Walkman, and loan his extra set of headphones—to me. We both loved the Clash. "The only band that mattered" mattered to Christopher, and he was thirty-two! As a nineteen-year-old who could have passed for sixteen my mind was blown. *He's thirty-two and cool music is still important to him? Who is this fucking guy?*

On those drives home we would go over the show together, constantly trying to improve, listening to tapes of the improv sets, trying to figure out how to best entertain, how to lead an audience without alienating them, and how to please a crowd without pandering to them.

One day he told me that he had been offered the chance to fill six hours of programming on a local Toronto TV station called Citytv. A station made famous in Canada by figuring out a way to show pornographic films late at night. Very rock 'n' roll. Christopher's show on Citytv would be called *City Limits*. *City Limits* was on the air from midnight until six o'clock in the morning on Friday and Saturday. Coming up with six minutes of entertaining television once a week is a difficult endeavour. Coming up with six *hours* of entertaining television twice a week is a Herculean task. But Christopher was up to it. And in true Christopher Ward fashion he took on this task without a peep of hesitation, with only the glimmer in the eye of an artist who sees an opportunity and is grateful for it. Christopher would show music videos, weird short films, and interviews with local musicians and artists.

Christopher asked me to perform on his show. *City Limits* was the first time that I did the character Wayne Campbell on television. The premise was that Wayne was Christopher's annoying cousin from the not-so-prestigious suburb of Toronto called Scarborough. Scarborough is the New Jersey of Toronto, and in the depths of winter it can get so bleak that locals call it "Scarberia." I wore a cheap, long-haired women's wig underneath a baseball cap covering my short punky haircut. Wayne would often "interrupt the show, unannounced." Rumour had it that, because of Wayne's "unannounced" appearances on the show, Citytv received viewer complaints for letting "Scarborough ruffians" into the studio. I still cherish that as my greatest review. There was never a script for Wayne's appearances. Christopher just believed in me, gave me the ball, and let me run.

Christopher himself had funny recurring characters, including a fictional Liverpool British Invasion band called the Double Deckers. Sort of a cheeky, chappy, Scouse Chad & Jeremy. Christopher allowed me to be a member of the Double Deckers; and as the son of Liverpudlian parents, I can tell you that he did a very good Liverpool accent. We would do interstitial pre-tapes, or "bumpers," that took you to commercial. Later when I wanted Austin Powers to have a band, called Ming Tea, Christopher was the first person I recruited to be a band member. And in the spirit of Christopher's show, Ming Tea became the "bumpers" between the scenes in *Austin Powers: International Man of Mystery*. Christopher is a brilliant stylist. He can catch the essence of an "anything" and distill it into a "something." The format of *City Limits* was quickly forged. Rules emerged, a style was born, Christopher's style.

When MuchMusic was created, Christopher was the obvious choice to be the majordomo of the new network's VJ stable. But beyond that, the style guide for MuchMusic owes much to *City Limits*. MuchMusic wasn't going to be MTV Canada, it was going to be a homegrown network with its own programming. And, like Christopher Ward himself, MuchMusic would be structured but loose, warm-hearted, funny, generous, entertaining and certainly always, always, always . . . Canadian.

Mike Myers, 2016

Introduction

It seemed, a few years ago, that almost every conversation I was having contained an affectionate reference to the early years of MuchMusic. While it amazed me how much people recalled, it also struck me that the whole phenomenon could fade from memory, living on in a few random YouTube clips and the greying recollections of those who worked at Much. Talking to people who watched during that time reminded me of how much it meant to them. And to me. I asked a few close friends what they thought about the idea of a book and I got enthusiastic support. I had no idea how extensive and rich an experience it would be.

I started on the road to writing the book in the fall of 2013 by returning to 299 Queen Street West, not to the studio floor but to the tape library in the basement. Bell Media management had given me access to the archives, and from there, I followed my memories and curiosity to see what records existed of that time, now thirty years in the rear-view mirror. Simultaneously, I sought out and began recording conversations with my old colleagues (many of whom started with me on Day One at the network) in cafés, living rooms, bars, offices, restaurants, backyards, at parties, in groups or solo, on the phone and by email. As I continued to unearth our shared history, recollections conflicted, as you might imagine, but the one thing almost every conversation had in common was the laughter that accompanied those memories. There was pride in the handmade, rough-around-the-edges, loose and unpredictable nature of the beast; marvel at the challenge and opportunity we had to create so much live music television; joy in the happy accidents that resulted on a daily basis; and a satisfaction in the knowledge that we were involved in something truly unique, in a set of circumstances that will never be replicated. We didn't really stop at the time to consider how rare our opportunity was because there was always something new to respond to—something going on outside on Queen Street that should be shot, a video effect that had to be experimented with, something in the news deserving of mockery and a voice cutting through the studio din saying, "Coming to you in five . . . four . . . three . . ."

As I rewound the old analogue tapes I saw Natalie Richard's expression while Tony Bennett danced her around the control room. The young girls' faces as Jon Bon Jovi waved from the balcony to the fans in the parking lot below. The kids in the street when Iggy Pop took an acoustic guitar and climbed through the window and began improvising songs.

I spoke with the VJs, producers, camera people, record-label reps, artists, video directors, and the man whose vision made it all possible,

Moses Znaimer. The one person I missed interviewing is the late John Martin, the originator of *The NewMusic*, MuchMusic's first director of music programming, and many would say the spark that started the whole thing. I take comfort in how frequently John is cited by so many of us throughout this book, how we hear his voice through these stories.

When Much launched in 1984, it was a time when people were obsessed with music. Your favourite band was how you found your tribe. You talked about the band, wore their T-shirts, waited for the next release and shared it with friends on vinyl, cassette, a Walkman with two headphones, mixtapes, or a ghettoblaster in the rain (see John Cusack in *Say Anything*). And with the dawn of the music video, you anticipated your next glimpse of the band. If you wanted to know about your favourite artist — when they were putting out a new record, a new video, when they were coming to your town — and if you wanted to see what everyone else was listening to, wearing, and talking about, MuchMusic was it!

A band's image could become so dominant that sometimes the music of this era has paled in comparison and been dismissed as inconsequential, but if you came of age then, the music is indelible, and important. Out of a nostalgic haze of hairspray, music that seemed like a colourful interlude between punk and grunge, is revealed to have amazing staying power. International acts like Prince, Tears for Fears and Eurythmics wrote brilliant, original and memorable songs. So did Loverboy, Luba and Glass Tiger in Canada. And the image creation that was part of the video-making process has had a sustained influence on fashion, advertising and filmmaking.

Much came along at a time of a brilliant creative outburst in Canadian music. We represented that perfect counterpart to ambition: opportunity. Some grabbed it. Some missed it. Some rejected it. In speaking again with the biggest Canadian artists from that era, we talked about the music, but soon moved on to fashion, the challenges of career-building in a formative time in the business and, of course, music videos. Artist after artist spoke of their time in front of the camera and how dramatically it changed their careers. Many look back at the early days of video with bemusement and self-deprecation, but what they created mattered, even if the hair was at times regrettable and the special effects ridiculous.

In the conversations I had with my old colleagues, a recurring theme was the enormous freedom we had. There were no restrictions — it truly was a fresh daily, seat-of-the-pants rock 'n' roll world unto itself that we were blessed to be part of. As programmers, we could play what we wanted without the conventional restraints of format and niche, ratings and phone requests. As presenters, Moses gave us space to discover who we were and how we could connect with our audience. And John Martin absolutely encouraged the rebellious, risk-taking approach to making television that was at the heart of what drove him daily.

Much was a place with no wardrobe, no makeup, no script, no rehearsal, no pre-record, no fix-it-in-the-mix, no wake-up call, no stylist, no day care, no free lunch, no dog-sitter, no back-patting, no troubleshooting, no researcher, no net—no kidding!

To millions of viewers, MuchMusic was the heartbeat of pop culture in Canada in the '80s and '90s. It was amazing to be part of a period that changed music in Canada forever. If you were one of the millions of viewers watching back then or if you tuned in later, I think we'll have a great time recalling the day-to-day craziness at the Nation's Music Station.

Christopher Ward with Magne Furuholmen, Pål Waaktaar-Savoy and Morten Harket of A-ha

1 Greetings, Limitoids

In September 1983 I performed in my last show as a member of the Second City touring company at the Old Fire Hall theatre in Toronto. I received the traditional send-off of a pie in the face along with an Elvis bust and a hint of an offer from my old friend John Martin, of Citytv, who was in the audience that Saturday afternoon.

"Come and see me on Monday. I've got something for you." Coming from John, this was a detailed proposal.

In his office, John told me that Citytv was applying for the licence for a 24-hour music channel that was to be Canada's answer to MTV, which had launched to great success in the U.S. three years earlier. They felt that with the groundwork of *The NewMusic*, a Sunday evening news-magazine-style show that had been on City since 1979, they had the experience, the credentials and the library to secure the licence, but wanted a prototype up and running to show the CRTC. And John wanted me to host it.

I wasn't sure. I'd just quit Second City to return to my first love, songwriting, and was developing the career of my then-girlfriend, Alannah Myles. Nevertheless, I agreed to shoot an audition tape and a few days later John offered me the gig—two nights, Friday and Saturday, midnight till 6:00 a.m. live, $25 thousand a year. By City standards, and in 1983 terms, it was a generous offer. I said no. John looked at me with that "must you be so tiresome" expression and countered with two points in that clipped Mancunian accent, which I can still hear.

"You need the money, right?"

"Umm, yeah."

And sealing the deal with his trump card, "And you can do anything you want on air."

Still, I said I had to think about it. A few days later, after my friends had impressed upon me what a raging idiot they thought I was, I accepted and did the demo. I found out much later that John had put all his chips on me when he presented my audition to Moses Znaimer—co-founder of Citytv and executive producer of all original programming—who had been expecting a stack of possible hosts. Moses watched the tape, liked it and turned to John.

"Okay, good, let's see the others."

"That's it."

"What do you mean?"

"He's the guy."

Moses was pissed off but, remarkably, he bought it and I became the host of *City Limits*, Citytv's all-night video show, launched in October 1983. John introduced me to Michael Heydon and Anne Howard, who were to produce the show, and true to his word, he let us do whatever we wanted. Chaos resulted.

"Greetings, Limitoids." These were my first words coming out of the opening that Michael had cut to Eddy Grant's "Electric Avenue." I remember being very short of breath but surviving my first intro or "throw," as the crew referred to it. My first interview was with Kim Mitchell, legendary lead singer from Max Webster, who was embarking on a solo career. As the countdown reached five . . . four . . . three . . . Kim shoved his finger about two inches up my nose. The other guests that I can recall included the late Frankie Venom of the band Teenage Head, and a musical gang of Citytv cameramen and producers called the Booze Mothers.

It didn't take long for us to get bored with our tiny, not-really-a-studio in the lobby of 99 Queen Street East. Shots and silly intros were set up on the fire escape, on the roof, on the street, in the basement, in the sub-basement beside a nineteenth-century boiler—anywhere a cable could reach. My Second City pals came by—Bruce Pirrie and Don Lake as the video police, arresting me for playing a video where someone danced on the ceiling (I'm guessing Lionel Richie was the guilty party). Ron James reprised a sketch as a Greek waiter that had killed in the touring company and Mike Myers became a regular as my cousin Wayne, the first TV appearance of the Wayne Campbell character, later of "Wayne's World" on *SNL* and in the movies. Wayne arrived unannounced and caused havoc, interrupting interviews and messing with the equipment.

We had a motley bunch of guests from bands showing up after their gigs—while some, like Stuart Adamson of Big Country and Jim Carroll, author of *The Basketball Diaries*, are no longer with us, others, like the band Bon Jovi, seem to be hanging around forever. With Bon Jovi, we got a call from PolyGram rep Karen Gordon, who we all liked and respected, asking us to "please have the guys on. They've got one video, they're doing a show at the El Mocambo and nobody knows about them, but they're a lot of fun." "Sure" was the answer.

KAREN GORDON They were playing at the El Mocambo in front of probably thirty people. Their first record was just out and it hadn't found an audience. It was a fairly generic American rock record, but when the band hit the stage it was obvious that there was something else going on. They blew me away. I had floated the idea of going to do [*City Limits*] after their show and after all the backstage blah blah that goes on. They were high from the show— and young and full of energy, and so when I suggested that Jon and one other guy come down to the studio with me, everyone wanted to get in on the action. As I recall, they all crowded into my car and their tour bus followed. We got to the station and it was

like five guys in a candy store. They were at the beginning of their career and at an age of eternal optimism.

(Above) The Bon Jovi BBQ

They did a fairly brief interview with you. What was there to talk about? They had one album and one video. But they loved being interviewed and after they got off air they wouldn't leave. They said, "What else can we do?" I remember that they taped every single holiday greeting that anyone could think of and that it still wasn't enough. Then I can't remember who came up with this but I think it was Jon, that they should go to the offices and pretend that their video had gone missing and they were determined to get it on the air. So your cameraman and a producer went upstairs to the main office and they basically did what was a skit—of a rock band searching for their video. It was pretty high school. And finally, after everything had been exhausted in terms of what they could do, they were persuaded to leave!

City Limits ran from October 1983 to August 1984. The CRTC approved the licence for the music channel that spring so *Limits* had done its job. The offices were being packed up for the transition to MuchMusic's first home, on the fourth floor. My recollection is that because of this we *actually* lost the video! The band seemed unconcerned, so we suggested they help us try to find it in the confusion of the move. Enthusiastically, they emptied desks and boxes and ransacked storage rooms, skulking through the building like rock 'n' roll Marx Brothers. My favourite image from this occasion is keyboardist David Bryan drinking beer from a woman's shoe that he had pulled out of her desk. Happily, we found the video before too much damage was done. The epilogue to this story is that three years and eleven million copies of *Slippery When Wet* later, Bon Jovi returned to play Maple Leaf Gardens and agreed to do only one press appearance—on MuchMusic! We set up a barbeque on the balcony overlooking the parking lot, which was filled with excited Bon Jovi fans. The boys insisted on doing the cooking.

One of the most infamous interviews on *Limits* was with Platinum Blonde, a teased-up trio who were causing teen hearts to flutter wherever they went. In those days my interview skills were scant, and in particular, in deference to the artists, I had no idea how to move the conversation along, or, when necessary, bring it to an end. Case in point was the Blonde's rambling interview, and when my friend and boss, an inebriated John Martin, rolled in, straight from the Bamboo Club on Queen West, he saw fit to holler "booow-ring," loudly and repeatedly, until the interview was brought to a merciful conclusion. Unfortunately, Moses had been watching and called me into his office on Monday to explain. I'd been pretty upset with John in the moment but I'd had time to cool off. I sensed Moses was after blood, so I lied to his face and said that the whole thing was a sketch we were doing, that the band was in on it and so on. John was crazy, but fiercely loyal to his people, and deserved the same, I felt. Moses knew I was covering for John, gave me the "you little fuck" stare and waved me out of his office like a mosquito.

Recently, I reminded Mark Holmes of Platinum Blonde about the incident.

MARK HOLMES That was awesome. *Boring! Boring!* You were beside yourself but in a way it bolstered us. At the time I was mortified just like you were. But I made sure people got better interviews out of me. It's etched in my memory but it's not a very clear etching.

To this day, a certain small group of friends will respond to something dull or tedious with a loud "booow-ring!," delivered in our best John Martin accent.

When we did the all-night show, we had a sense that no one was really watching, and a lot of the nutty things we did were done in order to stay awake and amuse ourselves. But to this day I still run into people who tell me how addicted they were to *City Limits*. Many would tape it on their VCR and watch later. When I was a kid, we would get together and sit around and listen to 45s. My daughter gets together with her friends and watches silly YouTube videos. Maybe *City Limits* was somewhere in between.

Booow-ring
Booow-ring
Booow-ring

With *Limits*, we would program the show earlier in the week, so the tapes could be pulled and ready. There was a running order, but it was definitely subject to change if someone showed up or we had a thematic inspiration or got a request.

Simon Evans started as a volunteer on *City Limits* and went on to produce shows on MuchMusic as well as being a VJ.

SIMON EVANS They wanted to get across that it was live so we took calls. It was, "Hey, its Jeff in Scarborough, I wanna see Motörhead." So we'd go to the tape library where all the videos were on compilation reels. We'd find the video, cue it up, time it and run it down to master control. Then you'd go, "This is for Jeff in Scarborough."

James Woods, who ended up working in publicity at Much, remembers *Limits* as a viewer.

JAMES WOODS I'd just moved to Toronto and I'd come home and watch *City Limits* and I'd think, "My god, this is the best thing I've ever seen in my life. I don't know what's going to happen, but I know I'm gonna watch these great music videos and shit is gonna happen.

Exhibit A—we had a contest to give away something substantial, which was rare, and we decided to award it to the first person who could show up in a wetsuit with a fish. No reason. Very soon, people were zooming up to the front of the building in the middle of the night. One enterprising contestant had a box of frozen fish sticks and was wearing a suit, which he proceeded to douse with water to create a "wet suit"! Would you have given him the prize for sheer ingenuity or, like us, waited a couple more minutes till someone arrived in a wetsuit with a fish?

(Top) Del Velure, the world's oldest VJ
(Bottom) Christopher Ward and Alannah Myles on the set of *City Limits*

There were a bunch of recurring characters that I did—a couple based on high school teachers, an unctuous nightclub manager, and a gangster stereotype. I think my favourite may be Del Velure, the host of the "Fireside Videos" segment and reputedly the world's oldest VJ. Del's taste ran to WWII-era chanteuse Vera Lynn, so we chopped up a City interview with Dame Vera to make it appear that Del was doing the interview. There was also a gossip columnist who was a parody of a judge on a local TV talent show that Alannah Myles had been on. He snottily pronounced her performance "just a tad bland." Now, you could say many things about Alannah's performances, but "bland" wasn't one of them, so we got him back by calling the character J. Todd Bland. Bland was cheerfully killed off at one point.

In some ways, it felt like a bunch of misfits who stumbled into a control room at the same time every weekend and emerged blinking into the morning with another TV show under our belts. I remember fondly sitting around with the *Limits* crew after 6:00 a.m., cracking a case of beer and jamming out ideas for the next night's show. If we were particularly excited and had lots to talk about, we'd go for breakfast to St. Lawrence Market and carry on until mid-morning or until we nodded off over bagels and cream cheese.

In a manner that would carry on once MuchMusic was launched, Moses and John Martin provided us with enormous freedom to play. Moses saw the longer-term possibilities in the chaos.

MOSES ZNAIMER I knew once I saw *City Limits* that we could do this; we could do it easily. We could do it in a way that was not simply a mimic of what that guy in the States was doing.

CITY LIMITS. THAT WAS THE FIRST TIME I DID WAYNE ON TV.

HOW AMATEURISH IT WAS. HOW CHEESY SOME SEGMENTS WERE. HOW BAD THE VIDEOS WERE . . .

2 Dollar-Ninety-Eight TV

Cheap *rocks*! Just ask fans of *SCTV* and the Shopping Channel. "Dollar-ninety-eight TV" is how John Martin described it, with pride. John, who had developed and produced *The NewMusic*, where a lean-and-mean approach to making television was honed, loved creativity born of chaos, and he had little interest in planning. While shooting in Jamaica, John spotted a waterfall he liked, stopped the car and instructed the crew to shoot Regina band the Waltons in the waterfall. Among other improvisational elements, a car battery was involved in powering the event. John wanted shoestring, seat-of-the-pants, spontaneous television, and hired people who were comfortable with disarray, inspired by anarchy. Budgets ran from tight to non-existent. It didn't feel like a constraint, but in hindsight I see that so much of what we did and who we became was dictated by expediency.

Laurie Brown became co-host of *The NewMusic* in 1985 and joined MuchMusic as a VJ around the same time.

LAURIE BROWN John's only directive to me was, "Do what you want, just don't spend any money."

Moses Znaimer is regarded as a broadcast visionary. He broke rules, ignored conventional wisdom, and along the way developed his own philosophy that led to the blueprint for MuchMusic. He's also a polarizing figure whose accomplishments are recognized at times begrudgingly, perhaps out of envy or because he's the first one to tout those accomplishments. In Canada, we like at least a little "aw, shucks" from our stars. Moses doesn't play that way.

His love of "process" was well known to the worker bees at Much. It was built into the "environment," as Moses referred to our workspace. As to how we used that environment, he knew what he *didn't* like.

DENNIS SAUNDERS, Much technical director It was hard to know what Moses wanted. What you could say in five easy words, he would say in twenty-five difficult words. But he did take me aside once and said, "I don't ever want this to be confused with CBC." And I said, "No chance." . . . That was the only imperative I was ever given.

So, did the monkeys really run the zoo, or was there an invisible hand guiding us from above?

MOSES ZNAIMER My management philosophy is benign neglect. I'm intensely there when something is forming . . . once that's done, "see ya." I'll let you know if there's a problem. Otherwise, keep going as fast as you can.

Where did the on-air style come from? It's been suggested that it was a natural outgrowth of the Citytv newsroom approach, but it was after we moved to 299 Queen Street West from our original location at 99 Queen Street East that *CityPulse* news debuted the open concept with mobile anchors, breaking free of the traditional guy-at-a-desk-with-a-phone style. Maybe the most prominent antecedent was the early version of NBC's *The Today Show*, which was broadcast from a storefront studio in New York and featured a mingling of the on-air talent and behind-the-scenes staff. We involved the crew on *City Limits* because they were in the shot, or close at hand, and to ignore them would have been like being at a party with a bunch of cool people and doing a monologue. On Much, the VJs were the faces of this new music video phenomenon, but soon it became apparent that what you saw was a collaborative creation. You not only could see the strings—we wanted to show you how they worked and who was pulling them.

David Kines started as an editor on *The NewMusic* and became director of music operations at Much, eventually moving up to vice-president/general manager. His take is that there was more expediency than philosophy at work on *Limits* and Much.

DAVID KINES MTV had launched in 1981. It's not rocket science to say let's play music videos in Canada. What turned out to be the genius of the [*City Limits*] control room—was that a function of "we don't want to build a set"? You can look back and say, "It's about the connection with the audience and the interaction." But was it really just a cost[-cutting] measure to put the VJ in front of the control room? You don't need a floor director because the PA just turns around and says, "You're up!" You don't need a lot of lighting; you've got an active background. Once we got the licence, we're going to do this full-time—let's do the same thing.

SIMON EVANS Moses's philosophy was to show behind the scenes. And one of the reasons we used the control room was because it was a ready-made set. I think on the very first show, you had me on air while I was taking requests.

The "$1.98 look" of Much grew out of *City Limits*.

City Limits was the prototype for a national music network. Previously, the CRTC had invited petitions for a movie channel; Moses had applied and lost out on the licence and he wasn't going to be denied again. A Citytv-produced music show, *The NewMusic*, had been going for four years, growing an audience, winning awards and creating a tape library filled with great content. It was also hipper by miles than shows like *American Bandstand* and *The Midnight Special*, which, at the time, were the places to see your favourite acts.

MOSES ZNAIMER I was irritated that we had to go after the Americans because I was ready to do it in '77, '78, '79 and '80, and it was the dullness of a regulator not to be able to see what seemed obvious, and so we had to wait while MTV became a phenomenon and then the Canadian regulator could understand it.

MTV had established a model, but it wasn't one we followed. The VJ intros or "throws," as they are known, were recorded in a studio, and then the MTV shows were programmed and packaged and aired. It was years before *MTV Live* and *Total Request Live* were shot in a street-front studio in New York. And some of those shows were pre-recorded!

MuchMusic launched on August 31, 1984, and, of course, we had a party. J.D. Roberts, Jeanne Beker (also the hosts of *The NewMusic* at the time) and I tried gamely to conduct spontaneous interviews and introduce upcoming videos through the din of a building jammed with revellers. And those were just the people working there. Our first official video, an idiosyncratic choice made by John Martin, director of music programming, was an early music-to-film clip by Eubie Blake from a film called *Sissle and Blake Sing Snappy Songs*. That was followed by the world premiere of Rush's video for "The Enemy Within."

J.D. Roberts at the launch of MuchMusic, August 31, 1984

J.D. ROBERTS I remember how excited we all were as the clock ticked down to the launch. Between *The NewMusic* and *City Limits*, we had plenty of experience covering the music scene and putting on a live TV show. But we were breaking

Christopher Ward at the launch of
MuchMusic

new ground. And whenever you break new ground, you walk a fine line between unbridled enthusiasm and a palpitation-inducing fear that you'll walk out on stage and promptly fall off the edge flat onto your face.

Compared to where television production is today, the whole thing was laughingly low-tech, particularly when Chris and I broke through a wall of chroma-key paper to greet the audience. We took a razorblade and made a small cut in it to ensure that we'd be able to get through. Can you imagine if the debut of "The Nation's Music Station" was delayed because we couldn't get past the paper?

I asked Jeanne what she remembered of the event.

JEANNE BEKER Well, I remember the outfit. Isn't it always about the clothes? I've seen footage of me interviewing Eugene Levy and someone from Platinum Blonde, wearing a very Michael Jackson–inspired outfit, militaristic, navy crepe, double-breasted jacket with big, gold-fringed epaulets on the shoulders.

In the course of the interview one of Jeanne's questions to Eugene Levy was, "The Pope is coming to Canada. Do you think he's going to be able to outdo this party?"

DAVID KINES I possibly did the first on-air screw-up of what would be many, many, many, about seventy-five minutes into the show. I was editing something that had to be on air and I ran into the control room with the tape and I brushed against the wheel of a VTR and stopped it on air and then quickly started it again.

I remember very little beyond the moment that J.D. describes of the two of us behind the chroma-key screen (an image-layering technique also referred to as blue screen) waiting to burst through. Looking back, I seem twitchy and earnest, with no sign of all that experience of live TV on *City Limits* in effect. We had a few station IDs from Geddy Lee, BTO, Little Steven, Annie Lennox and Rodney Dangerfield!

The voice-over on the main promo that ran through the show called it "The best in music videos from ABC to ZZ Top, all for less than the cost of a burger and fries." All hail $1.98 TV!

The guests included soap opera star Michael Damian, the Spoons, independent video artist Eva Everything, Kim Mitchell and Rik Emmett from Triumph. The highlights included a taped greeting from Klaus from Music Box Germany! Awkwardness reigned.

LAURIE BROWN We were playing videos and other people were doing that. But I do think it was the first real rock 'n' roll television, because it had the values, the culture, the style, the attitude of the music and it didn't have the attitude of television . . . watch *A Hard Day's Night* and that wonderful scene of them trying to do this TV show on the BBC and how the television culture couldn't be further away than what the Beatles were trying to do. I think that we broke that mould and we made it different and we made it okay for people to be on television. There were a lot of artists who did not want to be interviewed, who walked in reticent, defensive and not sure. K.d. lang was that way. She really really didn't want to do it; she was glum, quiet and we started to go and all of a sudden she realized, "These are my people, it's okay," and she opened up. A lot of artists were reticent until they got there and then they realized what was going on and that they could play.

Different people from the era have different ideas of what freedom represented. Here's Simon's take.

SIMON EVANS What amazes me, looking back, is that you didn't have to show a frame of anything you did to anyone before it went to air. There was no editing process, no one you needed to check with. We could have pulled our penises out and it would have been, "Oh well, no one saw that before it went to air."

So, how to sell this unruly brat? That was left to David Kirkwood, head of sales for MuchMusic, and his team, who quickly discovered that using unconventional tactics was perfect.

DAVID KIRKWOOD We . . . distinguished ourselves from others by resigning from the Bureau of Broadcast Measurement (BBM) and Nielsen audience measurement because diaries were not the way to determine our audience. Our young viewers were typically uncooperative and watched us differently from episodic television. So we worked out an average audience using the Print Measurement Bureau who was canvassing MuchMusic viewership along with magazines' readerships, giving us a healthy audience size. When I used this rationale in presentations, a typical buyer response was to say, "But you're not a magazine." Then they'd pause and say, "Well, you are sort of, because, unlike television, you target a very specific demographic *and* a specific interest." Unlike other sellers of television media, we could quantify the

consumption habits of our viewers For example, how many more times likely they were to consume soda than their same aged non-viewers. Buyers normally pay a substantial premium for such quantified, qualitative, targeted opportunities.

It was the most demographically targeted network on television available to advertisers. I didn't have much time for people who were doubters—there were a few, and they suffered for it—Coca-Cola had the weekends. The [*Pepsi*] *Power Hour* was Thursday and had the young male fifteen to twenty-four audience and they drink the most of that stuff. That's gold to them.

Former director of operations David Kines elaborates on the smoke-and-mirrors approach to wooing advertisers.

DAVID KINES Ratings and revenue. Maybe the first few years it didn't matter. Kirkwood went out and sold that thing without any ratings. He got a cheque from Coca-Cola for a million bucks with no ratings whatsoever. He sold environment and sizzle for years. Hence the ability to do whatever the fuck you wanted. Coke's happy.

I remember Kirkwood and the other sales people bringing in clients to the studio while we were on air and you could see their eyes widening as they stepped into the room. There was so much going on that they didn't know where to look. I'd always catch David Kirkwood's eye as he stood behind the camera while we were introducing videos or setting up an interview; it was client heroin he was giving out. The ambient sound level was clearly

unlike any other working situation they'd experienced,
unless they'd been on a construction crew, and it was
magic. Kirkwood worked to develop good relations
with the clients but also maintained a skeptical view of our benefactors.

**DAVID KIRKWOOD I think advertisers, left to their own devices,
will seek out and destroy the very thing they came to you for. . . .
I don't blame them for it. It's their nature; they can't help themselves. We used to do the MuchMusic video dance party and
Coca-Cola was the sponsor and when they realized we had trucks
to go out and do these dances, they wanted some identification on
the trucks, and while our backs were turned, they went to the
third-party management who designed the trucks and had them
painted Coca-Cola red with the name down the side and a small
'm' on the door of the truck. To a Coca-Cola person this looked
great but the reason [schools] came to us was the association
with MuchMusic and it's totally lost, so you've got another van on
the street and that's it. They're like children, they need you to say,
"No, I know what you want and I can understand what you want
but it's not for your own good."**

David describes how a bullish moment in early Much history became a
reminder to stay modest about our accomplishments.

**DAVID KIRKWOOD We reached that mark of a million subscribers
and we all thought that was pretty phenomenal because it was so
much earlier than anybody ever thought we could, so we thought
we need to promote this . . . so we had ten thousand copies of this
poster made before we realized that it said, *Home of One Million
Subscibers* (sic) . . . It was very MuchMusic—we tried to do something conventional and pound our chests in a conventional way and
we screwed it up . . . It kept us humble.**

The looseness of the daily doings at MuchMusic was creatively liberating.
You couldn't worry about messing up—it was inevitable and as it is with
improvised comedy we had a sense that the audience loved the mistakes
and enjoyed seeing how we'd work through them. I interviewed La Toya
Jackson, Michael's older sister. We were positioned directly under the big
fire bell at the old building, which chose that day to go off in the middle of
the interview at its usual deafening level, preventing any further conversation.
La Toya froze and the crew signalled me to ask if we should go to video.
"No," I indicated, "let's see where this goes." La Toya looked at the clattering
bell and back at me. "Is that a fire alarm? Is this live?" she asked, quite
reasonably. I nodded yes. Eventually, after a period of sitting there smiling
at each other (La Toya very nervously), *New Music* host Daniel Richler

stepped into the shot, leaned over us and held his trademark black leather jacket on top of the alarm, lowering the clang to a muted, repeating thud. On with the interview.

For me, working at Much was like being on a baseball team where there are 162 games in the regular schedule and if you get your ass kicked one day, you can't drag that with you into the next day's game. Whatever happened yesterday was so far in the past. I remember interviewing all these amazing people and I didn't even come away with photographs, which were always being taken, or copies of the interviews.

There was a legitimized wackiness at work in all corners of the building. Sarah Crawford recalls early days in the publicity department.

SARAH CRAWFORD There was a publicity manager named Kathy Hahn, and James [Woods] and I reported to her. Kathy was our boss and we came into work one day and Kathy said, "Sit down, guys, I have something to tell you," and we're thinking corporate restructuring, someone got fired . . . She said, "I've done the astrological charts for today and it is not a good day to be at work, so I'm officially giving you guys the day off." We didn't go.

JAMES WOODS I was still a volunteer and I thought it was a trap or a test, so I stayed.

From the beginning, we had lots of contests at Much. One of the first and most successful we did was a Loverboy contest. They wanted to take a picture of me with the entries and for some reason I decided, as the photo was being taken, to throw the entries up in the air. No disrespect to the people who'd sent them in, but you got a clear picture of the band's popularity at the time.

This approach was great as long we got thousands of contest entries. When Kenny Loggins visited Much, if I'd thrown the entries for his contest up in the air, it would've looked like a gust of wind blew across my desk carrying that day's handful of 3 ½-by-5 cards with it. It was a disaster, and of course, this was the one contest where we'd had the brainy idea of having the artist come to the studio to do the draw!

Steve on a bed of contest entries

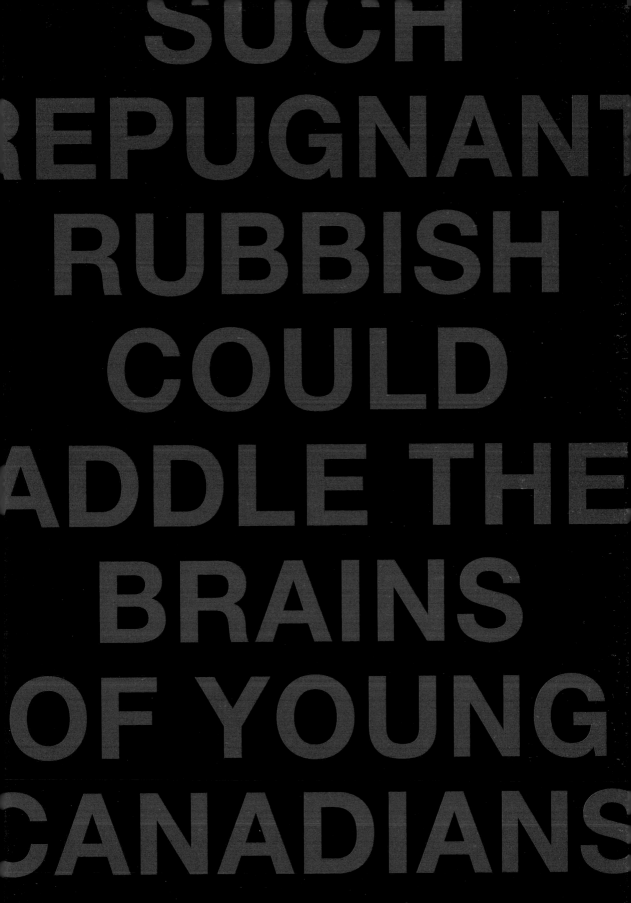

SUCH REPUGNANT RUBBISH COULD ADDLE THE BRAINS OF YOUNG CANADIANS

Saskatoon *Star-Phoenix*, April 24, 1989

JAMES WOOD We'd never had an artist do the draw. We would get twenty-thousand entries for a Bon Jovi CD.

Fortunately, someone came up with a brainier idea and taped a giant MuchMusic poster across the front of the barrel hiding the thirty or forty entries that idled at the bottom of the barrel, so to speak. Now, what to do about Kenny? Various suggestions ranging from postal strike to fire in the mailroom and other "dog ate my homework" type rationales were floated, but in the end we decided that Mr. Loggins would just have to roll with it. And he did. We did the interview; we spun the barrel; he reached deep, very deep into the barrel and pulled out the lucky winner. The customary fanfare was accompanied by applause from the studio audience, meaning the crew, and Kenny, smiled, I smiled and all was well. He didn't say anything; I didn't say anything. I thanked him and he could not have been more gracious.

Producer Morgen Flury has one further addendum to the Loggins saga.

MORGEN FLURY My father, when I was seventeen, had given me a Buick Century with houndstooth plaid seats, which he bought in Arizona. Kenny Loggins needed a ride from his hotel to the station, so I offered to go pick him up and he got in and snorted, "Nice car." I was offended.

Karma, Kenny, karma.

I recall another occasion when we gave away a Mr. T air freshener. Don't ask.

Live television provides so many opportunities to screw things up. David Kirkwood recalls one.

DAVID KIRKWOOD Erica [Ehm] did a live on-air draw for a Mars frozen ice-cream product, and I'd come down to the station to be with the client while they did it. Erica pulled the product out of the cooler and said, "Mmm, junk food!" I thought, "Oh, no!" and I apologized to the client and she said, "That's cool, that's what the kids call it."

Former head of publicity Sarah Crawford, recalls the cheap-and-cheerful origins of the network fondly while making a passionate point about the connection we made with the loyal viewers.

SARAH CRAWFORD We had two phones between four people [in the publicity department], we had one computer and one toilet, which if it jammed, you had to go to a whole different floor— because we had no money. But out of no money and no rule book was bred an incredible creativity. It was a magic time. We all remember how you get attached to music and to radio stations—

(Above) MuchMusic set, circa 1985
(Right) Jeanne Beker, J.D. Roberts, John Martin and Moses Znaimer at the launch of MuchMusic

that was your pipeline to a certain thing in your soul when you're a young person. MuchMusic was the first expression of that on a national level. We gathered all those little bits of energy from across the country and it all coalesced in a way that no one could have predicted, into this live, rambling, crazy thing that fed the young population of the whole country and fed us back because it was interactive before there was an internet.

Sarah! Yes! It's funny, all these years later, hearing these assessments that almost carry the risk of sounding pompous or like they're trying to give an overarching theme to something so loose and unkempt. Inflating the importance of rock 'n' roll is always dangerous. It turns *Wizard of Oz* on itself so readily and its cheapness shows through. It works best when you're not trying too hard—like sex appeal. But what Sarah says is eloquent, powerful and rings true. At the time, I didn't think of it that way for a second, but I did have a sense of the significance of what we were doing for the viewers, the way that radio gave me that fix of pop music, my one true drug growing up.

At the risk of sounding all "when I was your age I walked six miles in the snow to get to school," the tech level we operated on was primitive. Janice Groom (it was her shoe that was sipped from by a Bon Jovi band member), who worked as a director/producer and assistant director among other gigs, recalls the set-up.

JANICE GROOM [We had] one computer between six people. How do you get rundowns done for your live shows when you gotta spin the computer? . . . we called them bunk desks—six people at one big piece of wood with a drawer. You had one keyboard and one monitor coming out from the centre and it spun around and if you were sitting over here you had to yank some cords to get the keyboard over there.

It was one thing as an on-air person to learn to adapt to a chaotic environment, but what was it like for an office person, who would regularly have a camera operator standing on their desk, adjusting lights, or find themselves on national television at any time?

JANICE GROOM I put my blinders on and just did what I needed to do. I would have students or interns who would be all agog at everything that was going on there . . . "I need your ass over here. Just because George Harrison is over there doesn't mean we don't have work to do."

I asked music journalist Larry LeBlanc what he thought about Much when he first tuned in.

LARRY LEBLANC How amateurish it was, how cheesy some segments were, how bad the videos were. . . . It took about a year to shake out.

WILL SOMEONE ANSWER THE PHONE?

Jim Carrey

3 John Martin

John Martin is the reason I ended up working at MuchMusic. John, who died in 2006, is not around to tell his side of the story and I'm not sure that if he was, he'd be very helpful at doing so. I suspect he'd wave me away, as he did so often when we worked together, saying, "Christopher, Christopher, you'll figure it out." He was an unforgettable character, to be sure, rumpled and good-natured, born in Manchester, with an impatient and at times dismissive manner, and an affection for the three basic necessities—coffee, cigarettes and beer. An occasional meal would be thrown in. Trips to the dry cleaner's were optional and visits to the barber infrequent. But he cared about his people and the work we were doing. Even when it seemed like he couldn't be bothered, or looked at you with that "you are so annoying" expression in dealing with your pressing concern. A master of bluff and bluster, wily and worn, John made up his own rules as he made his way to the next beer, but he was beloved and got things done in his own way. He could be cuddly and offensive at the same time. Jeanne Beker, co-host of *The NewMusic* from its launch in '79 until '85, remembers her first encounter with John.

JEANNE BEKER John was a little disgruntled that he had to use me. I was foisted upon him by Moses and CHUM. He didn't want me to host *The NewMusic*. John did a pilot with J.D. and someone else and they all looked at it and said, "No, we're going to bring in this girl, Jeanne, who does the 'good news' reporting at CHUM. We want to cross her over into television." He wasn't happy about it. I remember meeting John for the first time at the Montreal Bistro and I thought, "Who is this guy?" "Hair by Ontario Hydro," he used to say. A mouthful of rotten teeth. I absolutely adored the man and he drove me totally crazy.

J.D. Roberts referred to John as "singularly the most brilliant and most frustrating person I have ever met . . . John also wanted to win. He felt that he had been disrespected by his former colleagues at the CBC, and others in the television establishment. He wanted to show all those people that he was the one who was right, and the only one who could do what we did. It took a long time, but John earned the respect of most everyone in the music and television industry."

If you wanted a meeting with John, or an answer to something important or you were just curious where the hell he was all day, the person to go to was John's right hand, Nancy Oliver.

NANCY OLIVER John was director of music programming and I was director of operations, or something like that. I took care of the nuts and bolts of scheduling and budget and that sort of stuff while John did the creative.

The "Chateau de Gonzo" was the name given to the house on Macpherson Avenue in Toronto where I lived with six others in 1976, including my friend, the journalist, high-rise window washer and sometime elephant trainer Paul Baran, who'd gotten me a gig washing dishes at the legendary Riverboat Coffee House. When Paul and I got home from a night at "The Rubber Boot," as he referred to it, where Murray McLauchlan, Roger McGuinn, the Good Brothers or Phil Ochs had been playing, we'd sit in the kitchen at the chateau, drinking beer and listening to "Sailin' Shoes" by our favourite band, Little Feat. Like clockwork, John would come down the lane from his place on Yonge Street for his nightly assignation with Tammy, who lived upstairs and would later become his wife. He'd always have time for a beer before heading upstairs. When he got the gig producing segments for *90 Minutes Live* (a late-night CBC TV talk show with host Peter Gzowski that lasted two years), he put me on a show where I had to sing to a track for the first time, standing on a little fuzzy cube, grooving solo. The best part was the after-party at the flagship Roots store where I witnessed Tom Waits and Hunter S. Thompson meeting for the first time and falling deeply into conversation.

When *90 Minutes* folded its tent, John drove cab and dreamed of a television show all about music. Nancy Oliver introduced the two men who would forever be linked in the creation of, first, *The NewMusic*, and then MuchMusic.

NANCY OLIVER I met John at CBC working for *90 Minutes Live*. He wanted me to introduce him to Moses because he had this idea for *The NewMusic*, which was right up Moses's alley. I was afraid to introduce John to Moses. They were both ladies' men, both pretty arrogant; I just didn't think they'd hit it off, which of course, they never did.

The contrast in personal styles could not have been more dramatic with Moses and John, but both had a rare comfort with hitting "play" and then letting things roll. Jeanne Beker gives both men credit in the way Much unfolded.

JEANNE BEKER Without question, both John and Moses were visionaries, but John in an especially hip way because he was riding that crest of rock 'n' roll music and it was such a part of who he was. He really understood it. He spoke that language effortlessly. He was this guy from Manchester who really got it. Truly a genius. I remember just before the launch of MuchMusic, Moses even said

You can do anything you want on air, just don't spend any money.

John Martin

to me, "Wow, that guy is really brilliant." For Moses to admit that someone else is really brilliant, they really have to be!

The NewMusic was a smash, launching in 1979 and eventually running for twenty-nine years.

At Much, Nancy tried to keep the proceedings buttoned down as best she could.

NANCY OLIVER I remember things would be going sideways . . . and I'd say what are we going to do and John would say, "Well, I think we should panic," which would just take us right out of the panic zone. Mike Rhodes [*Toronto Rocks* producer, later co-host of *Mike and Mike*] said he knew things were really getting bad when I pulled out my nail polish. This was the point where there was nothing I could do. I'd done whatever I could and now I just had to sit back and see what could happen.

Jeanne Beker and J.D. Roberts, hosts of *The NewMusic*

Mike Campbell, the other Mike in *Mike and Mike's Excellent X-Canada Adventures* remembers the origin of their show with amusement.

MIKE CAMPBELL We thought John Martin, Much's program director, would want us to do something along the lines of a rock 'n' roll survivor's guide to Canada. But no, John wanted us to do a show that was a cross between *Real People* and *That's Incredible*. [*Real People* was an early reality show that aired on NBC from 1979 to 1984; *That's Incredible* was the ABC version.] His example of something we could do was, "Get on the roof of a school and get the whole student population outside to spell MuchMusic with their bodies." No kidding, that was our direction.

It's worth recalling that John, while filling in as producer on the CBC current affairs show *Viewpoint*, had the Cambridge University Choir sing the Canada Elections Act in harmony.

Technical director Dennis Saunders, who was there from day one, remembers a significant role that John played for all of us.

Ultimately you're doing an advertisement for a song. That's really what the music video business was. You try and elevate it above that and make it an art form. It's like commercials. Ninety percent are garbage but some amazing pieces of art are made that way as well.

Video director Don Allan

DENNIS SAUNDERS John did something very important. He kept Moses away from us. And he kept the labels away from us, as far as what we played, and most importantly, he kept the CHUM guys away from us because they wanted to run the programming so badly. That was a battlefield that John chose to live and die on.

VJ Steve Anthony, recalls an occasion when John stepped up for him.

STEVE ANTHONY This defines John Martin. Guns N' Roses, in June of 1991, at the peak of their career, were playing at the Ex [the Canadian National Exhibition], very close to Much, as part of the epic Use Your Illusion tour, and we suspected that Axl Rose was going to come for an interview. We were waiting for them, but couldn't say so, so I was killing time and eventually started saying, "If G&R were coming . . . if they gave a crap . . . if they'd get off their high horse." I found out later that Axl Rose, in his trailer, was watching, got pissed off at me, phoned his manager in L.A. who called the record company in L.A., who called the record company in Toronto, who called John Martin to say, "Tell Steve to back off," and John told them to fuck themselves.

DENNIS SAUNDERS Much lost the plot when they tried to create a plot. When John left.

TERRY DAVID MULLIGAN, DJ, actor and host of MuchWest John reminded me of a carny, trying to sell you white liquid in a jar, with a moustached lady, and "guess the weight," stuff like that, because usually, I saw him in the pub across the street. He was so full of shit and yet he sold us that shit and made it work and we all bought into it.

MARK KEYS, former Much producer Working with John Martin was akin to having an internship with the Hunter S. Thompson of television production. He was a fearless leader, brilliant storyteller and chief of the gang . . . and the team would follow him into a burning house if John felt it would make the product better.

Dave Tollington, a former senior VP at Warner Music Canada had this story to tell.

DAVE TOLLINGTON John, for me, was a guy that used to hang around shows. I didn't know what he did or who he was . . . but he seemed to be connected. How else would he show up back-stage at Maple Leaf Gardens? I think he was driving cab at the time. Rod Stewart was playing the Gardens. He had a pretty tough publicist and he gave me one interview for Canada. I gave it to CBC TV but whoever was supposed to do the interview didn't show up. I'm sweating bullets . . . so I saw this guy who seemed to have a bubbly personality, who was English, hanging around there and I said, "John, would you mind interviewing Rod Stewart right now?" It went off so well that Rod said it was one of the best interviews he had ever done in his career and the last time I saw those two together they were playing soccer backstage at the Gardens.

Denise Donlon was hired by John to anchor the *Rockflash* desk, delivering short hourly live music news segments. Some years later, she replaced him as director of music programming.

DENISE DONLON John and Moses were totally salt and pepper . . . [antagonistically] jousting with one another all the time. Moses, the

When name bands are in town they drop by to have a good time. It's interesting trying to make a phone call with Chris Ward dancing on your desk and Twisted Sister throwing smoke bombs, but we try not to take ourselves too seriously.

John Martin to *TV Guide*, August 18, 1986

John Martin and Moses Znaimer

more precise, orderly, shrewd personality and John the bohemian, rock 'n' roll alchemist. It needed both to be magical, but it was never a marriage that could last forever. John's underdog, British, punky mentality was the spark of the place. He never gave us any direction. He'd say, "You're going to Hong Kong because we're part of the World Music Awards and we're going to do a throw from Hong Kong." I'd ask, "What do you want?" And he'd say, "Just shoot the shit out of it."

Morgen Flury and Simon Evans, who started on *City Limits* fresh out of Centennial College, share a recollection. John hired singer, and later radio host, Bob Segarini to be a Much producer, a role that proved short-lived.

MORGEN FLURY Bob . . . got canned because, while hosting an all-night movie show, the producer's cat got its head stuck in a yogurt container on air and people complained. Simon and I were PAs on *City Limits* and when Bob got fired I went to Nancy and said, "Why not, instead of hiring another producer like Bob Segarini, why don't you hire the two of us and split the $24,000 salary between us?" John hired people that he trusted.

SIMON EVANS Or hired people who just happened to be in the office at the time.

Simon recollects the night of the launch of MuchMusic, August 31, 1984, when John was responsible for programming our first show.

SIMON EVANS John had been at the Friar all day and he showed up with only one-and-a-half hours of a six-hour show and we wondered where the rest was. You, Ward, were pissed off. Viewers outside on Queen Street were pressed against the glass; it was so crowded. I lost it and put my hands around his neck to strangle him, and he said. "Oh, you've lost your sense of humour."

NANCY OLIVER [John] may not have finished the last four hours of videos—he would consider that grunt work, which he never wanted to do—but he spent a lot of time working on that first video [Eubie Blake from the 1920s singing "Snappy Songs"], tracking it down, getting the rights. He wanted to set the tone with that, a choice that nobody else would have made.

LAURIE BROWN That was the brilliance of Moses and John. Every other bit of rock 'n' roll on TV, what had happened was that all the rock 'n' roll had to walk across the street to TV but what John and Moses did was they took television to rock 'n' roll and gave it the same kind of personality, and the same kind of values and the same kind of spontaneity and nobody else was making

television like that. That's why the artists loved it, because anything could happen here.

When John left, it was sad, the end of an era many said, but it also provided relief from a long-building tension. Here's how Nancy saw it.

NANCY OLIVER It was way, way, way long overdue. I'd covered for John for a long time and I'd watched him spiral out of control. When he couldn't smoke in the office anymore, he just stayed at the Friar. If you wanted to talk to him about anything, you had to go there.

I don't think John wanted to be an old man anyway—he was pretty self-destructive.

John died February 24, 2006, at fifty-seven.

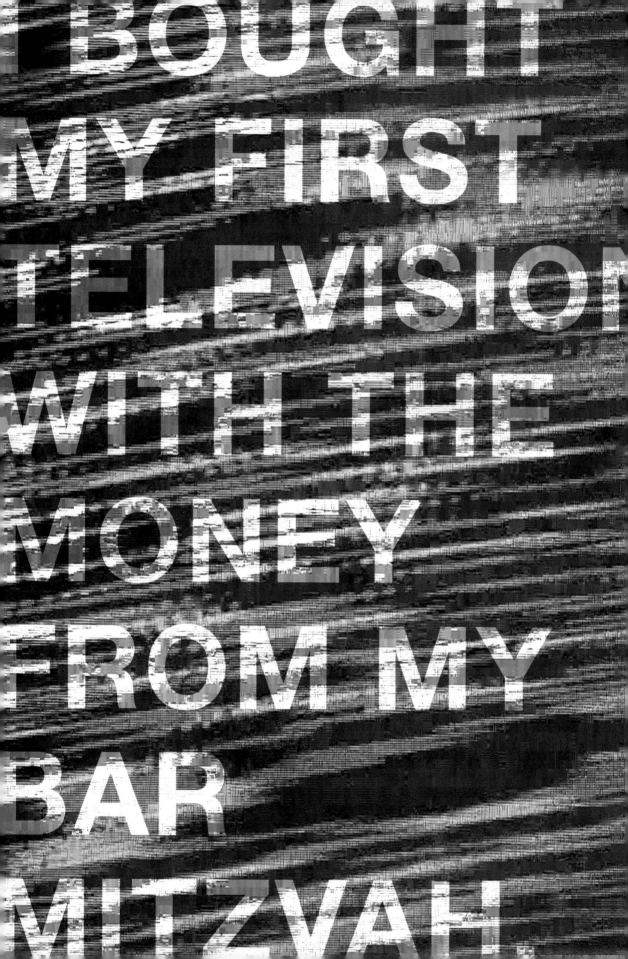

4 Mister Z

The man who made MuchMusic a reality is a giant in Canadian broadcasting who sees himself as the perpetual outsider, the giant killer. When people speak of Moses, it's almost always with respect, but seldom with affection. He's brilliant, cagey, funny and narcissistic.

When I recently met with Moses to talk about his memories of MuchMusic at his new HQ, the "Zoomerplex," he wasted no time in raising an issue that was top of mind—the credit that John Martin was receiving for the creation of MuchMusic.

MOSES ZNAIMER **It is important to distinguish between an early participant and a founder. A founder raises the money, gets the licence . . . A founder writes the original mission statement. A founder designs the look and feel. John did many things but he did none of those . . . John was NOT a founder.**

Moses's vehemence surprised me, until later, when I googled John Martin and found entry after entry referring to him as a founder of MuchMusic. John had pushed for me to host *City Limits* and I felt a deep loyalty to him. His shambolic style was all over MuchMusic and it would have been something entirely different without him. But, it still would have been something, even without him. Moses had a point. It's worth looking at Moses's history pre-Much, pre-Citytv. He reflected back to 1970, when he was in his late twenties.

MOSES ZNAIMER **I ran the country's first 24-track recording studio called Thunder Sound. I became inured to the fact that people in the music industry were really out there at times, and while they were doing whatever they were doing in the studio, which they were paying me $100 an hour for, and doing whatever they were doing in the basement because we were clever enough to put a sauna in there, which probably had more to do with why people hired the studio than the technology, I would be in my office listening to Hebrew liturgical music from the fourteenth and fifteenth centuries.**

An extraordinary amount of Canadian broadcast history has been written by families that grew small businesses into empires—the Shaw family, the Slaights and, of course, the Rogers family. MuchMusic was owned by the Waters family who had started their radio empire with one station on Yonge Street in Toronto. Much was an anagram of CHUM. Long before the launch of MuchMusic, Moses joined forces with the Switzer family in starting Citytv, the local station with big ambitions.

Jay Switzer, president and CEO of CHUM Limited from 2002 to 2007, tells the story of the birth of Citytv, which had four co-founders, including Moses and Jay's mother, Phyllis Switzer.

JAY SWITZER It was my mother's idea. She applied for the licence; it's in her name; it was signed in our kitchen . . . it was my father's idea that with the exploding cable TV business, which had just started in the late '60s in Toronto, being a UHF station with a bad frequency and small coverage that nobody could pick up over the air was not a disadvantage because on cable you were just as big and bright as the CTV station or the CBC. People hadn't caught on to that.

Despite having musical taste a little out of the mainstream, Moses was ready to launch an all-music channel before there was openness to it at the regulatory level. He told me a story that I'd never heard before.

MOSES ZNAIMER I got so frustrated with trying to get the commission [the CRTC, the regulatory body that oversees broadcast in Canada, and unofficially, the guardian of Canadian culture] into it that I thought, "Why do I have to wait for them, why don't we just do it because we're on the air, we have Citytv." I had met Bob Pittman [who started MTV] and I thought I would bring in MTV and play it after midnight [outside of regulatory control] on Citytv just to stake out the ground and take control of it. We worked out a deal and when it came time to sign, the business affairs guy from Warner [who owned MTV] came and the contract had a number that was a million dollars more than I had agreed with Pittman. I looked at it and looked at him and then I invited him to leave the building. And I said, as he left the building, "It's no big deal, we're going to do this ourselves."

When that day came in 1983 and the CHUM team had to go before the commission with their application for the licence, the odds were not in their favour. Jay Switzer remembers it well.

JAY SWITZER We were underdogs. We were this Queen Street, *The NewMusic*, anything goes, absolutely legitimate, authentic, young people talking to young people about what's important to young people, in their vernacular. Who the hell would give us this valuable, exclusive, single licence? You're going to trust the next three generations of teenagers to John Martin and Moses Znaimer? We were up against an Astral application, a Rogers application, a Donald K. Donald CPI application—three groups that

had old guard, old money, long history, no risks. [They had ten lawyers and days of rehearsal and rehearsal budgets of $100,000 and entire floors of hotels.] With us there was perceived risk that we weren't predictable and it might occasionally go off the rails but it would be true, and I think that's ultimately why we won it.

By this point in the summer of 1983, the groundwork for MuchMusic had been laid with the after-school video show, *Toronto Rocks*, the award-winning short film, *I Am a Hotel*, that Moses produced for Leonard Cohen, and most importantly, with *The NewMusic*. Moses credits John with the idea for *The NewMusic*. Sort of.

MOSES ZNAIMER Nancy [Oliver] said, there's a guy here who spends a lot of time reading *Rolling Stone* who wants to talk to you about the possibility of a program that would be as *Rolling Stone* is to print, in TV. John came in and began to do a pitch. I listened to a couple of sentences and said, "I agree. We'll do that." He kept pitching. I said, "I get it. I like it. We'll do it." Sometimes the hardest thing is to take yes for an answer. He was so fascinated with the minutiae of the industry and so in awe of some of the figures in the industry, I felt he was a good guy to have around. He was the first guy who came through the door with an articulation of what I was headed for.

The bottom line? John had a great idea and Moses said 'yes.' *The New-Music* lasted twenty-nine years, won many awards and a loyal audience and represented a commitment to music that no other petitioner could approach when it came time to seek a licence for a 24-hour music channel. The other factor in the petition was a scrappy little misfit of a show that aired weekends from midnight till 6:00 a.m., called *City Limits*.

SARAH CRAWFORD, former head of publicity MuchMusic was the love child of *The NewMusic* and *City Limits*.

City Limits was a perfect encapsulation of what Moses liked—fast moving, unpredictable television with all the strings showing.

MOSES ZNAIMER I believe that process is exciting. And there was the question of economics.

We can't let that word "economics" slip by too quickly, in our fascination with "process."

STEPHEN STOHN, president of Epitome Pictures and former head of CARAS (the Canadian Academy of Recording Arts and Science) The thing I think of most when I think of Moses Znaimer

is his crowning achievement really is hiring young, energetic, creative people and giving them vastly more responsibility and freedom than they ever should have, and paying them almost nothing.

By then, Moses had a philosophy about hiring on-air talent that was fully in evidence on Citytv, one that can now be seen everywhere you look on television.

MOSES ZNAIMER **I used the word "casting" and it outraged people, particularly when I applied it to the news. I wanted personality, preferring memorability to smooth. I wanted a cast of characters big and small, thin and fat, male and female and anything in between. I thought this could work doubly so for a station that dealt in music. I wasn't looking for a professional presenter. I was looking for people who lived the life of music.**

JEANNE BEKER **I think Moses's great gift was as a casting agent. He really knew what people would carry out the mission, who would irritate, and he loved that. He always said, "Let them either love you or hate you, don't be milquetoast."**

MONIKA DEOL, **host of** *Electric Circus* **The great thing about Moses was he let you be who you were. When I went on air I had a diamond in my nose . . . people didn't do that then; people thought it was a punk rock thing. I had a pierced nose because my grand-mother did.**

Moses explained his rationale for hiring me.

MOSES ZNAIMER **You clearly had more of the intellectual about you, which I thought was important because we were facing this stereotype of "it's a medium for people who are ugly and stupid." People were very dismissive of [music television] because so many of those early videos were about motorcycles and chains and scantily dressed women . . .**

Before I could relish my identity in the eyes of the boss, he elaborated.

MOSES ZNAIMER **I considered you part of my intellectual arsenal as opposed to the big-knocker part of my arsenal.**

A few short months after receiving approval from the CRTC for the licence, MuchMusic was up and running and never looked back. Moses could rightfully see his philosophy in action and feel satisfied.

MOSES ZNAIMER It worked quickly. It proved we could make a channel, which is entirely different from making a program, as even Oprah found out. Our "free form" communicated the spirit of rock 'n' roll with the ancillary benefit that it was inexpensive. All that structure, all that prep, all that desperation for smoothness and control costs big money. High cost, high delay. I like real time.

If viewers expected a Canadian-style replica of MTV, they would have been surprised.

MOSES ZNAIMER In the early days of MTV, they did it in a box studio outside of New York's jurisdiction so they could escape the unions. It was nothing but video and very stiff and very formal. I remember [MTV's Bob] Pittman said to me, "How much research do you do?" I said, "None. I'm it, the research department." He said, "We do five million [dollars] a year and what we learned is all they want is the music." I said, "I don't care, I want context. I want to know who's doing it and why they're doing it." He said, "You're nuts."

Moses didn't feel he needed audience research to understand the viewers (nor did he want to pay for it). He did believe in richer content than what MTV was offering, expecting the VJs to provide knowledgeable background on the artists, the music and the videos themselves. Moses's management style allowed for an incredible freedom in what producer Joel Goldberg called "a building full of misfits."

JOEL GOLDBERG There was a real feeling of adrenalin and creativity in the hallways of both buildings [99 Queen Street East, original home of Citytv and MuchMusic, and 299 Queen Street West, our second and permanent home]. And everyone really lived there, not just worked there. The budgets were incredibly small and the hours were long, but you really felt like you were part of something special. Most of my friends and girlfriends at the time came from those two buildings. We would go out in mobs to the Friar after work and drink and socialize and a lot of us would go right back to the building to work afterwards! A magical time as far as I'm concerned.

That extraordinary freedom at the heart of the story of MuchMusic started with ownership, as Jay Switzer explains.

JAY SWITZER Alan and Marge [Waters] were very involved and yet hugely respectful of the differences between what drove radio, which was their first love, and what drove television, and the differences between what drove television and what drove MuchMusic. There was this moment, where you look at the application where [on paper]

MuchMusic is going to lose money for four years. It's going to turn around in year four; it's going to have a total trough of maybe ten million dollars. You have to have a bank letter and an owner that says, "We believe in this, we stand behind this." The commission wants someone to be accountable, and the controlling share at CHUM was the Waters family . . . they had the smarts and the guts to say, "This is the future," much like they did with FM back in the AM days when FM didn't make sense.

As Much burst into life and found its feet, Moses and John had to make their strikingly different styles work together. Moses talks about life with John.

MOSES ZNAIMER We were very tolerant of him. He spent a lot of time elsewhere across the street in that bar. I felt it was part of this idea of a little zoo.

Jeanne Beker saw how the dynamic between the two men operated.

JEANNE BEKER Part of Moses's brilliance was recognizing that John really knew what he was doing and giving him pretty much carte blanche in the early days to run with it. I know things got a little treacherous as the years went by.

Denise Donlon, who also had a front-row seat, made this observation about Moses and John.

DENISE DONLON Moses had a lot of balls in the air but he could still be an acute micro-manager. When I was running the place he'd leave me alone for six months, then he'd suddenly appear and find something tiny to panic about. Or he'd find a junior PA who was smoking too close to the doors or who had a messy desk and he would suddenly have them up against the wall, yelling at them. I think it was partly to let everyone know that he was the man in charge even though he wasn't really there, and partly because Moses is a man of fairly fine aesthetics and he likes things to be orderly. If you looked at his desk, everything was at right angles to each another, carefully placed. His approach of precision versus John's "let's just throw this together and see what happens" was naturally going to be fractious between them.

Laurie Brown remembers Moses's involvement this way.

LAURIE BROWN "Most of the time he was hands-off at Much but all of a sudden he would swoop in and get very hands-on, very micro-management. He didn't understand why everyone working on that main floor wasn't wearing a Much T-shirt. Every once in a

Most people have . . . a bit of humour and they'll remember that was precisely what was said about Elvis Presley and Frank Sinatra before him. In both cases Christian civilization managed to withstand the onslaught and I think the same thing will hold true now. With as much sensitivity as we can, we will take serious note of what people say . . . but we're not going to be stampeded by some Mrs. Grundy.

Moses Znaimer (to *Videomania* magazine who asked about videos corrupting our children)

while he'd swoop in on *The NewMusic* and declare, "No voice-overs! That's regular television." We'd veered from the tablet and sounded too much like real television.

Simon Evans, who had to deal with John and Moses both as a producer and an on-air talent, has this recollection.

SIMON EVANS John would only step in if there was a big problem—like Moses had seen something and wanted an explanation. But Moses would call down and want to speak with you directly, usually to do with something he didn't like, occasionally something he did like. He used to have an assistant deliver a little piece of paper, folded over, with some cryptic message on it. You'd try to figure out what he meant. I asked John about it and he said, "Don't take it seriously. The next one you can take seriously, but the third one you really have to go and see him."

If you thought Moses wasn't paying attention to detail, you could be surprised by his reaction to something minute. Simon remembers an instance of a promo that Moses flagged.

SIMON EVANS I got called into Moses's office because of Guns N' Roses, who we didn't even interview. One of the roadies [in the promo] gestures with his backstage pass and it says "Glastonbury, Guns N' Roses," and in the band's insignia somewhere is the Luftwaffe symbol, with the wing and the bird holding the swastika in his claws. So I get a call from Moses asking, "What's this Nazi festival you're promoting on my air?" I have zero clue what he's talking about. I said, "The guy who runs [Glastonbury] is a hippie, the money goes to charity. It's been going on for twenty-five years; there's not a Nazi in sight." He puts the tape in, presses pause and says, "What's that at the bottom of the screen?" I'm backpedalling, saying, "It's Guns N' Roses. Slash is half black, half Jewish." They took the promo off the air.

It might not have been evident, given that Much rolled along on a conglomeration of wildly different personalities, multiple musical styles and an "expect the unexpected" approach, but make no mistake, there was a philosophy underpinning the whole mad enterprise.

CRAIG HALKETT, VJ and programmer One of Moses's directives was, "It's flow not show."

JEANNE BEKER Much was born from the same mind that imagined *The NewMusic* and it was very much all about kind of smash, grab, being vital, being relevant, of the moment, and being irreverent enough that no one could ever accuse you of taking yourself or your subject matter too seriously, which was one of the great, appealing things about it.

I asked Moses about his love of the medium.

MOSES ZNAIMER I bought my first television with the money from my bar mitzvah.

And what was on his mind the night Much launched?

MOSES ZNAIMER That very night, I remember thinking, "Can we still be doing this in twenty years' time?" I remember in my mind thinking, "Well, I can, I don't know about the rest of these bums."

Moses Znaimer and Christopher Ward

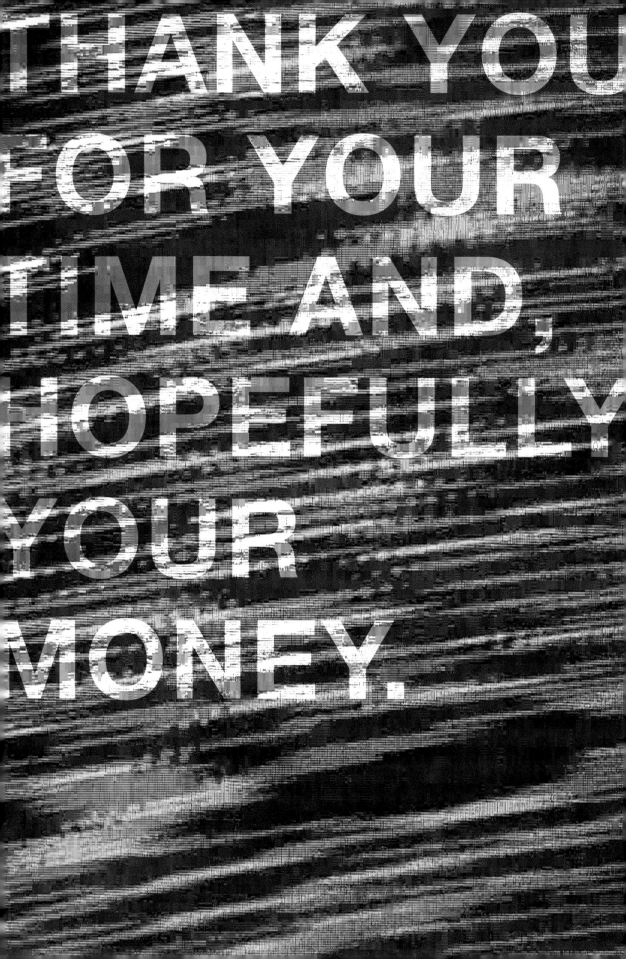

THANK YOU FOR YOUR TIME AND, HOPEFULLY YOUR MONEY.

5 The VJs

J.D. ROBERTS

"MUCH WASN'T GOING TO BE SOME FLUFFY, COTTON-CANDY SHOW."

It's strange for me to recall now that when we launched the network there were two VJs—two! J.D. Roberts and I split the six-hour broadcast day for about the first six weeks, seven days a week, until Michael Williams was hired. Also strangely, I don't remember being tired or wishing for relief; maybe I was as enamoured of the whole experience as the viewers seemed to be. And J.D. was still doing *The NewMusic* and would continue to do so for another year. But he was a machine!

Looking back I realize what a blessing it was to work with J.D. I knew it then too. He was a classic case of someone extremely talented who made their work look effortless, and whose diligence made everyone else's easier. After starting his career in radio, J.D. moved to TV in 1979 as co-host, with Jeanne Beker, of *The NewMusic*, where his presence was that of a rock-solid pro with major sex appeal. Behind the scenes he was a voracious learner of television skills—in those pre-union days, it was acceptable for an on-air person to get their hands on the gear.

DENNIS SAUNDERS, technical director [J.D.] wanted to know everything—how the cameras worked, what the editors were doing; he knew how the audio board worked—he was insatiable. He absorbed everything like a sponge.

The NewMusic was not only one of the key reasons CHUM/City was granted the licence for the video channel, it was also a foundation for us to stand on. J.D. talked about what he brought to Much from that experience.

J.D. ROBERTS A familiarity with the music and the people who made it. By the time Much went on the air, I had interviewed hundreds of artists. We were there when many bands came through Canada for the first time. The Police, the Clash, U2, Echo and the Bunnymen, Psychedelic Furs, Depeche Mode, Eurythmics, and so many more. We had also covered the Canadian music scene extensively—Rush, Triumph, Rough Trade, Jane Siberry, Bryan Adams, and others. We knew these musicians and their music.

Pat Benatar and J.D. Roberts

Simon Evans, who was one of the first producers at Much, remembers J.D.'s work with admiration, something not easily given by Simon.

SIMON EVANS I remember J.D. never wrote a question down but could give back the perfect re-asks. [When you do a pre-recorded, one-camera interview, at the end of the interview you have to ask your questions a second time with the camera focused on the interviewer rather than the subject. Subsequently, the two elements would be cut together. Good re-asks were essential for the piece to look credible.] He had that photographic memory. He edited the story in his head before he came into the station so he knew exactly what he wanted.

J.D. could clown around in the new spirit of Much, but he had a serious intent that underlined his work.

J.D. ROBERTS *The NewMusic* had also produced a few documentary shows, including the Bob Marley funeral, Reggae Sunsplash and coverage of Hurricane Gilbert, which devastated Jamaica. We weren't just doing a music show. Everything we did had a journalistic foundation. When we brought all that experience to Much, viewers knew that the channel wasn't going to be some fluffy, cotton-candy video show. There was going to be substance.

When J.D. made his move to news in 1987, there were a lot of scoffers who felt that he would never be accepted as a credible source for news. He segued smoothly to *CityPulse* news, followed by co-anchoring CTV's *Canada AM*. As John Roberts, he's been seen on CBS News, CNN and, most recently, Fox News Channel, winning three Emmy Awards along the way. I asked him recently what he learned at Much that he was able to put to use later.

J.D. Roberts's last day at MuchMusic

J.D. ROBERTS Technically, Much taught me a hell of a lot about live TV and how to stay focused in the midst of chaos. It was crucial in helping me through coverage of the bombing at the 1996 Atlanta Olympics. I was on a roof by myself for hours after the bombing, carrying our coverage

on the CBS network. A producer kept holding a sign up under the camera that read "they want you to keep going." Thanks to my experience at Much, I could.

MICHAEL WILLIAMS

"THANK YOU FOR YOUR TIME AND, HOPEFULLY, YOUR MONEY."

Michael Williams, a Cleveland native, was living in Montreal working in radio when Much came calling. Or, to put it correctly, when Mike called Much.

MICHAEL WILLIAMS I did a demo for Much while I was on the radio and signed off with "thank you for your time and, hopefully, your money." I put it on a VHS [tape] and sent it to Toronto. Apparently, they didn't have a VHS machine in the building, so John and Nancy went next door to Henry's camera shop to watch my demo.

Like J.D. and me, Michael was a music fanatic and knew his stuff. He also had the best scarf collection this side of Mick Jagger.

MICHAEL WILLIAMS I came down for the launch party in my Chevy Monza and I found myself standing next to Rush and I'm from Cleveland where everyone knows every Rush song. We felt that, although Rush was from Toronto, they got discovered in Cleveland.

Michael Williams with Angus Young and Brian Johnson of AC/DC

As the first black VJ, there were a lot of expectations for Mike from Day One. Fans of black music in Canada and the artists who created it looked to Michael to be the national voice they'd been missing. A reluctant spokesperson, Mike was still proud of Much's support of black music.

(Top) Michael Williams and Celine Dion
(Above) Michael Williams and Ice-T

MICHAEL WILLIAMS I'm from Cleveland where it's not about the colour of the music; it was about the feel and the sound. I think Canadian radio always saw black music and musicians as less-thans. John Martin didn't look at it that way. We had Grandmaster Flash, New Edition, Run-DMC, LL Cool J—all live on Much.

Behind the scarf there beat the heart of a stone-cold rock 'n' roller too! Mike talks about a couple of his favourite interviews.

MICHAEL WILLIAMS Lars from Metallica came in and said [after the interview], "I had such a good time, I'm coming back tomorrow." And he did! Another time, Angus Young from AC/DC played that purple prop guitar we had with the four strings. He broke another and kept going."

Fellow VJ and former camera operator Tony "Master T" Young recalls Mike's interview with Def Leppard.

MASTER T I was a cameraman on that interview and I was so impressed because they were impressed. [Mike] asked a question and one guy said, "How the bloody hell do you know that?" It was the respect that you guys as interviewers gave the artists, by doing your homework. It was a blessing for them, knowing they were stopping in Toronto, Canada, and someone would interview them who understands who I am and what my music is about.

Recently, I asked Michael if he felt pressure to represent the black community in Canada when he first came on air.

MICHAEL WILLIAMS Representing the community was a difficult thing for me . . . I wasn't their man because I wasn't from the West Indies, and that was a big thing. Master T was West Indian so they gravitated more to him than they did to me. People would tell me I had this aloof intellectual thing going. I represented the Quebec music community. I got asked to be a presenter at the **ADISQ** [Québec Association for the Recording, Concert and Video Industries] Awards; not many Anglo guys get that."

Michele Geister, co-producer of *RapCity* and *Soul in the City* describes Mike's strengths.

MICHELE GEISTER Michael was a serious musicologist who could go deep into music history across the spectrum . . . Michael came from Montreal with a fashion *savoir faire* that was European [combined] with rock 'n' roll; he had a much different aesthetic with his signature scarves than the caps and sneakers of the hip-hop crews.

CATHERINE McCLENAHAN

"EXCEPT FOR MOSES, I LOVED WORKING THERE."

If I asked a hundred people on Queen Street West today, or in Coquitlam or Shediac for that matter, who the first female VJ on MuchMusic was, I would wager that a hundred of them would say Erica Ehm. And they would all be wrong. That distinction belongs to a Canadian actress from Ottawa, now living in Los Angeles, Catherine McClenahan.

Catherine recalls where the idea of being a VJ came from.

CATHERINE McCLENAHAN I was at the MTV New Year's Eve party in New York with my then-boyfriend, Paul Farberman, who was vice-president of CBS Records at the time. I knew a few people, including the guys from Duran Duran, because my friend had gone out with Simon Le Bon, and I knew the guys from General Public because I'd done a movie with them in Toronto. Paul at one point turns to me and says, "You should be a VJ on MuchMusic." I said, "What's that?"

Paul, who knew everyone in the business in Canada, called John Martin and set up a meeting for Catherine, who did not lack confidence.

CATHERINE McCLENAHAN I had a meeting with John and we got along great and he said, "Now you have to meet Moses. Don't take anything he says personally." [Moses] kept me waiting for almost an hour. He calls me in and says, "You, you with your lawyer father. I already have my WASP with J.D. Why do I want you? Because I want a red-haired, French-speaking Eskimo." I said, "Well, that's not me. You should hire me because I go to every concert there is. I hang out with musicians. I know what's going on in the music scene. I'm funny; I'm smart; I'm good-looking. You should hire me."

Catherine did get hired, but the honeymoon was brief.

CATHERINE McCLENAHAN I worked there for about six months and I got a musical called *Yuppies*, and I asked John and Nancy if I could do it. I would work around my on-air schedule. They said, "Yes, it's fine, go ahead and do it." As soon as Moses found out, he fired me, so I sued him for wrongful dismissal and I won. Soon after I was hosting a video show on CBC called *Romantic Rock*.

She laughs thinking about what is more like a brief episode than a chapter in her life and career.

CATHERINE McCLENAHAN It was a creative and fun environment. It was a brilliant experience for me—except for Moses, I loved working there.

George Thorogood and Catherine McClenahan

ERICA EHM

"MY NOSE WAS BIG; I WASN'T PERFECT.
I DRESSED FUNNY."

She'd been a club DJ, a band manager, worked in a record store and been on CHOM-FM radio in Montreal while she was a teenager, but in the eyes of many, Erica Ehm was a neophyte who had no business being on television, particularly as the lone female on the nation's music station. Erica went from being "that girl on the phone" in the background of the shot to being a full-time VJ in what seemed like a heartbeat and she got savaged for her temerity. She talks on her Yummy Mummy Club blog about the hate mail she received.

ERICA EHM [The mail was] mostly from girls telling me how stupid, ugly and useless I was. There seemed to be a letter-writing campaign to bully me into getting a nose job—every third "fan letter" addressed to me reminded me that with a nose like mine I had no right to be on TV.

Even in this pre-internet bullying era, people were not reticent about expressing how they thought Erica must have gotten the gig.

ERICA EHM [They said] I must have slept with the boss. Or, the boss was my father. Or I slept with the boss who was also my father. Yep, I heard it all, behind-my-back whisperings and insinuations. I hate to disappoint, but the boss and I never did it.

They say careers are made in the confluence of talent, ambition and opportunity. Erica had them all. She researched like a fiend for interviews and from the beginning did the tedious work of looking back regularly at her day's efforts with a critical eye.

Moses remembers the reaction to putting Erica in the hotseat on Much.

MOSES ZNAIMER Why did I keep Erica Ehm when she was "umming" and "ahhing" and not smooth in her delivery? I had to explain that it's presenting someone the audience could aspire to. The typical letter would be, "I'm Suzie Q and I'm writing for all my friends in Grade 7 and we're horribly upset—she's a terrible representative and she trips over names and she doesn't know what she's doing and besides, if she can do it so can I."

Jeanne Beker had a similar experience with the painful process of growing up in the public eye, and sympathized with Erica's experience.

Erica Ehm and Jim Carrey

JEANNE BEKER **You don't know what you're doing. They just let us go out there, mercilessly, to sink or swim. We were making it up as we went along. What had gone before us were the helmet-headed, turned-up-nose girls, the blondes with WASP names. These were quirky people that [Moses] cast. He knew that was how to get people's attention. It didn't matter whether they liked you or not as long as you were passionate about it.**

SHERRY GREENGRASS, **producer We all knew Erica from the office and she was put on-air with no experience. She put the bone in her hair and all that stuff. In retrospect, I really admire what she accomplished. Out in the world, it was like with Jeanne, people would tune in to see the mistakes.**

Producer Morgen Flury sees Erica and Jeanne's shared experience from a somewhat different perspective.

MORGEN FLURY **All power to them, Erica and Jeanne—successful businesswomen, entrepreneurs. I don't feel bad for them— it was part of the ride, and it was an exciting ride.**

Michael Hutchence of INXS and Erica Ehm

ERICA EHM When I worked at MuchMusic I had no direction [from management]. . . [And] I was . . . repeatedly reminded how insignificant I was and that I was easily replaceable. I was paid less because I was a girl. I said to myself, if I ever run my own company I will do the opposite.

Ziggy Lorenc, who hosted a romantic video show on Citytv and Much called *MushMusic* got her share of heat while she was on air.

ZIGGY LORENC People will skewer you because they want to do what you do and they think you're living the high life.

Ziggy's insider view of Erica differs from that of the armchair critics.

ZIGGY LORENC I thought Erica was incredibly smart. She had that hat business [designing and selling hats that she wore on air]. I thought she was beautiful, smart. I adored Erica. I felt inferior.

Technical director Dennis Saunders had no problem working with Erica.

DENNIS SAUNDERS Guys would call in going, "Who's that girl answering the phone over J.D.'s shoulder?" We got to watch her grow up and (become) real good, tough . . . She fumbled, but she loved music. She was another one of those mirrors that got held up. I remember having a conversation with Erica, stammering, "You know, you're starting to dress kind of conservatively," and I'm getting really embarrassed. She says, "Dennis, you're trying to tell me to show more tits, right?" And the message was from Nancy Oliver—John's second-in-command, straight-laced Nancy. "No problem," [Erica answered].

Neil Finn, Paul Hester and Nick Seymour of Crowded House

Nick Seymour, Neil Finn and Paul Hester of Crowded House were, hands down, the favourite visitors to MuchMusic. They brought joy and mayhem and always performed, usually improvising something along the way. And they did their laundry at Erica's place.

Erica's time at Much lasted ten years, a time during which she truly grew up in public.

ERICA EHM When I started on air, I was twenty-three, and I was interviewing a lot of very interesting people who had, in many cases, led much richer lives than I had, and I wish that I could go back in time and ask them different things. . . .

Stop! Stop! I'm actually singing this part. Why is the camera on those two guys? Is there a director in the house?

Paul Hester, Crowded House

I only have one regret and that's not having video [of the time there]. I never really thought I'd like to hang on to this because I knew there'd always be more tomorrow. When it was over I thought, "I'm so glad I'm gone." I wanted to distance myself from my time at Much and redefine, reinvent Erica, and once I was reinvented, I wanted to enjoy what I had created. So if anyone has anything on tape, email me!

I asked Erica how her notoriety has changed over time.

ERICA EHM I'm a Canadian ex-celebrity, so I win. Sometimes I get good seats in restaurants and if I happen to go to a bar, people who are of my generation get excited to see me, but for the most part I've reinvented myself so thoroughly that people look at me more as a businesswoman now. I look much older, but they always go, "Oh my god, you look the exact same." And I go, "You are such a fucking liar . . . but thank-you!"

And despite the looseness at Much and the lack of constraint, I think we each applied the toughest expectations to ourselves.

ERICA EHM I understood that I was a role model. I was careful of every word that I spoke and made sure that I was so "me," and I was showing girls that they could be not perfect and cool enough to be on MuchMusic. My nose was big; I wasn't perfect. I dressed funny; I didn't always speak perfectly.

LAURIE BROWN

"I DIDN'T HAVE AS MUCH FUN WITH THE JOB AS I COULD HAVE."

Laurie Brown's entrée into life as a VJ was engineered with a typical John Martin pitch.

LAURIE BROWN I was doing *The NewMusic* very happily and John called me into his office and said, "We'd like you to do MuchMusic as well as *The NewMusic*." I said, "Are you nuts? I'm working really hard, out two or three nights a week with bands and to add live television . . ." John said, "It's not going to be hard. It's just videos. You'll get to a point where you'll be sitting at your desk working on a *NewMusic* script, and you're just going to turn your chair and look at the camera and introduce the videos for two minutes, then you're going to go back to working on *The NewMusic*. It's going to be nothing."

John also used the same magic expression with Laurie that he used with me. Here's Laurie's take on it.

Laurie Brown with DJ Jazzy Jeff and the Fresh Prince (Will Smith)

LAURIE BROWN "You can do anything you want." But there was the other half of that sentence, "You can do anything you want . . . as long as it doesn't cost anything." Which wasn't a problem. Go ahead and do anything you want. It was the most unbelievable gift.

I REALLY, REALLY REALLY HATE MY JOB.

Laurie Brown (eating an egg fried on Queen Street)

I wondered what direction, if any, Laurie had received from Moses.

LAURIE BROWN **Watching Much, [Moses] became very concerned that both Erica and I were brunettes and he thought that that was a problem. He called me into his office to talk about the possibility of me going blonde or wearing a wig. The conversation didn't go very far. I was dumbounded that this was what [the meeting was] all about, that he was watching Much and thinking, "Two brunettes, that's not good."**

The lack of direction or job description might be viewed as negligence by some, but to those of us who did it for a living it was a tacit form of approval, the nod that told you that you were doing just fine, carry on! Laurie had a strong sense of what a successful VJ needed.

LAURIE BROWN **Passion for music . . . If the audience knew that you were a lover of music, a lot of things could be forgiven. Here I was getting such proximity to people that were huge idols for most of the people in the audience, and that's why they were tuning in and I thought, I have a huge responsibility. I have to be sure that for the biggest fan of this artist, who knows way more about this band than I do, I have to do them proud, because I am their representative. I took that really seriously . . . probably too far. I didn't have as much fun with the job as I could have. And I felt a responsibility to the artists themselves, to give them an opportunity to talk about what they were passionate about . . . what was important to them. Those were the two people I was concerned about—the artist representing themselves in a way that they felt really good about and being there for the audience and giving them what they were craving. I was right there; I was the one to do it.**

In a medium where your job is to speak directly to the audience, there is by definition no fourth wall, but just as with news journalists and the events they are covering, there is usually an implicit separation between the on-air host and the things we cover. We don't normally get on stage with the band, get interviewed by the artists, or make our own videos. What am I saying? We did all of those things. In that spirit, Laurie had what she calls "the most perfect TV moment."

LAURIE BROWN **Right across the street they were shooting a TV movie with Debbie Reynolds . . . and I said I'm going to go over there . . . and see if I can get an extra part while I'm on Much. So they followed me across the street and I went up to some guy and told him what's going on, that we're shooting. Then we played a couple of videos, came back and that's it, I'm in the scene, and**

I had to walk past Debbie Reynolds on the street and do this little scene with her; so while they were shooting the movie, I was live on Much! That, to me, broke down all the walls and rules and showed the wires of everything at the same time. That was one of those perfect moments that you never could have orchestrated in a million years. It would have been too hard but it just happened.

The best part of Much was that I got to be myself on television.

It's amusing to learn what former VJs hear from the viewers who remember them well. For me, it's quite frequently in the form of a one-word exhortation: *Fromage!* Here's what Laurie gets.

LAURIE BROWN **The line I get the most is "Laurie Brown, I used to be so in love with you." I say, "So what am I now, chopped liver?" They'll tell me about the crush that they had and say, "Can we time travel back so that I can tell my friend that I met Laurie Brown, and here we are sitting and having a glass of wine together or whatever?" I say, "Yes, you have my permission to time travel back."**

DENISE DONLON

"I THINK I WAS WEARING SUSPENDERS."

Denise Donlon has had one of the most extraordinary careers in the Canadian music business. Starting as a concert buyer at the University of Waterloo, she moved to Vancouver to work for the Sam Feldman Agency as a publicist for the bands Doug and the Slugs, the Headpins and Trooper. When Much was looking for interviews with her clients, they came to Denise and she struck up a relationship with John Martin and Nancy Oliver. John offered her the *Rockflash* gig, doing hourly live music news segments, replacing Jeanne Beker who was launching *FashionTelevision.* Denise had her own reasons for wanting to return to Toronto.

DENISE DONLON **My parents were getting divorced and I wanted to be closer to them, and I was getting no dates in Vancouver and I thought maybe there might be someone in Toronto.**

Denise had been watching Much.

DENISE DONLON **I thought it was *Looney Tunes* but very exciting. It wasn't a trainwreck because no one ever got hurt, but you never knew what was going to happen.**

Steve Earle and Denise Donlon

John, as usual, knew what he was looking for in on-air talent, even if he or she didn't fit the established television mould.

DENISE DONLON **John wanted someone who could sniff out a story and who knew who to call and who would know what was bullshit and what wasn't. I never wanted to be a VJ. In fact, I never wanted to be on camera. I actually hated being on camera. I loved doing the work, the research, staying all night in an editing bay, putting things together, and who doesn't love meeting all the stars?**

Denise, like the rest of us, was given the "throw her in the deep end" treatment on her first day at Much.

DENISE DONLON **I was a stuttering maniac, deer in the headlights, lots of hairspray and big earrings. A terrible outfit—I think I was wearing suspenders.**

As someone who had promoted Canadian talent, Denise easily adopted the Much attitude toward the artists.

DENISE DONLON **We were playing Canadian content, of course, as a condition of licence, but we also played the Canadian artists because we really liked them and wanted them to succeed. They were our friends; they came by all the time. We didn't worry if "oh, we've already seen Alan Frew this month." It was, "There's Alan Frew walking down the street, let's go talk to him." We were excited about playing a $400 Pursuit of Happiness video. MTV had a more fraught relationship with the labels. There was a lot more, "You need to play this band and this video because it's a priority for this label." Profit wasn't the prime directive at Much.**

Denise points out another key distinction between Much and MTV.

DENISE DONLON **MTV wanted their VJs to be as big stars as the people they were interviewing. Our attitude was that we were a vehicle for our guests to shine.**

As the *Rockflash* anchor and later as a co-host and producer of *The NewMusic*, Denise had the opportunity to interview some musical superstars. Of course, superstars sometimes get up on the wrong side of the bed.

DENISE DONLON **I interviewed Don Henley at Kingswood Music Theatre [an amphitheatre at Canada's Wonderland theme park that hosted many major acts in the 1980s and '90s]. He was notoriously cranky, and he arrived thirty minutes late. He was *so* not into this interview. He crossed his arms and legs and stared at the floor and then the manager had to say, "He's ready," and I thought, "He doesn't look ready," because he wouldn't look at me. I had to work him for the first fifteen minutes and finally, his arms came down and he started to engage and the last twenty minutes, we had a great interview. He was very politically minded, very forceful in his opinions, smart, and you could take him on and he'd take you on. At the end, we said thank you, and he said to his manager, "That interview was really good, not at all what I expected from MTV," and the manager said, "Well, it wasn't MTV."**

Seven years after her debut at Much, Denise replaced the man who hired her, as the network's director of music programming.

DENISE DONLON **John's relationship with Moses had deteriorated to the point that John knew he was out the door and he was the most generous person about it—he said, "If anybody has to replace me, I'm glad it's you." He gave me the permission and the wings to**

carry on the vibe that he put into the place. We were in a place where the line between church and state was getting a lot thinner. We were doing a lot more product placement on air. We needed the advertisers to pay for the dance mixes [a series of dance music compilation CDs released beginning in 1990] that we were doing and the SnowJob [concerts] and the MMVAs. What John gave me, and I think I kept, were the looseness and the principles around not selling out. We retained our viewer loyalty because they saw us as them. Even when we tried to sell them something we'd mock it with the sounds of cash registers. That's what the advertisers wanted— to be in this rock 'n' roll circus.

Denise had a vision for Much that went beyond what had been the original blueprint. Not everyone bought in, but Denise had the power to make the changes she believed were necessary.

DENISE DONLON On Much we did a lot of activism—we did AIDS PSAs [public service announcements], we did election coverage, the Kumbaya Festival [an annual music and arts festival in the '90s benefitting HIV/AIDS charities]. We weren't cramming political ideas or education down the audience's throat but we were using the videos—like Madonna or REM or Sting with a rainforest video . . . as a way to talk to the audience. . . .
I thought we were engaging with the audience on a deeper level than just entertainment. We were culturally and socially making those connections.

Given all that she had been part of at Much, and all that she had accomplished, I asked Denise what she was most proud of.

Listen to me, Lewis. Let me finish.

Prime Minister Jean Chrétien (to Avi Lewis)

(Left) Prime Minister Jean Chrétien in the MuchMusic studio
(Opposite) MuchMusic VJs

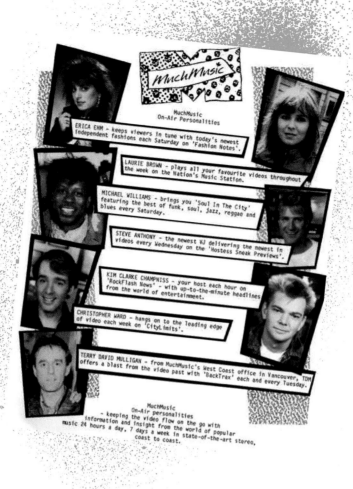

MuchMusic
On-Air Personalities

ERICA EHM – keeps viewers in tune with today's newest
independent fashions each Saturday on 'Fashion Notes'.

LAURIE BROWN – plays all your favourite videos throughout
the week on the Nation's Music Station.

MICHAEL WILLIAMS – brings you 'Soul In The City'
featuring the best of funk, soul, jazz, reggae and
blues every Saturday.

STEVE ANTHONY – the newest VJ delivering the newest in
videos every Wednesday on the 'Hostess Sneak Previews'.

KIM CLARKE CHAMPNISS – your host each hour on
'RockFlash News' – with up-to-the-minute headlines
from the world of entertainment.

CHRISTOPHER WARD – hangs on to the leading edge
of video each week on 'CityLimits'.

TERRY DAVID MULLIGAN – from MuchMusic's West Coast office in Vancouver, TDM
offers a blast from the video past with 'BackTrax' each and every Tuesday.

MuchMusic
On-Air personalities
– keeping the video flow on the go with
information and insight from the world of popular
music 24 hours a day, 7 days a week in state-of-the-art stereo,
coast to coast.

DENISE DONLON I'm most proud of championing Canadian artists' careers.

She recalled an *Intimate and Interactive* [a series of live in studio performances featuring interaction with home and studio audiences] performance given by the Tragically Hip, featuring lead singer Gord Downie.

DENISE DONLON The interviewer asked Gord what he thought was surprising about Canada that he learned on tour. He said, "It's surprising to me that people think we're unpatriotic." And the audience spontaneously started to sing "O Canada" to him.

Oh, and how did that move to Toronto work out? Denise and Toronto singer/songwriter Murray McLauchlan are happily married, over twenty years later.

Kid Rock: Do you want to have sex with me?

Michael Williams: Not on this chair, baby.

MUCHMUSIC WAS LIKE ELECTRICITY BEING CREATED.

6 The New Popstars

Building a career in music in Canada had long been a challenging proposition. Tiny budgets for recording, labels that were for the most part distribution outlets for U.S. major labels, a shortage of experienced managers, and a potential audience that was spread out across daunting swathes of geography all contributed to making it an uphill slog. The CRTC's Canadian content regulations, created in 1971, had helped, to be sure, by requiring minimum percentages of Canadian music be played on radio stations, giving artists exposure and support, but as much as anything they'd created a cottage industry of turntable hits, songs that radio played to meet their requirements, but which rarely got turned into retail action. It's a simplification, but by 1984, the Canadian music business had gone through a couple of significant growth spurts, post-regulation. In the '70s, we heard a lot of the Guess Who, Anne Murray and Lightfoot on the radio, and these domestic acts became legitimate worldwide stars. Next up came Rush, Triumph, April Wine, the Stampeders, Chilliwack and Max Webster as rock, Canuck-style, emerged.

Then came Much. When we got behind a band, it made a difference to careers overnight, because a band could go from being a local phenomenon to having instant visibility nationwide. And unlike radio, whose programmers frequently resented the Canadian content regulations, feeling that they were obligated to play inferior songs, Much embraced homegrown artists, believing that supporting their careers was a collaborative effort. We believed that the talent was there and that there was an audience appetite for Canadian music. It made sense that as the star system became healthier, more money would pour into the business and the quality of what was produced would improve. One of the first priorities was the creation of Videofact, an annual fund started by MuchMusic in 1984 as a condition of license that gave grants to Canadian recording artists to help them make videos. Artists from K-os to Celine Dion to Great Big Sea received Videofact grants.

COREY HART

Corey Hart was Canada's first video superstar. The songs were hits and the pout was gold. Director Rob Quartly, who helped define the look of an entire generation of Canadian acts, including Gowan, Platinum Blonde, the Spoons and Glass Tiger, said that Corey "was the best artist I worked with at making

a personal connection with the camera." Together they created a consistent character for Corey that ran through a string of high-rotation videos.

(Top) J.D. Roberts, Corey Hart and Michael Williams
(Bottom) Director Rob Quartly and Corey Hart on the set of the "Sunglasses at Night" video shoot

COREY HART **The lone wolf persona is true to my actual personality, so it was easy for me to play this solitary character.**

It was the video for "Sunglasses at Night" that established the template for Corey's version of the "James Dean loner guy" and it spoke to millions of teenage girls. For the video, which Corey describes as having a "*1984 Orwellian theme*," Quartly chose Toronto's Don Jail for the location, and for the female lead role of the stern, but beautiful warden, he cast a young singer/actress and future VJ named Laurie Brown.

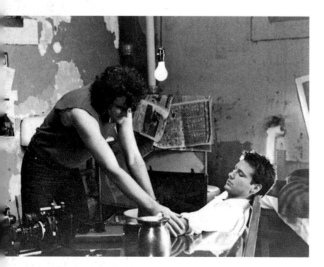

LAURIE BROWN **My agent said, "You're going to get $750 to do this and it's a night's work." We shot at the old Don Jail, which was very spooky and amazing. I remember I heard the song so many times that night and I thought, "I'll remember this song for a long time," but I had no idea that it was going to be a hit. It seemed kind of dorky to me. I was slightly older than seventeen, so maybe I was missing the point. I remember watching it later and thinking,**

[COREY] COULD SPIT UP A STORM. HE SOLD IT; HE WAS TOTALLY IN IT.

Rob Quartly (on Corey Hart's singing)

"This is very slick." It had some beautiful lighting; the production quality in it was really, really good.

COREY HART I was incredibly nervous before the filming of "Sunglasses." It was my first time shooting a music video, and the night before, I royally sucked running through some of the scenes.

Corey Hart in a train station in Japan, with expectant fans at the window

To make it even more challenging, Quartly wanted Corey to shoot the phone booth scenes singing at double speed, slowing it down in post to get the dreamy effect. Corey said, "It was weird to go at it like 'Alvin and the Chipmunks.'"

"Sunglasses at Night" won the first Juno for Video of the Year in 1984, and helped establish Corey Hart as a superstar in Canada and internationally.

COREY HART Between '84 and '88 I couldn't really go anywhere without being mobbed by fans. Wearing sunglasses was obviously no disguise!

PLATINUM BLONDE

If ever there was a Canadian band that was tailor-made for the video era, it was Platinum Blonde. They were charismatic; they had the *au courant* sound, deftly mixing strains of Elvis Costello, the Police and Tears for Fears with big sing-along choruses, and they were nicely bankrolled by Sony. The debut video for "Doesn't Really Matter" cost $40,000, a modest budget by Michael Jackson standards, but for an unproven Canadian act, a serious commitment. Like Corey's label had done, Sony turned to the top director of the day, Rob Quartly, to work his magic with their new act. Singer Mark Holmes talked about their first experience with video.

MARK HOLMES We're at our first video shoot and I always thought they were very glamorous, "Wow, *we're* doing a video." We'd see videos like Duran Duran's and they made themselves look really rich, really successful. I was excited "there's going to be girls in the video" and of course the girls have got white painted faces, I don't know what they look like—it wasn't exactly what we were expecting . . . I had to sit in a chair with a massive fan blowing in my face trying to keep my eyes open while smoke and debris was flying all around me.

Rob Quartly also directed the follow-up, "Standing in the Dark," and had to accommodate an unusual request.

ROB QUARTLY CTV had a show called *Thrill of a Lifetime* and someone's thrill of a lifetime was to be in a Platinum Blonde video. The video was "Standing in the Dark" and I remember people were having their heads shaved, and there was a lot of weird stuff going on, and there was a war room with a Plexiglas table and these people underneath the Plexiglas table. So I thought, what a perfect place to put someone for *Thrill of a Lifetime.*

The financial aspect of making videos was something few acts thought about. Videos were paid for upfront by the label, but the "recoupment" clause of an artist's deal would show whose money was ultimately at stake.

MARK HOLMES The record label was spending money and of course we had to pay for it with our royalties, and of course they

Chris Steffler and Kenny MacLean of Platinum Blonde with Michael Williams

owned the video afterwards. . . . That was quite a scam the labels had going for a while . . . but then again, where would we be without it? It was a necessary evil. If someone were to say to you, "I'll make you a video that makes you famous, however we're going to own the video and you're going to pay for it eventually," I think ten out of ten people would still say "absolutely."

Be careful what you wish for. Mark recalls the band attending a Psychedelic Furs concert at Massey Hall as fans.

MARK HOLMES We didn't have security or anything and getting down the street to the car was a madhouse. We were literally being torn apart, people grabbing at us . . . it was mayhem; we were the Beatles. It wasn't just fan adoration like the Psychedelic Furs show, it was fanaticism similar to the Beatles and the Stones when they first came out. . . .
   It really hit me that our videos pushed this reaction right over the edge. It was seeing us—we became film stars in music.

Platinum Blonde's shows were hormonefests, and due to the screaming fans in the crowd, the band's hearing was at risk.

MARK HOLMES We would literally finish a song when we were playing live and then cover our ears.

The comparison to iconic acts like the Beatles and the Stones may be accurate with regard to the decibel level, but not when it came to remuneration.

MARK HOLMES Fame before the fortune is a tough, tough pill to swallow because . . . everybody knows you and you're still poor . . . and you can't afford to have a special car and bodyguards to protect the asset that you are. [Lead guitar player] Serge had hundreds of people camped outside his parents' house. In this country the fortune, the minimal fortune, doesn't come until much later.

HONEYMOON SUITE

One band that arrived at virtually the same time as MuchMusic was Honeymoon Suite. Despite this, drummer Dave Betts recalls that there wasn't a lot of enthusiasm on the part of their label for the new medium.

DAVE BETTS "New Girl Now" was the band's first video, and if I recall, the idea of doing a video was not totally embraced by our

label, WEA Canada. They viewed it as a potential waste of money with the assumption that it may or may not get airplay and if it did, it would be minimal.

Their debut video for "New Girl Now" came out in the fall of '84 and Much jumped on it while the band toured the U.S. Their manager, Jeff Rogers, talked about how things played out for the band.

JEFF ROGERS We weren't on the road in Canada, but we came back [from the States] and we had a gold record because MuchMusic kept us alive and we had the cachet that we weren't [in Canada], we were on the road in America.

The band soon went for glamour—cars, girls, the beach!—with "Wave Babies," another song from the debut album. Guitarist Derry Grehan has the real story.

DERRY GREHAN We shot it in Picton, Ontario, and it was just after they had this tornado up in Barrie that year . . . and it was chilly. We made it look like it was all sunny and eighty degrees, but that's the "magic of Hollywood," as they say.

Well at least they'd get to hang out with the "wave babies," wouldn't they?

DERRY GREHAN I remember management making us all leave and go to another town for the night after we wrapped for the day so we wouldn't get into trouble. . . . Probably a good idea . . . we were a pretty restless bunch at that time.

Michael Williams with Derry Grehan and Johnnie Dee of Honeymoon Suite

A feel-good story came out of the "New Girl Now" shoot for one of the extras, who was a runaway from B.C. Derry remembers the story well.

DERRY GREHAN **Her mother was watching the video one day and recognized her daughter in one of the crowd shots. So somehow she got hold of the record label . . . and got re-united with her daughter. I remember even seeing a little article in *People* magazine about it later on.**

Echoing what Mark Holmes said about the Blondes' experience, Derry sums up the effect of video for Honeymoon Suite.

DERRY GREHAN **It kind of made little movie stars out of musicians, and gave them this kind of mystique. We had to learn really quickly about getting our look and image together.**

THE SPOONS

A musical and fashion movement known as New Romantic began in the U.K. at the start of the '80s, where it seemed all the happening movements were beginning, and was spearheaded by synth-pop bands like Spandau Ballet and Culture Club. Initially it was seen as a reaction to the minimalism of punk; the music was lush and the look was flamboyant.

The band that best epitomized that style in Canada was the Spoons, a group from Burlington, Ontario, begun in 1979, featuring the charismatic front duo of Gordon Deppe and Sandy Horne. Gordon spoke about the importance of video to the band.

GORDON DEPPE **Videos and MuchMusic played a huge part in our careers. We arrived just as they did and we walked through the '80s, hand in hand. I recently read that the very first show began with, "Welcome to MuchMusic. Coming up we have brand new videos by Duran Duran, Howard Jones and the Spoons." I'm pretty proud of that.**

In common with Corey, the Blondes, and later Gowan and others, the Spoons turned to director Rob Quartly for their breakthrough video, "Nova Heart."

GORDON DEPPE **Videos were such uncharted territory back then, I don't think there really was a plan. Working with Rob Quartly was a matter of putting ourselves in his capable hands, like you would the director of a movie. But because the video for "Nova Heart"**

J.D. Roberts with Gordon Deppe
and Sandy Horne of the Spoons

was so different, so un–rock 'n' roll, when it was aired everyone knew exactly who the Spoons were.

And fans wanted to look like their favourite acts. Gordon talks about the effect of having your style broadcast across the country.

GORDON DEPPE With the all-white outfits . . . in the "Nova Heart" video, a lot of fans started showing up at shows dressed like that . . . Never before in the history of music was physical appearance so critical, so out-there for everyone to see. Truthfully, I wasn't very comfortable with it. One fan even cut her cheek . . . to emulate the scar I've had since childhood. That was more fan adoration than even I could take.

Occasionally, there was a price to pay for all the glamour and adoration as the band found on the Quartly-directed "Old Emotions" shoot.

GORDON DEPPE One of the most ridiculous scenes we ever did in a video ended up being the most horrendous. At the end of "Old Emotions," the director put us in a small room having a pillow fight. He convinced us that the effect would be quite striking played back in slow motion. Only thing is, we almost choked to death on the bags of feathers the crew rained down on us. Every few minutes one of us would jump out of the room, hacking our lungs out. I guess it was fair punishment for agreeing to such a ridiculous idea.

MEN WITHOUT HATS

Another band that briefly predated Much's arrival, but who became mainstays on our early playlists was Montreal's Men Without Hats. I asked leader Ivan Doroschuk about the English-language music scene in that city.

IVAN DOROSCHUK It was tight . . . with the obvious rivalries, but it produced a lot of bands like Men Without Hats, the Box, and Rational Youth. There was a strong community, especially in that period of the late '70s, early '80s. We were tapping into something new so we felt like it was a secret club. Our goal was to get out of there anyway.

Ivan offered a formulation for the origins of New Wave that was new to me, but immediately made sense.

IVAN DOROSCHUK I was in the disco scene front and centre. That's why for me New Wave was an easy transition because I've always said that New Wave was the marriage of disco and progressive rock. I was a huge fan of Genesis and Pink Floyd and my mother was a music teacher at McGill for twenty-five years and I took piano lessons all my life.

As for the origins of Men Without Hats, Ivan added this:

IVAN DOROSCHUK We formed Men Without Hats in the student union building at McGill University. It was all guys from Ontario.

And in the "small world" department, Ivan spoke of a face familiar to Much viewers.

IVAN DOROSCHUK One of the people in that scene was Erica Miechowsky [a.k.a. Erica Ehm]; she was the DJ at one of the first punk/New Wave clubs downtown called The Blues, where we played.

Even now, I play 'The Safety Dance,' and at the end I break into the move and the whole audience goes along with it. I almost see it as my responsibility to play them for as many people as I can while I still can.

Ivan Doroschuk, Men Without Hats (on performing "The Safety Dance" and "Pop Goes the World")

The band's breakout hit has an amusing backstory.

IVAN DOROSCHUK It was in the late '70s and I was hanging out at a club in Ottawa. In those days it was top 40 disco playing in the clubs, but every now and then the DJ would slip in a New Wave tune like "Rock Lobster" or "Heart of Glass," or maybe if you were lucky, a Devo song. So we'd get up on the dance floor and start jumping up and down. Nobody knew what we were doing and they thought we were looking for a fight and we'd get tossed out. It happened quite a few times; every time we'd start pogo-ing . . . we'd get told to stop. That was the inspiration for the lyrics to the song.

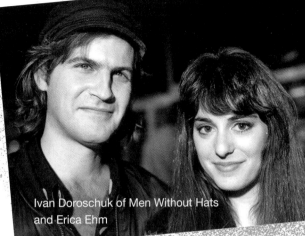

Ivan Doroschuk of Men Without Hats and Erica Ehm

Certain songs of the era are inseparable from the videos that accompanied them, and I think "The Safety Dance" is one of those. Ivan got paired with director Tim Pope, who lived in England and had done some very popular videos for the Cure. Their means of communication seems primitive now.

IVAN DOROSCHUK It was before the internet and long-distance calls were cost prohibitive, so we sent each other a letter saying what we thought should be the script of the video. Our letters crossed paths, but we both had this Pied Piper idea and almost the same idea for [the type of] location. I was going to do it on Mount Royal in Montreal, coming out of the forest early in the morning, going to the Mordecai Richler bandstand.

In the end the shoot was booked for the town of West Kington, Wiltshire, in England.

IVAN DOROSCHUK I was on tour so I flew there on the Concorde and shot it in two days. It was seriously overcast the first day and the second day it was pouring rain. Every shot I was back under the umbrella blow-drying my hair . . . it all got shot in this little town and the . . . extras were from the village. I came into the town one morning and danced through it and at the end everybody in the town was dancing in this courtyard. Fans have sent me pictures recently and it hasn't changed one single bit.

I asked Ivan about the universality of the song and video, in an era when a band's look and sound often shaped, and sometimes narrowed, who their fans were.

IVAN DOROSCHUK I think the fact that I had long hair and it was a medieval kind of a thing—that's what caught people off guard. They said, "He doesn't have the whole New Wave look with the zippers and the pointy shoes and spiked hair." It just told people, "There's no uniform for this song." It doesn't fit into any category— everybody can dance if they want to.

LOVERBOY

Although they may be associated with a slightly earlier era than Much, one of the Canadian bands that benefited most from video was Loverboy. Lead singer Mike Reno talked about shooting their first videos.

MIKE RENO [Video] was an amazing tool [for breaking Loverboy]. We couldn't believe it. They didn't even know what to call it; the word "video" wasn't even created. They said, "We need some music clips with you guys performing live. We're going to put a montage together." They said, "You guys are on tour; we want you to drive to Albany on your days off. There'll be a crew waiting for you at [the Palace Theatre]." We got there and all they really wanted us to do is play our songs over and over again all day long and every once in a while they'd have me sit at a table with a girl, stare in her eyes and smoke.

These "montages," or early music videos, shot beginning in 1980, worked wonders for the band, getting them in on the ground floor with the fledgling network. When MTV launched in the U.S. in August of 1981, Loverboy had videos for "Turn Me Loose," "The Kid Is Hot Tonite" and "When It's Over," all in rotation.

MIKE RENO [MTV] had a 24-hour music station and they didn't have nearly enough to fill the time. They would play a dog taking a pee on a fire hydrant. They had to play something. We were just lucky. Even if the video was no good, you'd still get played.

And soon there was no doubt about the power of the new medium.

MIKE RENO When [MTV] came out with all these videos, [we] really couldn't go out of [our] hotel room anymore. It was almost panic Beatlemania time. It put a face on everybody. That was the

major change and I remember it like it was yesterday. One day you could go get a newspaper at the 7-Eleven and the next day you couldn't leave your hotel room.

Loverboy may have benefitted from the novelty of music video, but this was a band that built their success the old school way—on stage, in rehearsal rooms and in the studio. And they had the rock-solid support of managers Bruce Allen and Sam Feldman.

MIKE RENO We worked our songs out with a crowd. We used to say to Bruce Allen, "Get us some shows on Vancouver Island to get away from the mainstream Vancouverites who are a little picky." Gotta head up to Nanaimo and Comox where people don't give a shit; they're just happy to have a live band. Sam Feldman would say [to the local promoter], "They're top 40." And when we started playing all our own material, the promoter would call Sam and say, "These guys aren't top 40," and Sam would say, "listen, dude, they will be top 40 so just fucking play 'em or I'll never send you another band."

Listening to the tightly constructed Loverboy songs made me wonder if Reno and co-writer Paul Dean took the same workmanlike approach to songwriting that they took to building their stage act. Mike elaborates on their process.

MIKE RENO We rewrite songs more than anybody I know. We write a song, Paul takes it and rewrites it about ten times, and asks me to come back and sing it again. After about a month I don't even recognize the song anymore. Then he plays me a finished song and it's three

Christopher Ward with Mike Reno and Scott Smith of Loverboy

different songs put together that I don't even recall singing. Paul is a Frankenstein creator.

On subsequent albums, the videos became more involved and the budgets rose along with the record sales. I was curious about the video for "Queen of the Broken Hearts" where the band are seen wandering around the Mojave Desert until some girls show up.

MIKE RENO **They flew us in by helicopter . . . it was super hot, as you can image in the Mojave Desert . . . and they had us clad in leather. They had all these wind machines because they wanted to shoot a sequence . . . [the director] said, "I want to light it and shoot it in the dark," and as soon as it got dark out the wind came up and it was almost like a hurricane . . .it was blowing the wind machines over, they weren't even being used anymore. The other scene [was] where we had to walk over this hill and they'd shoot from a mile away so you'd get that ripply effect from the heat. At the end of the day, everyone fell asleep in the helicopter on the way home.**

Oh the glamour! If you recall the video for "Lovin' Every Minute of It," it's interesting to hear Mike explain the rationale behind the visuals.

MIKE RENO **That was the most fun for me. We all got to write our own fantasy sequence. We rented the whole Holiday Inn by the Hollywood Bowl so the cranes could be put up alongside the seventh-floor windows. The cranes had the cameras on them and they'd go up and down in the parking lot and film all the rooms separately. Each room or two were these things that were people's fantasies. Mine was to have a party with craziness with midgets and lizards and dancing girls . . . Fellini-type stuff. Paul's was to be in a music factory building guitars. He's always been that way, clinical. I think Scotty wanted to be playing strip poker with the girls. Doug, of course, had the candelabra on the piano because he'd taken fourteen years of piano lessons and . . . he was an A student. He could play circles around everybody and just had to play "dun-dun-dun-dun-dun" with one finger in most of our songs.**

At the Juno Awards Hall of Fame presentation Mike said, "Thanks to MTV and Much for playing our silly videos."

MIKE RENO **They were no sillier than anybody else's but in reality, we were on motorcycles, we were in hot-rod cars, we were in Porsches. We did anything to look like whatever was happening. We kind of took our fashion sense from shows like _Miami Vice_ . . . Then someone would say, "We got to get you all dirtied up for this**

one because you're going to a biker bar." And you had to laugh—
they were silly little three- to four-minute fantasies of what rock
stars do when they're singing their songs.

As for that legendary fashion sense, Mike laughs looking back.

MIKE RENO Look at the back of our first album . . . red leather
pants and the yellow V-neck shirt tied in the front. God! Did I
actually do that? It's kinda funny because people actually want you
to dress the same, they want you to look exactly the same as you
did thirty-six years ago. I say, "Really? Then why don't you come to
the show in your prom dress?"

Throughout the '80s Loverboy was one of the biggest bands on MuchMusic.
And they never forgot how important the medium was in launching and
sustaining an amazing career.

MIKE RENO MuchMusic. It was like electricity being created. It
was that powerful . . . it saved careers. It created careers; it was
everything. To be on TV was huge; it took you to the star level . . .
Everybody could see you. It was that powerful. We took it very
seriously in that respect. We knew that once you get on TV it's a
whole different game.

I did ask Mike his favourite part of watching Much in those days.

MIKE RENO I had the hots for Erica Ehm. Who didn't?

BRYAN ADAMS

In the decade that saw the birth of MuchMusic, the country's biggest-selling
rock artist, Bryan Adams, built his career on a bedrock of timeless songs
written with his collaborator, Jim Vallance. The records, like the shows, were
seamless and featured great singing, playing and production.

Bryan arrived just as video was becoming an essential tool in establishing
an artist. Manager Bruce Allen had seen the effect of the medium on
Loverboy's success and was eager to utilize it with Bryan, despite some
reluctance on Adams' part. They arranged through Bryan's label, A&M
Records, for hit director Steve Barron to come to Vancouver for an unusually
intense shooting schedule.

BRUCE ALLEN We did five or six videos in three or four days
throughout Vancouver—"Summer of '69," "This Time"—we tied

them all together. Bryan struggled with it, but he did embrace it because he saw what happened with "Cuts Like a Knife" in the U.S.

The *Cuts Like a Knife* album, released in January '83, went platinum in the U.S. and three times platinum in Canada. The video for the title track was a major contributor to the record's success.

Bryan talks about how Steve Barron was chosen.

BRYAN ADAMS He was an influential director because he had made some cracking videos like the A-ha video ["Take on Me"] and Michael Jackson's "Billie Jean." We hit it off straight away; he's Irish and we are the same age approximately. The breakthrough video was "Cuts Like a Knife," everyone talked about that video at the time.

I asked about the process for the artist and director.

BRYAN ADAMS I'd speak to him and discuss whatever the concept was . . . Depending on the video, so much of what happened on them was made up on the spot and from performance. There were always script ideas like, "Get a car, get a girl, Bryan walks with girl, girl gets in car, girl drives away, Bryan stands there watching," that sort of thing, most of which had nothing to do with what the song was about.

Adams' 1984 album, *Reckless*, was released a couple of months after Much launched and Bryan became the most-played artist on the channel. Looking back we see a parade of hit songs, videos and sold-out shows, but amazingly, it might not have happened if certain choices had gone another way. Bryan's co-writer Jim Vallance explains.

JIM VALLANCE There are three songs that Bryan considered deleting from the *Reckless* album: "Heaven," "Summer of '69" and "Run to You." Bryan had previewed the album for music mogul Jimmy Iovine [Tom Petty, Meatloaf, U2 and Dire Straits producer], looking for feedback. Jimmy's suggestion was, "Leave 'Heaven' off the album." Fortunately Bryan ignored Jimmy's advice. "Summer of '69" was a problem from the beginning. We re-wrote it three times, and we still weren't happy. Even when it was mixed and mastered, we debated if it should be on or off the album. Strangely, thirty years later, neither Bryan nor I can remember what we didn't like about it!

The song that kicked off the album and became a massive hit, "Run to You," also had a bumpy road to inclusion on the record. Vallance, who co-wrote the song with Bryan, tells the story.

JIM VALLANCE "Run to You" was originally written for Blue Oyster Cult, at the request of our friend Bruce Fairbairn who was

producing the band. The signature sound on "(Don't Fear) the Reaper" [the band's biggest hit] is the guitar riff at the top of the song. Believing that was the key to getting our song recorded, we inserted a guitar riff at the beginning of "Run to You." We sent the song to Fairbairn but the band didn't like it. We sent it to another band, but they didn't like it either. So we forgot about it. A year later, when we were finishing *Reckless*, someone pointed out that the album only had nine songs. We needed one more, so Bryan suggested "Run to You." His band nailed it in one take, and it became one of Bryan's biggest singles.

I asked Bruce Allen if there was any concern about separating Bryan from the teen idols of the day when it came to making the videos to accompany the album.

BRUCE ALLEN **Not a problem, because he was rockin' hard with the band so I never had to worry about the teen idols . . . As far as I was concerned, we were always competing with Springsteen, with real bands . . . He might have started that way with Sweeney Todd, taking over for Nick Gilder. You could have said that was a poppy little teen band, but he didn't embrace that. He did it because he was trying to get ahead . . . Bryan was a hit songwriter and not ashamed of it, and to have hit songs, you needed video.**

The video for "Summer of '69," one of the many memorable songs from *Reckless*, was part of that group of videos that were shot at the same time. I asked Bryan about the making of that one.

BRYAN ADAMS **It was mostly made up of a little set where we're supposed to be a young band practising and the set falls over and the rest was just "Bryan stands next to girl, girl and Bryan fade from black and white to colour," which I suppose was to represent the past and the future. There are some moments of stomping out a fire, falling out of a hammock and running through a warehouse, which have nothing to do with the song at all. In fairness to Steve, it was shot as a five-song video compilation over a few days . . . as a sort of film that went with the release of the album. There wasn't much thought put into it.**

Like almost every artist, Bryan had a story of how things can go wrong on a video shoot.

BRYAN ADAMS **The biggest disaster was on the video for "Run to You." The set designers couldn't find a real tree anywhere that would match the description of the script vision, so they decided (at some expense) to build a fucking tree in a studio, and the plan**

was it was going to be hit by lightning. **The big moment to test the lightning came and the fake lightning hit the tree, and being that it was made entirely of Styrofoam and some other massively flammable substance, it naturally burst into flames and burnt to the ground within about thirty seconds. End of prop, end of shot. Luckily for everyone concerned, the cameraman ran film to test the camera. The tree was central to the theme of the video, but because it was gone, we resorted to my spinning around in the rain with a guitar (something one always does with a guitar) and getting soaked to the bone and eventually catching a cold.**

Another common theme was the high price-tag for video making, rarely part of the discussion in the planning stages. Again, Bryan's videos were no exception.

BRYAN ADAMS I suppose the biggest "production" we did was for "Heaven," with all the TV screens. I don't want to think what we spent to do that video, but it thankfully got played.

All three songs were top 10 in the U.S. and in many countries around the world, but "Heaven" gave Adams his first *Billboard* magazine #1 song. Maybe this makes it easier to justify the cost of making the video! Bruce Allen has no regrets.

BRUCE ALLEN Video gave Bryan Adams a face, but the most important thing it did was let people know that this guy was a real live act and he could sell some tickets. He had the hits; they knew they were going to see a rock show and away we went and I've got to attribute a lot of that to MTV and MuchMusic without a doubt.

Seven years later, with the release of *Waking Up the Neighbours*, Adams topped his own previous success in all respects. "(Everything I Do) I Do It for You," the theme song from the film *Robin Hood: Prince of Thieves,* was #1 on the Billboard charts for seven weeks and was the top song of 1991 according to the industry publication as well.

Bryan had this amusing recollection from the video that accompanied the song.

BRYAN ADAMS Julien Temple [who had directed videos for David Bowie, Culture Club, Depeche Mode and others] was hired by the film company to direct the video of "Everything I Do." I'd never worked with him, as his videos were always quite dance oriented/ choreographed, and my vids needed to be a bit rougher. Anyway, his script had this elaborate detail of a storm with lightning, which sounded good. Lightning storms were a thing with directors back then. So after a day of shooting random shots of me wandering

At first I hated [video]. I thought how dare this medium put pictures in people's minds of a song when, to me, the music was a thing where you'd close your eyes and form your own story. But then I got to the fact that, "Wait a minute, this is going across the country," and it's actually helping sell records. So quickly I got to like it. Kim Mitchell

aimlessly on a beach (not in the script), and me walking around here and there in the English countryside (also not in the script), I asked him what was happening with the lightning scene. He pointed at one of the lighting grips, who was hanging off a ladder with a large PARcan [a type of electric light used in films] with a diffuser [for spreading light to soften it] attached to it, which blinked on and off like a navy Morse code light, and he said, 'It's right there." The grip waved at me.

Bruce Allen's perspective differs from Bryan's own view of what Bryan refers to as "my dreadful videos."

BRUCE ALLEN Now some of those videos bother him; he looks back . . . he judges them too harshly; I thought they did a helluva job for us. When we go out now on the road and we play "Kids Wanna Rock," and the video plays in the back on twenty panels and you see what he was like when he was that age. It's cool for the fans because they grew up with him. You can't be precious about that; I tried to tell him this is great stuff to these people. Just like your songs are great stuff.

I asked Bruce about seeing Much for the first time.

BRUCE ALLEN As Canadians do, and we're hard on our own, I thought it was a poor copy. It's like the CFL versus the NFL—it's kind of okay, but it's a poor copy.

Adams has a clear-eyed take on what distinguished MuchMusic from its American counterpart.

BRYAN ADAMS Much became a progressive video channel more than MTV, playing different content and . . . broke videos and played unknown artists before anyone else.

7 The Power Hour

LAURIE BROWN Hosting the *Power Hour* was the last thing I saw myself doing at Much.

Laurie had been called into John Martin's office. "John grinned at me. This was exactly the kind of trickster move he loved. I protested that I didn't really know the music, and the sexism and blatant female exploitation and degradation made me crazy. He said, 'That's why you should do it.' They were willing to put metal and Laurie in the same room and see what happened. So I did it."

The *Power Hour* was one of the original specialty shows, along with *City Limits* and the *Coca-Cola Countdown*. It became the *Pepsi Power Hour*, allegedly because Pepsi, jealous of Coke's naming rights on the countdown show, said, "We want a show, we don't care what kind of music it is." The following was large, loud and loyal, and the music was a perfect way to reject your parents' music, whether that was the Doors or Neil Sedaka. There was a strange combination of ultra-dark themes (Iron Maiden, Judas Priest, Metallica) and buffoonish theatrics (Twisted Sister, Alice Cooper) delivered by the crunch of all those Marshall stacks of amplifiers. Bulging leather pants, studded bracelets and bullet belts were featured in a fashion parade that owed its roots to the military, biker culture and a taste for all things Viking. Every serious metal act now toured with a pyro specialist, responsible for handling an array of flash pots (small containers used for creating bursts of flame and smoke onstage), flame projectors and strobes. This was show biz with bite! It was made for the arena, and being a hockey-loving nation, there was one of those in every town. Mike Campbell, co-host of *Mike and Mike's Excellent X-Canada Adventures* explains it like this.

MIKE CAMPBELL Metal was a mainstay in every nook and cranny of the country. Metal was, and is still, a rite of passage for a lot of mostly male Canadian teens. Meat-and-potatoes, party-hearty, have a good time—it is kind of a Canadian motto after all.

Metal fans relied on Much, as Sean Kelly, guitarist and author of *Metal on Ice* explains.

SEAN KELLY Growing up in North Bay—the music I liked, I wasn't hearing on my local radio station. I was relying on MuchMusic to

(Above) Brent "The Doctor" Doerner, Brian Vollmer,
Daryl Gray and Greg "Fritz" Hinz of Helix
(Right) Christopher Ward, Crüeton-for-a-day, with
Nikki Sixx and Tommy Lee of Mötley Crüe

**tell me what was good. What
MuchMusic did was show me that
the Canadian acts were every bit as
good as the American ones. To me it
was a revelation to see a band like
Helix—and they're from Kitchener—
and I'd been to Kitchener! And
they're playing these big polished
tunes, and they're coming to my
arena. Mötley Crüe aren't coming to
my arena. And neither are Twisted
Sister, but Helix are.**

Although metal itself was a branch on the family tree of rock, there were many
species of metal that sprang up in the wake of Zeppelin and Sabbath—
sub-genres like thrash, speed, death and glam metal. They were all
featured on the *Power Hour*, but the one that dominated the airwaves was
glam metal, referred to by a term that was then considered derisive, but
which since has been nostalgically adopted by many of the bands' fans:
hair metal.

Now, no self-respecting act in the '80s would have referred to themselves
as a 'hair metal' band, but from the post-millennial high ground we smirk a
little, downplay our earlier affection and slap a label on them. But who doesn't
recall fondly a time of global aerosol shortages and girlfriends calling out
from the bathroom, 'Honey, have you seen my mascara?'

In this land where leather gave way to spandex, the music itself was built on a foundation of crunchy guitars, a thick layer of power chords, and musical structures not unfamiliar to country music. A healthy dollop of attitude, accompanied by some flamboyant and muscular drumming (see Tommy Lee), and voila!

KISS-style party-posturing dominated lyrically. Think Quiet Riot's "Cum on Feel the Noize" (even if it was a Slade retread from the '70s), or Canada's Helix and "Rock You." These bands made their bones touring, taking the party to all the towns along the Trans-Canada Highway. As leader Brian Volmer recalls, Helix earned their stripes on the road,

BRIAN VOLLMER On six or seven nights a week in bars across Canada on lots of alcohol and lots of amphetamines. We made a hundred-and-fifty bucks a week, maybe. We knew sixty different ways to cook macaroni-and-cheese on a hotplate in the hotel room.

Have you ever looked at some of these reviewers? These guys are in bad shape. They don't exactly have groupies, right? They might be a bit frustrated.

Nikki Sixx, Mötley Crüe

J.D. Roberts with Dee Snider
of Twisted Sister

For the "Rock You" video, Helix's label turned to the omnipresent Rob Quartly.

ROB QUARTLY I had just done an Anne Murray video earlier in the week, so Helix was the perfect juxtaposition. We were at the Brickworks all night—fire, water. I thought, "What does heavy rock look like?" I remember shooting the lead guitarist; he would go underwater, wait for the water to settle and then come bursting up out of the water with his guitar. We had a nurse there just in case.

Despite the popularity of the party anthem, it was often the cheesy "power ballad" that took an act to another level. I'm inclined to pinpoint October 12, 1988, as the apotheosis of this trend, the day that Poison's "Every Rose Has Its Thorn" was released. In the video, our tattooed but sensitive hero, lead singer Bret Michaels, laments his outcast state in the song's tortured lyric.

There's a substantial lineage in the mighty power ballad, going back to "Stairway to Heaven" (yes, I recognize the heresy in this assertion), Nazareth's "Love Hurts" and Lynyrd Skynyrd's "Free Bird." But Poison, I believe, was its death knell, followed by many tepid variations on the form, like Winger's "Headed for a Heartbreak." and "Still Loving You" by the Scorpions.

The cascading ringlets of Dee Snider should be emblematic of an entire subset of hair metal. But as original VJ J.D. Roberts found out, the band took their rough-and-tumble attitude quite seriously.

J.D. ROBERTS Twisted Sister was at the height of their popularity when they stopped by Much. They didn't want to just show up on set when we came back from commercial, so we orchestrated a Hun-like attack on our studios to bring them in. We had a camera out in the hallway when we came up live. Dee Snider led the charge as they stormed the set. I figured that as he got close to me, he'd put on the brakes and hop into the interview position beside me. Instead, blond curls whirling, he executed a flying tackle on me. We all went over the back of the desk together, a mass of Oyster Bay flesh and heavy metal fashion. Snider is not a small guy. When he landed on me, a spike on his studded belt dug deep into my elbow. The hook-shaped gash oozed blood all the way

Lee Aaron and J.D. Roberts

through our interview. For years after, I had a badge of honour and a great story to tell. But looking at my elbow now, the scar has finally faded. It's remarkable that the band outlasted the wound.

Metal holds a powerful place in late '80s, early '90s musical memory, at least partly because it's gone and it's easier to be nostalgic about something that has a tombstone on it, even if it's one with umlauts and that weird gothic script. Grunge came along and said 'see ya' to hair metal. What could Warrant, Ratt and Cinderella say when Pearl Jam and Nirvana showed up? It was like the "Bobby" era of early sixties pop music, as Bill Wyman of the Stones referred to it, that washed out to sea in the wake of the British Invasion. Bobby Vinton versus the Beatles. Hmmm. Bobby Vee versus the Kinks. Bobby Sherman versus anyone. You see what I mean.

In a genre of music where most of the guys looked like women, where were the heavy metal femmes fatales? The ones who actually looked good in lipstick and platform shoes? The women—who are they? The Runaways? Lita Ford, maybe, but Joan Jett was always a punk, no? Vixen—c'mon, Richard Marx wrote their hit, "Edge of a Broken Heart." That's problematic. But hold on—in Canada we had a serious contender, one who could really sing, who was gorgeous and managed to balance femininity and a seriously fierce stage attitude.

LEE AARON I came from musical theatre, that's how I got discovered. But I was very shy and really intimidated by the audiences at first and I didn't have any idea what I was doing. My first manager took me to see the movie *The Rose*, and a lot of my original persona was stylized after Bette Midler's character in that movie. Then I realized the power of putting my foot on someone's table and I ran with it.

Her biggest hit, "Metal Queen," caused a major dust-up at Much.

LEE AARON You have to remember I was quite a young girl when I did that. I didn't have a huge political agenda at the time, but it was about female empowerment, women standing up for themselves, being treated as equals to men. For the video, we said, "Let's create this dream scenario where she's a female warrior." I showed up and they had this costume from Malabar [a longtime Toronto costume rental company]. I said, "Hey, I can do Raquel Welch in a fur bikini," having no idea the effect this would have. MuchMusic was in its infancy and they were looking for powerful videos to put in rotation.

Behind the scenes at Much there was a strong movement to ban the video with its bondage imagery, but some of us fought back to have it played, pointing out that the singer emerges in control at the end of the video.

LEE AARON All the bands of the ilk that we come from objectified women. When I made the video for "Whatcha Do to My Body," we tried to flip that coin and objectify the men on purpose and that gained us a lot of women fans.

Snakes, lizards and other serpents— representations of evil in Western mythology—coil through many videos. Simulated sexual activity, often of the perverse, unnatural kind—at least one hopes it is simulated—is depicted hourly.

Saskatoon StarPhoenix, April 24, 1989

Spiñal Tap, I believe, deserve a chapter or a book of their own, and several books have been written about the film. Even as a complete parody, they've influenced how we see the metal genre. And every musician since 1984, when *This Is Spiñal Tap* came out, has had to be able to quote major chunks of dialogue from David St. Hubbins, Derek Smalls and Nigel Tufnel, or risk scorn. The U.S. Library of Congress deemed the picture "culturally, historically, or aesthetically significant"! And it's been established through rigorous testing that D minor is, indeed, the saddest of all keys. There was an oft-repeated rumour at the time that German heavy metallers the Scorpions went to see the film and stormed out, deeply insulted. I guess someone had to be.

The question of legitimacy looms as large as a band's cool factor, and there were some tough choices to make regarding who belonged on the metal bus and who didn't. Sean Kelly, guitarist and author, says the distinction was completely clear.

SEAN KELLY Keyboards was the defining factor between what was metal and what was not. That was a faux-pas to have keyboards on stage, even though everybody had them on the records. I loved keyboards but I couldn't openly admit that. I couldn't tell my friends I was going to see Platinum Blonde. Of course, if you were lucky enough to have a girlfriend, you were listening to bands with keyboards!

In the pantheon of heavy metal bands, one stands above all. Not in sales, glamour or posturing, but in reputation, where it counts. Motörhead are revered. And there was no risk of seeing a keyboard at a Motörhead show. Although they formed in '75, it seems like they have been around forever.

Christopher Ward with Jon Bon Jovi

(Even today, the autocorrect on my iPhone adds the umlaut over the second 'O' in the band's name.) Formed and fronted by Lemmy Kilmister, the stated goal was that the music be so loud, that if they moved in next door, your lawn would die. I seldom hosted the *Power Hour*, but on one rare occasion that I did, the show was co-hosted, sort of, in the sub-sub-basement at 299 Queen Street, by Lemmy and Philthy Phil. Each of my co-hosts had a 26-ounce bottle of booze under his chair—Lemmy was drinking Jack Daniels, and I believe Phil favoured gin. Naturally, things deteriorated rapidly until it was time to give away the life-sized Motörhead poster. The boys, feeling a little peckish after the beverage course, decided to eat the poster, live on air.

A separation must be made between the men and the men-who-look-like-women. There might be a teased-up, frizzy dividing line that leaves Van Halen, Def Leppard, Aerosmith and Guns N' Roses on one side, and Dokken, White Lion and Hanoi Rocks on the other, but the difference that mattered was, and always will be, the songs. Def Lep, with the genius of Mutt Lange behind them (he produced the record, co-wrote all the songs as well as recorded many of the guitar parts and backing vocals on *Hysteria*), Aerosmith with some serious song-doctor hired hands and Loverboy, with the core writing team of vocalist Mike Reno and Paul Dean, aided by contributions from Bryan Adams, Jim Vallance, and producer Bruce Fairbairn, recorded hits that still sound great and have outlasted the visuals.

But if you had to pick the ultimate hair metal band, wouldn't it be the New Jersey cowboys, riding their steel horses to fame and fortune? They combined killer songs with big-time charisma and an attitude that said "it's all about our fans." And yes, Jon Bon Jovi had great hair.

By the end of her time hosting the *Power Hour*, Laurie had embraced the gig.

LAURIE BROWN Never have I come across fans so dedicated to their music. It wasn't a fad or a phase. It wasn't about how cute a band was, it wasn't even about how popular they were. In fact, the more obscure the better. They loved the music wholeheartedly. And they wrote me about it. Constantly. I received more letters from *Power Hour* fans than any other viewers of Much, and most of those letters were from Canadian prisons. These guys—and they were all guys—would lay their stories out for me and then talk about the music they loved. Heartbreaking stories and I could tell for many of these men, writing letters was not something they did often. I felt very honoured that they would make the effort to write. I still get cabbies giving me free rides because of hosting the *Power Hour*. That rocks. And so do they.

"Cave Girl"
Laurie Brown

8 Rock Royalty

Much never had any difficulty attracting the biggest international stars to come to the studio and sit down for an interview. Even the holdouts like Madonna came around, and had a great time in the wide-open, easy-going environment. It was an obvious call for the labels given that Much functioned like a national radio station, with a very engaged viewership, representing an efficient way to reach an act's target audience.

DURAN DURAN

A telegenic band like Duran Duran was made for Much and the crush of fans on the street confirmed it. A young and relatively inexperienced Erica Ehm was given the opportunity of interviewing one of the biggest bands in the world.

ERICA EHM I remember my interview with Duran Duran because I was freaking out. I'd been on the air for three or four months and everyone was going, "Erica is going to fuck it up," because I hadn't done many interviews. I wasn't actually a big fan of the band so I wasn't nervous to talk to them because I didn't really care emotionally, but I was on the spot professionally.

In the eyes of management, Erica was a representative of the young viewers, even if some of them were highly critical of her work. She bridged the gap deftly by asking the questions the fans wanted answers to.

ERICA EHM Simon, how did you meet Yasmin?

SIMON LE BON I'd seen her picture in a magazine . . . this is what rock stars do. They go through *Vogue* and other fashion magazines, picking out girls and phoning up the agencies. I did it once and I ended up marrying her. Oh my!

JOHN TAYLOR You tell them you want them for a video, that's really clever.

(Above) Erica Ehm with Simon Le Bon, Nick Rhodes and John Taylor of Duran Duran
(Left) Erica with Nick and Simon
(Opposite) Duran Duran fans

Duran Duran were exactly what you hoped they'd be—cute, cheeky, and a little out of touch with reality.

ERICA Why did Roger [Taylor, the band's original drummer] leave?

SIMON LE BON He got to a point where him and the music business just weren't working well together and he decided for the sake of his own piece of mind he'd be better off getting out of it. The pressure of interviews and photo sessions and going up and standing there in front of thousands of people was not the kind of life he wanted to lead.

So, there you have it. The departure of original band member, Roger Taylor, was due not to musical differences or personality conflicts or poor health, but to "the pressure of interviews and photos sessions"! Imagine the toll one of those babe-filled videos took on the man!

The band took to Erica immediately and when Simon and Nick Rhodes returned as Arcadia [a one-album side-project between Duran albums] the following year, Erica was the host again.

YOU READ ABOUT THEM.
YOU ONLY SAW THEM IN
BIG VENUES OR WHEN
THEY DID SOMETHING FOR
THE QUEEN BUT ALL OF
A SUDDEN THEY'RE
ON QUEEN STREET.
THEY'RE RIGHT THERE.

George Stroumboulopoulos (on Duran Duran)

She handled the interview brilliantly and a bit of silly but entertaining rock 'n' roll theatre took place. Erica recalls a layer that the audience likely wouldn't have seen.

ERICA EHM When I started to do the interview I saw that Simon and the guys wanted to fool around, have some fun and I was completely comfortable with that. Every time Simon did something that was a little bit kooky, he looked me in the eye and I could tell he was checking to make sure that I was okay with it.

NICK RHODES So, tell me, how long have you been working for MuchMusic?

SIMON LE BON (Pointing water pistol) Tell him!

ERICA EHM I'll tell, just don't shoot. It's been seven months.

Simon strokes Erica's leopard print jacket.

ERICA It's quite nice, isn't it?

SIMON Pussycats don't like water.

NICK You get to talk with some famous rock stars.

ERICA My favourite was a band called Arcadia.

NICK She's trying to be clever.

SIMON Either that or she's trying to confuse us, and I'm very easily confused.

Follies involving cake and water pistols ensue.

DAVID BOWIE

It seemed like no one wanted to play it straight when they came to Much, as Laurie Brown found out when she sat down with the legendary David Bowie.

DAVID BOWIE Hi, This is David Bowie. Welcome to my show. I have a special guest for us today, Miss Laurie Brown. The last time we met was in Paris.

David Bowie on Queen Street with fans

LAURIE It was Paris. It was June.

BOWIE How's the tour going? You look very good. It's such a strenuous tour, it must have taken a lot out of you.

Laurie also remembers what a friend to Much Bowie was and how engaged on his many visits.

Laurie Brown with David Bowie

LAURIE BROWN One of the best moments of my career at Much was when Bowie, somewhere in the states performing at some event, noticed a Much camera and turned to camera and said, "Hi, Laurie." That pretty much made my decade.

In the wake of his passing in January 2016 she adds this:

LAURIE BROWN I have been saying how curious he was—and how he was equally interested in what I thought, what I was listening to, what I was thinking. He was always curious, always courteous, respectful and always gave great interview.

ROBERT PLANT

One of the first major interviews at Much, a true encounter with a legend, was when Robert Plant came by in the summer of 1985. J.D. Roberts was stoked.

J.D. ROBERTS Led Zeppelin was an iconic band in my life. They were what I was listening to growing up. I remember dropping the needle on *Led Zeppelin II* and hearing the 'ba-da-da-da-dun' of "Whole Lotta Love." It was a total game changer. I had never heard anything like that before. As much of a fan as I was, I never had the chance to see them in concert, so meeting Robert one-on-one was an amazing opportunity.

If Mike Williams thought he had a shot at that interview, he soon found out how wrong he was!

MICHAEL WILLIAMS I remember Robert Plant came in on my shift, but J.D. was going to get that interview. He was like a puppy with a pork chop.

In keeping with the "nothing is sacred" philosophy that ruled at Much, a little buffoonery was cooked up for the occasion.

J.D. ROBERTS Our rooftop interview almost ended in tragedy, though. While we were on the air, producer Michael Heydon was to play the part of a bicycle courier and deliver a gold record for the Honeydrippers album, along with a bottle of champagne to celebrate the moment. The roof was topped in about two inches of pebble gravel. As Michael pedalled his way toward us in a [Flying] Wallenda–like attempt to balance the award and champagne, his front wheel dug into the gravel. He pitched left and nearly soared off the edge of the roof. He narrowly avoided a four-storey plummet to the alleyway below. The viewers were unaware that anything was amiss, but he was as white as a sheet when he pulled up on the set.

Michael did manage to sustain the gag and pretended to be in awe of meeting J.D., and completely oblivious as to who Robert Plant was. Robert was totally amused by this. During the interview, he addressed the issue of living with his famous past, and why he is driven to move on.

ROBERT PLANT I want to make everything, to some degree, dangerous because I don't like middle ground. I don't like half of what I hear and what I see. It's too easy. It's like somebody shelling peas. You can make a million versions of "Whole Lotta Love," and they can still be played, but there's no reason for me to subscribe to that and join the bandwagon.

> Heroes are made by saying nothing at all.
> Robert Plant

This is an artist who has had a remarkable post–rock God career by following his muse, whether it was with the Honeydrippers or Band of Joy or his collaboration with Alison Krauss, *Raising Sand*, which won an Album of the Year Grammy, an honour that eluded the mighty Zeppelin. Still, it seemed he wasn't yet ready to hang up his codpiece.

ROBERT PLANT I like the lobbies to be filled with women.

Iggy Pop performing on
Intimate and Interactive

IGGY POP

In stark contrast, Simon Evans, producer of *City Limits* and host of *The Wedge*, picked Iggfest, a wild, two-hour live event with Iggy Pop that he hosted and produced, as a career highlight. The venue was *Intimate and Interactive,* a series of live performances by artists including Alanis Morissette, Green Day, Mary J. Blige, Barenaked Ladies and Coldplay. MTV had the *Unplugged* series but *I&I,* as it came to be known, featured not only live-to-air performances in front of a small studio audience, but also questions from viewers via phone and fax as well as the audience in attendance. Iggy took it to a whole other level.

DENNIS SAUNDERS, director Nothing was planned. [We said] you've got two hours and a live network. What do you want to do? He loved it. In the paper the next day it said, "Best *I&I* ever." And there was critical acclaim from the industry.

During the two hours, they took calls, questions from the audience and invited people inside from the street. Simon held a mic for Iggy as he climbed out the window into a crowd on Queen Street and improvised a song that might be called "Out on the Street."

Iggy ran through various topics of conversation from the Sex Pistols' Steve Jones's sex habits to, in response to an audience question, Iggy's favourite hair colour.

IGGY POP Natural is my favourite colour of hair because it has a better shine, Ed.

And, in case you were wondering,

IGGY POP I really like Courtney Love. It's a cool name, sounds like a porno actress. I used to go out with strippers and porno girls years ago and they were always nice.

Throw in a little philosophy and you've got it covered.

IGGY POP When I got involved, rock 'n' roll was considered a sleazy, extended-boyhood occupation for greasers who were on a downhill slide.

And Simon summed it up leading into a commercial break.

SIMON EVANS We'll be right back after this if we still have a licence.

ROBERT PALMER

Robert Palmer represented a highlight for two on-air personalities for quite different reasons. Michael Williams felt there was a high fashion standard to live up to.

MICHAEL WILLIAMS I remember getting dressed in a Pal Zileri suit, which I got on loan, to interview Robert Palmer. I thought, "I can't look like shit." I was such a fan of his.

Palmer was relaxed, candid and self-deprecating.

ROBERT PALMER [I want to do] music that's not stadium rock; it's not showcases; it's not disco. It needs an environment to enjoy it, preferably with people dancing, having a romantic, relaxed, elegant evening. Now, of course it's a fantasy. (Laughs.)

You can see why Ziggy Lorenc, *MushMusic* host, describes him as her favourite interview subject.

ZIGGY LORENC Robert Palmer, one of the most old-school, elegant men in pop. But first he had to take off his suit jacket, roll up his sleeves and have a double Scotch. I felt like saying, "Can I do this interview on your lap?"

Kate Bush and Christopher Ward

KATE BUSH

I had a few encounters with rock royalty myself. One that surprised me by how passionate her fans were was Kate Bush. I asked about the story behind her video for the song "Cloudbusting," which featured Donald Sutherland. Here's the thoughtful answer I got.

KATE BUSH I really wanted it to be a short piece of film. I didn't want it to be seen as a promotional clip. Part of that was having an actor, hopefully a great actor, play the part of the father and myself playing the part of the young boy. The song was inspired by a book that's all about a very special relationship between the guy that wrote the book, as a child and his father. His father was a very respected psychiatrist and . . . had this machine called the cloudbuster that could make it rain, and together they'd go out into the dry desert and make it rain, and this was a very magical moment for the child. Unfortunately, the peak of the book is that his father's arrested. His beliefs were considered outrageous. It was very hard for the child to cope without his father and in some ways the connection with rain for him, every time it rains, he thinks of his father.

The rarity of this encounter was only reinforced with time, given that this was the last trip to North America the reclusive star made, and it was thirty years ago. This interview was one of a small handful that were awe-inspiring to many of my friends, including Mike Myers, who wanted to touch the hand that touched the hand and demanded a detailed account of my meeting, including how Kate smelled. Good, as I recall.

GEORGE HARRISON

The ultimate "holy shit" moment for me was when a Beatle came to Much in March of 1988. Technical director Sylvie Marcoux said it was like church in the studio when George Harrison arrived. I was once the schoolyard geek who did four separate Beatles impersonations, not just the generic one that we'd all been working on. The Beatles were the reason I became a songwriter. "Can't Buy Me Love" was the first song I learned from my cousin on guitar. The last show I'd lined up to get tickets for was the George solo show at Maple Leaf Gardens in 1974, the one with the Shankar family. How desperately I'd wanted Beatle boots with the Cuban heels. Denied by parents who were not thrilled with the fringe that was working its way down my forehead when I emerged from the rock 'n' roll sanctuary of my room. All is now forgiven.

We'd had a false start on this interview a few weeks earlier, but we'd been assured that it would happen this time. There was a major security condition that we not announce it was coming up. Can you imagine today, something like that not getting out somehow? When I think back, it's amazing that George even made this visit, given that the interview was live, if unannounced beforehand, and people could and did come down to the station once they saw him on-air. He was also the one member of the Beatles who described their fame as "a prison," an impression at odds with images of the hotel pillow fights, cheeky press conferences and happy group waves as they descended from yet another airplane to hysterical crowds.

I was nervous, as you would expect of a man meeting a childhood hero, but I was also prepared and the conversation flowed easily. He talked about writing songs with Jeff Lynne (record producer and leader of Electric Light Orchestra) in a new style for him, his regret at "Something" being licensed for a car commercial, the strange sound of the Beatles on CD as opposed to vinyl and his comfort with taking time off to be creative.

GEORGE HARRISON You don't always have to be in the public eye to exist.

George Harrison and Christopher Ward

There was a moment when I thought I was losing him to the minutiae of the topic when he dove into some serious esoterica about primitive studio technology. Of course the nerd in me was thrilled to hear how the lads had used tape loops.

GEORGE HARRISON The first one we did that on was a track on [*Revolver*] called "Tomorrow Never Knows." We all made up little abstract sounds on our home tape machines. You stick them together on a loop around the playback head and hold it with a pencil to keep it tight. We had all these things on different machines. And then we'd mix them all into the record.

But then a low-grade panic swelled until we got back on track. I asked if he'd heard that Paul was considering doing an album of John Lennon songs and we got a flash of the wry George wit.

GEORGE HARRISON Paul? Maybe because he ran out of good ones of his own. (Laughs.)

CHRISTOPHER WARD Well, now we've got that on record.

GEORGE HARRISON It's true.

We did return to the present day, talking about making videos, specifically working with Kevin Godley and Lol Creme (members of the band 10cc and later Godley & Creme, and the directing team behind Peter Gabriel's "Sledgehammer" and Duran Duran's "Girls on Film") on George's "When We Was Fab." For the video, they had George performing the nostalgic Beatles-style song in front of a brick wall while various sight gags took place featuring Ringo Starr and others.

GEORGE HARRISON I was a bit nervous because Godley and Creme are a couple of loonies, especially Lol [Creme]. They're very sweet but I wasn't sure if they knew exactly what they were doing. I found out they knew sort of ninety percent what they were doing and the other ten percent was a bit of a grey area. But it was very good, very funny. I approached them. I said, "Go home and smoke something, listen to this and come up with an idea." They came up with the idea and after a few days they started panicking. They said, "It's not going to work, it's not going to work." And they tried to get out of it and I said, "Don't panic now." I had to do it; I had three or four days before Christmas and it had to be done, so I said, "Just go for a walk in the garden, have a cup of tea, calm down, and then I'll talk to you in an hour." And I talked to them in an hour and they said, "I think it'll be okay."

After the interview George commented to me, "We got into stuff there which I never dreamed of. It's good. It makes it different to all the other stuff I've been talking about." He then looked around at the ongoing chaos that was MuchMusic, and in typical understatement, added, "This is a very casual program."

NIRVANA

Rock 'n' roll mints new heroes and new royalty with surprising speed. Sometimes the ascent and descent happen in a hurry and the fast fades of Falco and Ratt were likely not mourned by many. The early years at Much saw acts like the Beastie Boys and Duran Duran, seeming to be sure candidates for early burnout who turned out to have amazing sustaining power; and artists like Tina Turner, Don Henley and ZZ Top have second acts that many would not have foreseen. One band that seemed poised for a long run at the top, based on their startling originality and the deep connection they made with their fans, was Nirvana. The band formed in 1987 and their first release was *Bleach* from 1989, followed by the ground-breaking *Nevermind* in 1991. At this point Kurt Cobain was arguably the most influential artist in popular music.

In August 1993 Erica Ehm interviewed the band in Seattle on the eve of the release of their third album, *In Utero*. Cobain already had a remarkably clear perspective on what they were trying to accomplish.

KURT COBAIN This is the last chapter of three-chord grunge music for us. It was an easy and safe thing to do because we knew it's still popular. We had to get it out of our systems.

Erica talked about her interview with the members of Nirvana, and in particular Kurt Cobain.

ERICA EHM He was very reserved so when we started to talk, I thought, "He is quite different than I [expected]." There was little edge to him; he was very vulnerable and a very nice guy.

He acknowledged the challenge of entering the mainstream without losing loyal fans.

KURT COBAIN A couple of years ago when we were making these bold negative statements . . . we were really confused and afraid we would lose a lot of our audience, people that meant a lot to us, people that we hopefully feel we have a connection with, the

college students, people in the underground. I don't think we've lost them. I think they're still fans. I'm not worried about it anymore.

This was a band with massive success that still saw itself as a group of outsiders, a classic artistic conundrum.

KURT COBAIN I know that I'm too stubborn to allow myself to ever compromise our music or get so wrapped up in it and involved to where it'll turn us into big rock stars. I just don't feel like that. Everyone else accuses us of it. We're just not as popular as everyone thinks. We're not as rich as everyone thinks.

Knowing that Kurt Cobain would die a little over six months later makes what he said about family heartbreaking.

KURT COBAIN I was a lot more negative and angry a few years ago and that had a lot to do with not having a mate, a steady girlfriend. That was one of the main things that was bothering me that I wouldn't admit at the time. Now that I found that, the world just seems a lot better. It really does change your attitude. Four years ago I would have said the classic thing, "How dare someone bring a child into this life? It's a terrible way to go and the world's going to explode any day." But once you fall in love it's different.

Erica remembered her reaction when she heard of his death by suicide.

ERICA EHM I had to host a three-hour live segment [the day after he died] and I was so angry. I was angry at him because I also am very much aware of people's responsibility in the public eye to their audience, and I thought, "You selfish bastard, you are now potentially going to incite other teenagers to kill themselves." . . . Of course, my heart went out to him but I was very worried at the message he was sending out to kids.

Like anyone who was moved by Cobain's music, Erica tried to understand what had affected him.

ERICA EHM I think for the most part, rock 'n' roll is very superficial and I think that was one of the things, when I read about Kurt Cobain, is that he didn't like the facade of rock 'n' roll because he's down to earth; he was a normal guy and the trappings of fame really bothered him because it's hypocritical. You're wearing your plaid shirt and your ripped-up clothes and your greasy hair but you have so much money, you're living like Donald Trump. It doesn't make sense; how do you keep that lie up?

Erica asked Dave Grohl, Nirvana drummer, later of Foo Fighters, about the media scrutiny the band was under.

DAVE GROHL I don't pay attention to the media at all. If I was to pay attention to everything written about the band, it would break my heart because there's so many stupid lies and speculation, so I don't pay attention to it. Plus, everybody wants to write something about Nirvana. It's kind of stupid because we're just three normal people, relatively normal, who play in a band, and people have turned us into "the godfathers of grunge." It's just music. It's just a band. It's no big deal to us, I suppose.

Grohl, originally from Ohio, also addressed the influence of life in Seattle.

DAVE GROHL I remember before I moved here I always read these interviews with bands that said, "The reason there's so many bands is because you can't really do anything outside because it rains so much. Everyone's stuck in the basement and there's nothing better to do than start a band." I first read that and thought, "That's stupid, there's just a lot of good bands." But [now] I think it might be true.

Strangely, for a musician at age twenty-four, he was already looking ahead to a very different life.

DAVE GROHL I can sit here and say I'll do this for a few more years and then I'll have a normal life, but I know that in ten years I'll miss it. There's a lot of things I'll miss. There's a lot of things I'll be glad I don't have to deal with anymore . . . I'll miss being onstage with Kris and Kurt and some of the insane shit that happens when we play.

MADONNA

The sidewalk outside the station was jammed; the studio was full and there was a charge in the air. When Tony "Master T" Young was assigned the live *Intimate and Interactive* interview with Madonna in March of 1998 (minus the live music component that was typical of the show), he felt the pressure from "the street-corner critics" as well as from his boss, Denise Donlon. But not so much that he lost perspective.

MASTER T That interview changed everything in terms of my recognizability. That same week I had K-Ci & JoJo on, and Denise

kept coming to me, "Have you watched every interview ever done with Madonna?" I said, "No, that's not me." And she said, "We've got all these interviews in the library, you should go and watch them all." I said, "No, right now I've got to focus on K-Ci & JoJo because they're huge to my community." She kept asking, "Are you okay?" Terry David Mulligan wanted it, everybody wanted it, and I was thinking, "Oh fuck, I've got K-Ci & JoJo coming in, and they used to be in *Jodeci*."

Tony found a connection with Madonna that enabled the control freak in her to relax and enjoy the untamed atmosphere at Much.

MASTER T I knew I had her because Much was my house and she'd never done a live interactive interview like that, that close to her fans. She was nervous. These people kept coming up to me, talking in my ear and she said, "Why don't you just leave the guy alone?" I said, "This is all part of it," and she said, "I don't know how you do it." I felt like her guard was down.

Perhaps inevitably, Madonna found a way to take the interview where she wanted it to go.

MASTER T She asked me, "Have you heard the new record [*Ray of Light*]?" and I said yes, and she said, "What do you think of it?" and when you get that question, you'd better have listened to it.
"I could see the level of transition you've gone through for this record; you've lost a bunch of people. I sat down and listened to this album in the dark."

Some classic Much-style spontaneity contributed to making the interview memorable.

MASTER T Madonna was getting more and more comfortable and someone asked if she sang in the shower. She replied that she sang Frank Sinatra songs and when I asked which song, she said, "'My Way,'" and I said, "Of course, how stupid of me." I asked her to show me some yoga. So I took my jacket and shoes off and got into some painful position and it was fun. I was not the biggest Madonna fan, which is probably why it worked.

YOU'RE
RIGHT UP
THERE
BESIDE THE
POPE AND
RONALD
McDONALD

A BIRD'S NEST WITH A HORSE TAIL HANGING OUT THE BACK.

9 The Look

Entire eras tend to get reduced to a few highlights and headlines. For the early years at Much, I can imagine the voice-over and see the parade of black and white images, like in the Billy Joel video "We Didn't Start the Fire": *The '60s were summed up as women's lib, the Kennedy assassination, the Beatles and the anti-war movement. Two decades later, the '80s could easily be reduced to Reaganomics, the fall of the Berlin Wall, and Cabbage Patch dolls.* The same reductionism happens with fashion: *In the '80s it was all about big shoulders and big hair!* Goodnight.

An hour spent watching MuchMusic would put the lie to that over-simplification. The basic jeans and T-shirt of Bryan Adams lived right next door to the parachute pants and fingerless gloves crowd. And then there were Devo and the B-52s.

Jeanne Beker saw rock 'n' roll and fashion from a unique perspective. Her TV career was launched on *The NewMusic* in 1979, which she co-hosted with J.D. Roberts. It was a syndicated hour-long, magazine-type show that dealt with music in a journalistic style. In 1985 she began what would become an amazing twenty-seven-year run as the host of *FashionTelevision*, later called *FT*.

VJs dressed for Halloween

JEANNE BEKER I think what happened is that the rock stars became a lot more image conscious. There was a rawness and authenticity that got lost, watered down as the importance of TV escalated. When I first started interviewing artists, I don't think they really gave a shit about TV. To them it was a bit of a nuisance, especially the New Wavers and the rockers. They didn't really know how to act on TV because no one had done that. They hadn't been interviewed in their hotel rooms and dressing rooms or in the studio. Some of them would have been on *Top of the Pops* and

done a standard "answer a few questions" interview, but we were really going into their lives and we wanted to capture them in terms of who they were.

The holdovers from the punk era had to adapt or get lost in the blur of the bright new medium. Some took to it and fashioned strong visual identities, like Talking Heads, Adam and the Ants, and Billy Idol. Others, like Blondie, even with the charismatic Deborah Harry, didn't fully make the transition to the video era, while iconoclasts like the Clash and the Ramones held on to their ripped-and-ragged roots, making that "the look."

Jeanne maintains that the spirit of punk carried on.

JEANNE BEKER It didn't die in 1980. I think it was Malcolm McLaren and Vivienne Westwood who set the tone, starting to take fashion more seriously, and starting to look back for historical references. The pirate thing, the New Romantics, Adam Ant— which was a backlash against the irreverence and non-fashion fashion of punk—it was all making a statement.

But fashion, like music, was ready for a change, as it always is, and the video revolution came along at the perfect time. The era of confrontational style featuring safety pins and razor blades, along with Doc Marten boots and Mohawk haircuts, was rapidly becoming passé (that awkward period before something becomes retro, and hence cool again). Bands with a sense of glamour and adventure emerged and combined powerful image-making with hit songs into big success. Think Duran Duran and Wham! Self-styled newcomers like Cyndi Lauper and Prince brilliantly mixed a sense of the visual with arresting musical moments. Interestingly, many of the biggest stars had a gender-bending quality to their look—Boy George, Annie Lennox and Michael Jackson.

Annie Lennox expressed her personal philosophy about where style comes from.

ANNIE LENNOX It's a natural thing. I've always been interested in clothes; I've always been a bit anti-fashion. I'm very interested in style but fashion for me is like High Street and that means hard sell and it means designers and it means lots of money and I'm a little anti that . . . I'm not very girly-girly, and I'm not terribly masculine, either, so it has to be a balance between the two things.

JEANNE BEKER When you talk about the zeitgeist, the spirit of the times, there is a commonality of attitude that you can identify by the decades. In the late '60s it was about liberation, in the '70s it was idealism and individuality, but by the '80s, it became about sexual liberation and gender identity and not just social mores like in the '60s.

Annie Lennox and Erica Ehm

One artist who straddled those eras cast a long shadow stylistically, both in sound and look. An entire generation of vocalists took their cue from David Bowie. The strangled croon of Human League, The Thompson Twins, David Byrne of Talking Heads and Robert Smith of The Cure became a hallmark sound of the time and it's hard to imagine Canadian acts like Blue Peter, Men Without Hats and Images in Vogue without Bowie as antecedent. And like Sinatra in another generation, Bowie inspired his contemporaries and those that followed with a distinct visual style as well.

One of the most image-conscious bands to emerge out of Canada in the '80s was Platinum Blonde. Mark Holmes talks about the origin of their look, and what the standard at the time was in Canada.

MARK HOLMES Bryan Adams . . . that was the look—the jeans and the T-shirt, the work boots and the "hey, let's play baseball" type thing . . . but I'm English, I came from T-Rex, David Bowie. I want makeup and glamour and glitter . . . Duran Duran, all the New Romantics, all the New Wave stuff was already available, but it wasn't coming out of Canada. So when we put the groovy New Wave image together with the hair and the makeup it kind of blew people's minds a bit.

I asked Mark who styled the band, and he laughed.

MARK HOLMES I did it all myself. I cut everybody's hair and I usually bought the clothes.

In an era where the emphasis was on the look, in some cases even more than on the sound, Platinum Blonde had to defend their choices.

MARK HOLMES Visual became such a huge part of the '80s music. People were trying the most outrageous haircuts just to somehow stand above the crowd . . . to people who'd say, "Do you think your hair and your image speaks louder than your music?" I'd say, "We went on tour with Bryan Adams. Do you know what's in his tour case? Ten exactly-the-same white T-shirts, the same blue jeans, a couple of pairs of those boots. He wears the exact same thing every night—it is an image!"

In the '80s Molly Johnson fronted the band Alta Moda, named after the Italian term for haute couture. Her band played up and down Queen Street in Toronto, which was also the heart of young fashion at the time. Although the look artists create for themselves is by its nature "of the moment," you can't usually define the transition of a trend into the mainstream so clearly as Molly does here.

MOLLY JOHNSON With Alta Moda I always had artists dress me. I had spandex suits with six arms. I had hand-painted shirts that

Mark Holmes of Platinum Blonde

melted and cracked as I performed, and then were auctioned off . . . We had backdrops painted by graffiti artists. We ran that way, lived that way, until the day Le Château opened on Queen Street. For a year there was a war between Le Château's windows and the punks. They would spray paint them every night and every morning Le Château would come and clean them. One day their windows were all punk clothes so the spray painting just enhanced them. It was at that point that we realized if you can manufacture a ripped shirt with a safety pin in it and you walk in the store and you see twelve of them in small, medium and large, we're done here.

In direct contrast to the minimalism of punk, an over-the-top attitude emerged in the mid-'80s. The opportunity that video afforded an adventurous artist like Peter Gabriel, a survivor from another age of British pop music, was a whole other canvas for his capacious imagination, along with those of the directors he worked with, like Godley & Creme. David Byrne of Talking Heads saw no limitations as the band's music developed and the accompanying videos became increasingly experimental and very entertaining. Here fashion went "big" in every sense. And it was fun—one of the most important aspects of the look of the era.

Perhaps the canniest artist of the time was one who was a master at appropriating, melding and disposing of ideas at will. Madonna began her career with a thrift-shop eclecticism that combined lingerie and bows, multiple necklaces, rosaries and crosses in a way that high-school girls could emulate and scandalize their parents. The pointy Gaultier bra and corsets came later. Jeanne remembers her first impressions of Madonna.

JEANNE BEKER In the first episode of *FashionTelevision*, we went to New York and interviewed Betsey Johnson. I knew Betsey Johnson's history with the Velvet Underground and Andy Warhol and I had incredible respect for her; she'd seen it all. She told me that Madonna was her idea of a true-blue woman who's got it down as far as image and knows what she's doing. I'd seen Madonna and she wasn't that impressive, but we always said, "She knows how to market." After that I started to look at Madonna differently, and soon she worked with Jean Paul Gaultier and she started to wear clothes that were empowering, not just the bohemian hippy-dippy look of *Desperately Seeking Susan*. She started wearing theatrical, powerful things

that made political statements in a big, bold way. In a gender-bending way, like Gaultier, she was saying that women can be as powerful as men.

I asked Jeanne who else she thought was influential at the time and got a surprising answer.

JEANNE BEKER The Stones. Jagger emerged as an older guy who had not lost his groove at all, as a performer, as a showman.

My first memory of the Stones is from the cover of their debut album in 1964, and it's one of anti-fashion; but of course, that makes its own statement. Bassist Bill Wyman talked about the origins of the Stones' look.

BILL WYMAN That wasn't an image. That was exactly what we were like. Everybody thought we or Andrew Oldham [the band's manager and producer] had created an image for the Stones, but we were like that when he met us for the first time. We were like that because we didn't have money for stage uniforms and [matching] coloured guitars and the same hair and everything. We just went on the stage the way we came off the street. We used to get out of a van or out of a Tube station or the bus, whatever we arrived in, and go straight on stage.

Was there ever a band where the look, the attitude and the spirit of the music were more in tune? Bill Wyman reflected on the earliest days of the band.

BILL WYMAN We used to sit on rusty old stools, which we carried around in the back of the van, and drink beers and smoke. That was unheard of in those days. We had the hair; we used to smoke on stage; we used to drink on stage and I used to chew gum on stage, which offended so many people when we did TV shows later. They used to ask me particularly not to chew gum on the TV in those days. We were the first band that never wore a uniform on stage. Now it's so accepted but then it was unthinkable that you would present yourself to the public without wearing a uniform.

Platinum Blonde's Mark Holmes affirms the impact of all that on a young musician.

MARK HOLMES I loved looking at photographs of the Rolling Stones smoking and drinking and the clothes they'd wear and the cavalier lifestyle—that to me was just alluring and it made the music even better.

Of course, by the time of the Ed Sullivan appearance, the Stones had graduated to fashionable suits and later to more dandyish outfits—because they could.

BILL WYMAN That was two years after we started, which is a long time in this business. And we had tidied up a bit. Without totally conforming, we had kind of smartened up. It was nice to buy nice clothes as well, once you had the money. You did want to wear a nice jacket and a great pair of boots, but you never strayed too far from that casual look.

As for the VJs, there was no expectation placed on us to come up with a look—no surprise, I guess—and there was certainly no budget for wardrobe. We all responded in our own way. To accompany her young, colourful outfits, Erica went for hats, and created a side business from it. Ever pragmatic, she offers this explanation for the choice.

ERICA EHM I started wearing hats because I've got shitty hair.

She does recall an earlier fashion choice as a teenage DJ in Montreal.

ERICA EHM I got the tightest handmade leather pants ever and I had to lie down on a table and they [needed] pliers to do them up.

Erica Ehm with Paul Langlois and Gord Downie of the Tragically Hip

Michael was all-in with the big scarves.

MICHAEL WILLIAMS I wore scarves because I didn't have the money . . . because they didn't give us a clothing budget . . . but a scarf served two functions. One: I'm from Montreal and you always had to have a scarf because you'd freeze your balls off outside, and Two: It was definitely a fashion statement. They were inexpensive Indian scarves, some had glitter, some different colours.

Laurie's look was eclectic, perhaps highlighted by two unusual outfits. One, "the rubber dress," was a singular fashion choice that is recalled with fondness by many male viewers of the time.

LAURIE BROWN The thing about a rubber dress is they're hard to get on and baby powder is usually involved, but once you get it on you need to spray it with Armor All to give it that nice shiny [look].

The second choice, no doubt celebrated by a large constituency of metal fans, was "Cave Girl."

LAURIE BROWN We did the prehistoric *Power Hour* chroma-keyed in front of Stonehenge. Where else would you be in a fur bikini? I was pregnant when I did that shoot but no one knew. I was feeling prehistoric.

Monika Deol, host and co-producer of *Electric Circus* made the bold choice of wearing traditional clothing on air.

MONIKA DEOL I always felt that clothes and fashion were not as superficial as people would like to believe. I think it's a sense of identity. I remember the first time I wore something Indian on air and everybody in the station asked, "Is it a special Indian holiday?"

The mullet
mistake. A
mean just f

Monika's choices didn't go unnoticed outside the building either.

Monika Deol with Tionne "T-Boz" Watkins, Lisa "Left Eye" Lopes and Rozonda "Chilli" Thomas of TLC

MONIKA DEOL **The shocking thing was the reaction I got from young Indian kids, writing to me, stopping me on the street, "I couldn't believe you wore a salwar kameez on MuchMusic . . . I don't dress Indian but now I'm going to." It made me think if people are going to pay attention to me because of what I look like, then I'm going to use that to break a few stereotypes. I want the Indian kids to realize we can do this and the non-Indians to realize next time you see somebody walking around in a turban or an Indian outfit, there's more to them than just what they're wearing.**

More conventionally, *I* went for the colourful shirt approach, knowing that most of the time, the camera was framed on my head and shoulders. Yes, there are some shirts that cause a head shake of regret, but by far, my most egregious fashion choices were made from the waist down. Early on there was a pair of plastic pants that I bought at Fiorucci, that epicentre of cool on East 59th Street in New York, that brought a certain amount of mockery from my colleagues, but nothing like those damned Issey Miyake black-white-and-blue knitted pants (see next page!) that I chose to sport for a VJ promo shot and which live on in infamy.

In the '80s it seemed that with the triumph of image, what was on top took on even greater significance. There was indie hair, which spoke of the

Christopher Ward, Denise Donlon, Michael Williams and Erica Ehm

free spirit who wore it. Robert Smith of the Cure was pure electroshock bed-head art. The fact that he looked like he'd had a head-on collision with a Lancôme truck just made it more weird and wonderful. It's hard to think of it as coincidence that Mike Score of A Flock of Seagulls quit his job as a hairstylist to introduce that golden waterfall look as a rock star. Gowan, Images in Vogue, the Parachute Club, Luba, the Spoons—don't try to tell me that these local heroes were strangers to backcombing and goo-in-a-jar.

When it came to hair, the VJs were as guilty of salon crimes as the artists in the videos we played. I went for purple streaks for a while, and got called on it by Tracey Ullman.

Denise Donlon went poufy; Steve Anthony swung from golden-maned rock hair to bedhead, but J.D. Roberts kept it basic. The *Toronto Star* referred to his "bushy mullet," and J.D. took his medicine.

J.D. ROBERTS The mullet was a mistake. And I don't mean just for me. It was a mistake for everyone who ever wore one. A few years back on CNN, I was interviewing Bono about meetings he was having at the United Nations. I reminded him that we had talked a few times in the early '80s when we were both sporting some awesome mullets. He told me he looks back on those days and still can't believe he did it. His mullet was much better than mine, though. Mine looked like a bird's nest with a horse tail hanging out the back.

Looking back, hair and music, like hair and fashion, have been bedmates forever. In the world of rock 'n' roll, think of the iconic looks fashioned by Elvis, the Beatles, Rod Stewart, Tina Turner, Cyndi Lauper, and Debbie

Harry of Blondie. From the Brian Jones bob to the Grace Jones flat-top, to the "boiled-egg look" favoured by Sinéad O'Connor, hair matters.

Canadian artists, for the most part, were not renowned for their fashion sense. Often it looked like a director had sent them to Le Château on a very limited budget. Looking back you can see the trends of the day in full effect in videos by Platinum Blonde, the Parachute Club and Glass Tiger. Taking on a classic, elegant approach like the one Bryan Ferry of Roxy Music featured, worked well for Paul Humphrey of Blue Peter. A few bands brought their own look to the videos. Gordon Deppe of the Spoons recalls how they came up with the wardrobe for the "Nova Heart" video.

GORDON DEPPE **The New Romantic all-white outfits and Sandy's tutu were already part of our live shows and I think that contributed quite a bit to the overall look.**

Gordon talks about watching videos as a fan himself.

GORDON DEPPE **Like a lot of people, I watched MuchMusic not only for the music, but also the look of the band: the hair, the clothes, what guitars they were playing. I may not have liked being under the microscope myself, but I sure didn't mind being a voyeur like everyone else.**

Video director Rob Quartly, who worked with the Spoons, Corey Hart, Glass Tiger and others had a golden rule for imaging.

ROB QUARTLY **I always pushed for the album cover to be done at the same time [as the video] for that glue from an image point of view. I remember with Platinum Blonde, after the album and video came out, seeing people on the street wearing the exact same wardrobe, worn the exact same way.**

Christopher Ward and
Tracey Ullman

10 The VJs—Take Two

STEVE ANTHONY

"I SOLD DAVID BOWIE'S CIGARETTE BUTT FOR TEN DOLLARS TO A FAN OUTSIDE."

The second wave of VJs began in 1987 with a splash. Steve Anthony was hired to replace the departing J.D. Roberts, the first of the originals to leave, and Steve wasted no time in making his imprint on the gig. Craig Halkett was there to shepherd Steve through his first day.

CRAIG HALKETT "Knock knock. Who's there? J.D. J.D. who? How quickly they forget." This was how Steve ended his first show.

Like J.D. and Michael Williams, Steve came to Much from a radio background, but one that was just a little less than conventional.

STEVE ANTHONY My expertise in radio, my attitude was, "Fuck you all, I'm going to do what I want to do." At [Toronto station] Q107 they let me do whatever I wanted, and that's what attracted MuchMusic, and that's what they encouraged. The accepted attitude was, "Do it and get your wrist slapped." They expected the unusual and would defend you if it went wrong.

Steve's chaotic style was engaging partly because it was so unpredictable.

STEVE ANTHONY At the end of the interviews we had a game, where some trust was required, called "Braino!" You'd march the artist over to the water cooler, which always had really cold water in it, and competitively, we would drink the cold water until someone got an ice-cream headache, and then you would slap your forehead with the middle of your palm and yell, "Braino!" and you would win. Confetti would appear on screen; it was ludicrous. All kinds of people did it. Jeff Healey did it. I have a much better idea of how far you can go now. Then, you'd have to get four or five questions into the interview, and the body language would tell you what you could get away with.

Jeff Healey and Steve Anthony

The style of humour was, I think, David Letterman–influenced. In the late '80s, Letterman was in his ascendancy on late-night TV and was known for recurring gags as well as an irreverent approach to interviews.

CRAIG HALKETT Steve was always thinking about the next joke instead of listening to the answer to the question he'd just asked. He wasn't just about the music.

The artists, the crew and anyone in sight were eligible for participation in the madness of the moment.

STEVE ANTHONY Whenever I needed a contestant, it was Mike the Cleaner. One example was a game called "Who Dat?" where we would take a picture of a celebrity and stretch the fuck out of it, so Bryan Adams' jaw takes up three quarters of the screen. We would go out on the street with a monitor and ask, "Who dat?" and Mike would always get it wrong.
    Another recurring character was Mary the hot dog lady, a Portuguese woman who had a hot dog stand on the corner and we referred to her as my mom. We'd stop by and have family conversations with Mary regularly.

Not every artist was happy to be part of the Steve circus.

STEVE ANTHONY Sarah McLachlan, years later, told me that she was afraid of me. I did a thing, which would be set-up in advance, where I would try to ask the stupidest question ever asked on TV, which I did with Sarah. Later, VH1 had a series called _Before They Were Stars_, including an episode on Sarah where they showed a clip from my interview, with me asking a deliberately inane question. ["If you could be any tree, what tree would you be?"] They took that question completely out of context and keyed me as "Mr. Annoying." That was it—my American television exposure on VH1 as "Mr. Annoying."

I recall Steve, during their interview, asking the Nelson twins "the stupidest question ever." He asked them, separately, how old they were.

STEVE ANTHONY It was planned. We had all this fanfare with a key flashing "the stupidest question ever." But they answered it!

(Opposite) Sarah McLachlan and Steve Anthony

We were the people that you could see every day that you got to know and that you actually could come and poke with a stick.

Steve Anthony

I'd interviewed Huey Lewis a couple of years earlier and found him humour-less and stuffy and not what I'd consider a good candidate for wackiness. Steve took up the challenge.

STEVE ANTHONY **We were waiting for Huey. It was a Saturday; I'd grown a beard, and he was not there, so I decided, "Fuck it, let's find out if I should shave my beard off or not." We started taking calls and faxes and people decided that, yes, I should shave the beard off. So, I'm in the middle of shaving it off in the makeup room, when Huey Lewis shows up. They ushered him into the makeup room, so I shook his hand with shaving cream all over it, and I'm shaving while I'm asking him, nonchalantly, "What's it like to be the number-one artist in the world?" He looked stoic. He was professional enough not to walk out.**

The best part of the Huey Lewis incident, aside from the fact that he was extremely unhappy and he was a huge artist at the time, was that a number of people from the station went out for dinner with the band and the label people and the band said that if they ever found Steve Anthony, they would kill him. And they were serious.

Michael Williams offered this wry recollection in a recent conversation with Steve.

MICHAEL WILLIAMS **I stopped a few people from killing you once or twice.**

LAURIE BROWN **When Steve arrived there was a shift. The VJ became the entertainment; the VJ became a star; the VJ became a celebrity. I never thought of myself as a celebrity. I thought of myself as someone in a very privileged position, but I didn't think I was a celebrity. I just had a great job and I thought everyone would want my job.**

Labels began to request that their artists be interviewed by other VJs. Producer Morgen Flury had her share of frustrations with Steve.

MORGEN FLURY **Steve had a lot of energy, he reminded me a lot of my Pomeranian, cute little blond with so much energy, who really needed a tranquilizer . . . I eventually said to Steve, and to John, "I can't work with this man." I think the kicker was when Huey Lewis came in—it was like pie in the face, only pie in the hand.**

Looking back, I appreciate Steve's fearless antics; the rest of us were positively buttoned-down in comparison. I'd done comedic stuff on air, influenced by my time in the Second City touring company, but nothing like this.

STEVE ANTHONY I used to run at the window like an emu running into a fence. People outside would jump back. I remember interviewing the teen actress from *Blossom*, Mayim Bialik, and she was talking, and this fog came over my brain as I was looking at the people on Queen Street, so I ran at the window and smashed into it, and people jumped back. I came back to the interview, sat down, and said, "Where were we?"

Steve and I shared a desk, and it was like having the King of Chaos as my next-door neighbour; his shit would come tumbling down in a daily tsunami of papers and cigarette butts and food wrappers and discarded clothing, so I created the Line of Death.

STEVE ANTHONY That was the only rule I followed and respected. You actually put a piece of masking tape down [the middle] with a hash-mark on it, like on a road, and you wrote on both sides, so I couldn't help but see it, "LINE OF DEATH." There was no mistaking or misunderstanding what this was.

And it worked!

Let's give Steve the last word.

STEVE ANTHONY Laurie was interviewing David Bowie. He was smoking, and at the end of the interview I went over and grabbed the cigarette butt out of the ashtray, and I ran outside and I sold David Bowie's cigarette butt for ten dollars to a fan outside. One of my smartest business moves ever.

MASTER T, A.K.A. TONY YOUNG

"WHEN I LEAVE, YOU'RE NOT GOING TO FORGET MY ASS."

Tony Young took the long way to becoming a VJ; one who was celebrated for his decade of work on-air. But long before that happened, he put in his time elsewhere in the building.

MASTER T I was first hired as a VTR operator. I had been avoiding City like the plague because my older brother was there. I eventually realized that [the salary] wasn't going to make me rich at Channel 47. While I was doing camera at Much, Gord McWatters [currently head of creative services for Bell Media] and I would have field days every Friday when we did a series of promos. The first

"Weird Al" Yankovic and Master T

MuchMusic Rap? Talk about a stereotypical brother, I was walking around with a ghettoblaster on my shoulder. It was my wife, Paula, who helped write it. It was a minute and a half promo for MuchMusic, a long ID that became popular and people thought, "Oh, he wants to be on-air."

T is being modest here. He was not only an important crew member who cared about every aspect of what he was doing; he also had a personality that everyone thought would translate naturally to being on camera.

MASTER T We wrote this "MuchMusic Groove," which apparently is the first rap video in the library. Gord and I worked on it for about three months.

The reception to the video was amazing, and it led to T's first show, *X-Tendamix* which later became *Da Mix*. John assigned Simon Evans to produce. Tony explains the set-up.

MASTER T I got an idea for a show with a keyboard as my co-host, so I got this W30 [Roland keyboard] sampler, with Paula's voice sampled. It was like,
> **"Hey I'm Master T, what's goin' on? How you doin', Roxy?"**
> **"I'm fine, T, who's on the show today?"**
> **"Bobby Brown."**
> **"Oh yeah."**
So we shot a pilot with the crew. The beauty of it was I was a crew member first and on-air personality second. I always felt connected to the crew. I was one of theirs.

Mary J. Blige and Master T

When it aired in 1990, the show was a hit. Master T was a hit, but still he had reservations.

MASTER T I didn't feel like I was a VJ. When Moses said, "Do you want to be a VJ?" I didn't feel comfortable in my own persona, my own look.

Eventually, the viewers decided.

MASTER T I was doing the show, three hours, once a week, and I was a cameraman. I remember shooting Steve at the Science Centre and when I'd put the camera down, the kids were coming

up to me, "Hey, Master T," and I'm signing autographs. I knew I had to choose and I thought, I'm going to stay with being a cameraman, that's where my base salary is.

As we know, it didn't go that way.

MASTER T After about three to four years, I got my full VJ licence. The challenge of being a VJ is that for many of us it was so close to who you are as a person. I had that Master T thing as another persona. It was easier for me.

Still, there was no avoiding the responsibility that went with being the lone black VJ after Michael Williams left Much.

MASTER T I always felt that I was separate from all the other VJs because the minute I walked out of the building, it was, "Hey, there was a shooting at Jane and Finch. How come you're not talking about that on MuchMusic?" The black community will not mess around; they'll tell you if they don't like what you're doing. At first I was a frustrated actor and I did a Scottish character and they'd say, "Hey, I saw you on air wearing a dress" and I'd say, "No, man, that's a kilt." And they'd say, "You gotta be careful what you wear on the TV." I was very conscious of bringing black culture to the station. They couldn't see their favourite reggae artist or R&B artist on any other network. When I travelled the country doing the Much dance thing, I realized the power of MuchMusic.

Tony called himself a frustrated actor. In the early *City Limits* days, we were doing sketches, one of which featured T as Tony Basiloni, the owner of a suspect comedy club called Moses Palace. Once he was on-air, he started using his characters, including Taurus T, the love god.

MASTER T We used to put my voice through an enhancer to lower it, "Ohhh yeah. It's Taurus T here ready to spread the love vibe to all you fellas out there." I'd give out love tips. I finally got to interview Barry White, and he's six foot five and wearing this $5,000 flowing black silk outfit. We taped at the Senator [jazz club] and I was nervous as hell. My brother Basil was shooting and Barry said, "Oh yeah, the Young brothers, stay together, work together, stay tight, don't ever change." I told him about the Taurus T character and said he's like a disciple of love, and I said would you mind if I did this character [now], and he said, "A lot of people wouldn't fuckin' do this; you should have sent me the script first; you shouldn't just come up to the man like that; you should have had me look it over, check it out at my hotel." I'm thinking, "This is

not going well." I apologized and thought, "What was I thinking?" while I take my shirt off to put on the Taurus T shiny silk shirt and hat, while I'm being scolded by Barry White. I'm saying, "I was so wrong." And he gruffly said, 'What's it all about?' and I said, "It'll just be a quick thing." And I said, in character, "Oh yeah, this is Taurus T here and this is an emotional moment for me. The one and only, the love god himself is with me," and he's over there laughing, killing himself. He starts going with the whole thing, saying, "You know, T, the fellas out there have got to appreciate their women." And I said, "Appreciate, that's with an 'a,' right?" and he says, "That's right, the fellas have got to be more sensitive." I said, "Yeah, the problem is that we fellas are always on," and I hit the piano and he replies, "Yeah, we never shut off," and hits the piano. It was the most magical two minutes.

There was another very brief interview, if you can call it an interview, that many people remember vividly.

MASTER T People identify me with doing one of Tupac's last, if not the last interview, in New York at the MTV Awards. I asked him one question and he went off on a whole diatribe about the East coming for the West. Two days later he was executed.

At the end of his time on air, Tony was ready to go.

MASTER T When I came off, it was a blur. There was a burnout factor. I turned forty.

In 2001, after more than a decade of work, Tony could look back on having done interviews with some of the most iconic artists of the day, including Britney Spears and Madonna. The send-off was huge, and the time was right for T.

MASTER T I got Lauryn Hill to perform. I'd interviewed her several times, I wanted to say, "When I leave, you're not going to forget my ass." Kardinal [Offishall], Michie [Mee], Maestro [Fresh-Wes] all performed in the parking lot. And Lauryn played acoustic guitar and riffed on these lyrics, very unstructured. We weren't allowed to promote it and [David] Kines [then-director of music programming] was losing his mind. She said, "If MuchMusic promotes this, I'm not showing up."

As a wacky coda to all this, there is one final moment worth mentioning, again more of an encounter than an interview. This one with former prime minister Brian Mulroney!

MASTER T I went to Denise because I had to interview a politician and said, "What do I ask?" and she said, "Just be yourself." I asked, "So if you get into Sussex what are you going to do, how are you going to change the crib up?" and he rolled with it. I also interviewed the finance minister. So I was starting to get more comfortable. So Mila and Brian [Mulroney] are coming out of the Convention Centre [in downtown Toronto] and there's a scrum, and I'm this close, and I said, "Hey, Mila, what's going on?" and I said, "Yo, Brian, whassup?" and my voice just cut through, and he kinda looked at me like, "Who the heck are you?" He was not feeling it. And everyone wrote about it.

SIMON EVANS

"I ALWAYS LOOK AT YOU AS A DIRTY SHIRT IN MY LAUNDRY."

Simon was another VJ who took a roundabout path to becoming an on-air guy and if you believe him, he was particularly ill-suited to the gig.

SIMON EVANS I'm a twitchy sort of individual to begin with. I never wore makeup. Moses wanted me to be just me, with the stammering and the twitching and everything else. It was like, "Now you're clowning around not just for the twelve people in your office, but you're clowning around for the nation and yes, maybe looking like a bit of a dick."

With roots in the all-night *City Limits* show, Simon was one of the first people hired, if "hiring" includes working without pay.

SIMON EVANS During my third year at Centennial College, the first term was an internship . . . and if there was a possibility of a job—"you don't have to come back. Stay with this company if they'll keep you, and we'll put together a little make-up exam." In typical fashion, [producer] Morgen [Flury] and I were hired [as interns] without an interview. We started September '83 and we were doing office work and going out with the camera crews. About three weeks in, director of operations Nancy [Oliver] came to us and said we're starting this new idea. We're doing an all-night show because we're going for the licence for an all-music station and we'd like you guys to work on it. "Yeah, absolutely," I thought, because if this flies, there are jobs at the end of the tunnel." There was no interview, you've got a pulse, you're in.

When they needed someone to do G5 [an early graphics generator], they asked me and I said "sure." I hadn't a clue how to do G5. It was a very rudimentary computer, but it was still a computer, and we had no idea what we were doing. We were excited because we knew it could turn into a network; this could turn into music television. MTV was chugging along nicely. We were huge music fans, so this was a dream come true.

Even more so, a paying job would have been a dream then, and it did finally come to pass.

SIMON EVANS **Nancy decided she was going to give us some money so it was our first official job, but she only had enough for one person, so Morgen and I had to split the cheque—it was $48 a weekend and we split it. In her eyes we were boyfriend and girlfriend, so that was the way to do it.**

There was such a free-form sense of roles and responsibility when it came to putting the show together that both Morgen and Simon assumed many producer duties when the need arose. Eventually that was recognized.

SIMON EVANS **We became associate producers. It was pretty straightforward—a guest might come in or we'd do some shtick, but basically, we were playing six hours of videos. The camera people came up with the interesting shots. Everyone was left to be as creative as they could be.**

Simon gave me his typically understated account of what I well knew was a challenging job with a lot of balls in the air.

SIMON EVANS **Now that I think about it, it was a lot of responsibility. Live television.**

If you saw Simon on-air, it won't strain credibility to say that he was caustic, and at times lacking in diplomacy. What do you want? Simon was from Liverpool. John Martin was from Manchester, so there was a sort of grumpy, mutual admiration that could veer into near fisticuffs at times. Simon tells how he came to be on-air.

SIMON EVANS **We had three VJs quit in a row and [we] were short-staffed. They thought they would bring on members of the crew to do a shift if they wanted to, and John said, "You're always criticizing everyone—you should do it." So, I did it and while I was on air, they were having a meeting in the boardroom, John, Moses and a bunch of other executives, and Moses sees me on and turns up the volume and I'm being an idiot and Moses says, "You see—**

Simon Evans with Stewart Copeland of the Police

that's the kind of guy you don't put on TV, so that's the kind of guy we *should* put on TV." I was wearing a band T-shirt, had stupid hair and had to do my first interview with Stewart Copeland of the Police. So then, I had to have my one-on-one with Moses, and he said I was now going to get laid a whole lot more, and as my agent he should take ten percent.

Did Moses regret this in-the-moment decision? He'd never admit to it.

SIMON EVANS I had a few encounters with Moses. They did postcards for all of us—I don't know why they did one for me; I was on the air a couple of hours a week, hosting *The Wedge*. So, I picked the shot—it was me holding a gothic candlestick and making a stupid face. Moses called me up to his office and I think he thought I was making a mockery of everything. I waited for an hour, as usual, and when I came in, he threw the picture at me, and said, "What is this? I always look at you as a dirty shirt in my laundry." I thought, I don't know what that means but I'm taking it as a compliment.

In some ways, despite his success as a VJ and the respect that he got from the viewers for his passion for music, Simon still never really adapted to the gig as wholeheartedly as the others did.

SIMON EVANS I didn't like being in front of the camera; I didn't like the extra attention. You'd be somewhere to see a band and there'd be someone tugging on your arm, wanting to talk to you because they'd seen you on TV.

Still, Simon took pleasure in those times when everything worked on the job.

SIMON EVANS A great one for me was being on the roof of Sam the Record Man, shooting Alice Cooper and singing "Under My Wheels" with him, one of the first records I remember as a kid. They were doing the whole performing on the roof and hoping the police would shut them down thing, but of course the cops didn't give a shit.

Simon's naturally combative nature worked wonders at certain times.

SIMON EVANS I'm one of the few people in Canada who interviewed Liam Gallagher [of Oasis]. He and Noel were scheduled to come in for an interview and to play an acoustic version of "Supersonic" as a single. They got involved in fisticuffs in the parking lot; blows were exchanged. Noel had stormed off in a huff so Liam came in. He's exactly what you'd expect—he's a lout and he was already fired up. I knew he was a Manchester City [football club] fan and I'm from Liverpool and I said, "I hear you're a Man City fan; well, I won't hold it against you," and he says, "You're a Scouser; I'm talking to a fucking Scouser." And then the interview was great. He launched off into this rant about Americans.

And if Simon made the most of his heritage, who's to complain?

SIMON EVANS I had a beer with Sarah Brightman at noon at my desk because she was on Ziggy's *MushMusic* show. She says, "You're British, aren't you?' And I said, "Yes, I am." And she pulls two beers out of her bag and says, "I haven't had my morning beer yet." She sang to me at my desk, too.

Simon Evans and Mike Myers

I TURNED
MYSELF
INTO
A CARTOON
CHARACTER . . .
MY LIFE-LONG
DREAM.

11 The Video Stars

By the mid-1980s a renaissance in Canadian pop music was in full swing. Canadian artists had the support of domestic labels, and access to a fanbase that embraced them with a fervour that previously had been reserved for stars from the U.S. and U.K. It was a glorious time to be writing, playing, recording and performing music in this country. Nowhere was this celebration of music in Canada more fully in effect than at 299 Queen Street West. A new generation of artists exploded on the screen.

GLASS TIGER

One of the faces of this new wave of stars was Alan Frew, the lead singer of Glass Tiger, a band from Newmarket, Ontario.

ALAN FREW [Video] was the single most important thing at the time. We had just watched what it had done for Duran Duran on MTV, and we started to realize that video killed the radio star. It was super important and along came MuchMusic and Glass Tiger and it was like a marriage made in heaven. It was vitally important in breaking the band.

When they debuted in 1986, Glass Tiger had the golden combination—a charismatic group of band members, a collection of memorable, anthemic songs and the support of a major label, Capitol Records. The first single from *The Thin Red Line* album, produced by Bryan Adams' collaborator Jim Vallance, was "Don't Forget Me (When I'm Gone)," and it was a smash. For their debut video, Capitol turned to the hot hand, Rob Quartly. The resulting video was a hit on Much, but not so well regarded by the band's lead singer.

ALAN FREW The video is very corny and difficult to look back on. The proof was in the pudding when the Americans said, "We love this track" . . . they insisted on an alternate video; they didn't like the corniness of the trumpets and the kids and the marriage so we just shot a live video of us performing "Don't Forget Me (When I'm Gone)" on stage.

The single featured a cameo from a very recognizable Bryan Adams, but only on the record.

ALAN FREW When it became obvious that we weren't getting Bryan for [the video] . . . I think it was Rob Quartly's tongue-in-cheek moment to say, "What if we had a kid do the Bryan Adams thing?" People ask about the embarrassment factor . . . looking back on your life . . . we all look back on it like a scrapbook from high school. I mean, can I look at my '70s high school yearbook with platforms and bell-bottoms and not cringe? . . . The saving grace is, just when you're looking at yours and thinking, "Oh my god, did we really do that?" then you see something that Duran Duran did or Rod Stewart or Luba and you realize it was a sign of the times.

Songwriter Jim Vallance talked about his first gig as a producer.

JIM VALLANCE I got a call from Deane Cameron, who was then head of A&R at Capitol Records in Toronto. He'd just signed Glass Tiger, a young band from Newmarket. He already had a producer in mind, but the band needed help arranging their songs. I play guitar, keyboards, bass and drums, so in some ways it was a "rock school" session, with me sitting in on various instruments while making adjustments to the arrangements. It wasn't quite songwriting, but it bordered on it. Maybe that's why Deane suggested I try writing with the band.

A few weeks later the band flew to Vancouver. We spent a productive week during which we wrote "Don't Forget Me (When I'm Gone)" and "Someday" [two of the band's biggest hits]. When Deane heard the demos, he asked if I'd be interested in producing the album. I felt bad, because I was stealing the job from another producer—someone I knew and liked—but I didn't feel bad enough to decline the offer!

After the "Don't Forget Me (When I'm Gone)" experience, Glass Tiger did develop a relationship with a video director that was built to last.

ALAN FREW The one [director] that really stands out for us is Don Allan who . . . eventually did eight Glass Tiger videos [including "My Town," "Diamond Sun," "I'm Still Searching" and "My Song"]. He brought cohesiveness to everything by involving us; he involved me behind the scenes in concept . . . it became more of a team as opposed to the way a lot of directors work where they go, "Here's my concept, love it or hate it, but this is it, you ain't changing it."

Director Don Allan, who has worked with k-os, Rush and the Tragically Hip, among others, brings a strong point of view to his work.

Erica Ehm with Alan
Frew and Michael
Hanson of Glass Tiger

DON ALLAN **I probably listened to a song more
than the artists [themselves] because I listen to it
hundreds of times as I'm writing the video. I then
listen to it hundreds of times on-set and then
hundreds more when editing it. When you analyze most songs,
they're quite trite and repetitive. There's not much there, so
often we would try and interpret what it was and give it more
meaning than it had. As a particular chorus repeats, you can't
just have the same visual idea over again. You can musically,
but you can't visually. So you're giving that same line other
visual interpretations, often writing into it stuff that the original
writer didn't intend. There's also the video hook, which is the
technique. . . . It has to have an arc like film or like a song does.
Some videos—they've blown their load in the first minute and
then they're just repeating for the rest of the song. To me that's
a channel change.**

I asked Alan, who is originally from Scotland, if looking back, there was one
video in particular that really stood out.

ALAN FREW My favourite memory would be getting the opportunity to go to Glasgow for the shooting of "My Town." Poor Don Allan. He put me in my environment and every time somebody would say "cut," I'd be in the pub or in the betting shop putting money on the horses. Don allowed me to be very involved in the concept, so there's a couple of very cool moments. One is, my cousin is in the video, hanging her washing out in the backyard. Two of my favourite soccer stars at the time did cameos. My son Gavin and [keyboardist] Sam [Reid]'s son Justin are in the video. And a very famous old Scottish actor, Jimmy Logan . . . we shot one of the pub scenes at my pal's pub in Glasgow, so it was like old home week. A lot of love, a lot of friendship [was] in the making of that video.

Director Don Allan shared in the family experience with Alan.

DON ALLAN "My Town" is about Glasgow and the idea of immigrating to a new country. The Scottish comedian, Jimmy Logan, who Billy Connolly credits with being the reason he got into comedy, is my uncle, so we used him in the video. Also my grandmother is in the video. In "I'm Still Searching"—both our dads [Don's and Alan's] are in it, sitting in a pub drinking.

One of the most visually arresting of the many hit videos that Glass Tiger did was for the song "I Will Be There."

ALAN FREW We were on tour with Journey. We shot some of the footage live from the Journey tour and on a day off, they took us up to Vancouver because the director had this idea of flying us up to the top of Tabletop Mountain on this pristine, untouched mountain so that the first footsteps made on it would be ours. Those were the days when the money was there and you could do those kind of things and it was a beautifully shot video.

The band had a remarkable string of high-rotation videos and Alan was very clear about the effect of all that exposure.

ALAN FREW Nothing beats coming right into the living rooms night after night. MuchMusic made us popstars. Erica [Ehm] was with us when . . .we gave a free concert at the Parliament Buildings for Canada Day and there were in excess of a hundred thousand people there and it took us three hours to get from the stage to the main road. She was trapped with us in the van.

Larry LeBlanc, the dean of Canadian music journalists had a unique insight into the making of a hit.

LARRY LeBLANC The music business is not about music; it's the right piece of music at the right time. The ultimate band in that era that was built almost singlehandedly by MuchMusic was Glass Tiger, from top to bottom.

This may sound like an indictment of a band that broke via video, but there were lots of good-looking bands with boatloads of money being thrown at them who could hire the best support team of publicists, producers and song doctors, but couldn't sustain a meaningful career. There's a reason why Glass Tiger's songs are still heard on the radio today that transcends nostalgia.

ALAN FREW We knew that we were solid writers, solid musicians. We had cut our teeth . . . we knew our craft. What happens when you become popstars, the industry [the critics] . . . it's the very nature of their job to hate everything . . . they were the ones that wanted to say, "This is all fabricated, it's all bubblegum." You pay a certain price for that.

To record companies, videos were a roll of the dice on acts that had already been gobbling up resources with ever-mounting recording budgets as well as other traditional promotional expenses. Former Warner head of marketing Dave Tollington who worked with bands like Honeymoon Suite, Messenjah, Blue Rodeo and the Odds addressed this issue.

DAVE TOLLINGTON From a business point of view, making domestic records, signing acts and doing all that, it effectively doubled the cost of doing business. Yes, they were fifty percent recoupable against the artist, but . . . the dirty little secret in the music business is if you have one profitable artist out of ten you've signed, you're considered a genius. So you made two or three videos for all the ones that didn't sell any records. It became really expensive and you couldn't sign as many acts and take as many chances.

Kim Cooke, who was a senior VP at Warner through the '80s and '90s, mentions another aspect of the challenge for a label in making videos for their acts.

KIM COOKE As the A&R guy, I found that making or commissioning videos was harder and much more stressful than making records because when you're making a record, there's a belief in an artist who has a bit of your soul and there's usually a communal vision on who's going to produce, where it's going to be recorded. When you're making a video, you've got this whole other person between you and the artist. Sometimes it turned out great and sometimes there were disasters. . . . Sometimes the directors wanted to make art.

In an effort to reduce risk, the labels wanted bankable directors and there weren't many of those in Canada. Okay, there was just one—the ever-reliable Rob Quartly. There were lots of other very creative people in the field, some doing excellent work, some directing videos for songs that became hits. But this was one guy who seemed to have the touch with hits for Platinum Blonde, Corey Hart, Glass Tiger and others. So when CBS was ready to shoot their wad on a video for singer Lawrence Gowan, Rob got the call.

GOWAN

Lawrence Gowan had waited his turn after emerging from the crucible of the ever-tough Ontario club scene with his band, Harlequin. Having learned a few things about keeping an audience's attention, Gowan was one of a very select group of acts who used video as an artistic vehicle as opposed to merely an advertisement for a single. He tells a great story of second, maybe last, chances, and the value of doing it your own way.

GOWAN I had a lot of failure prior to getting to make a record in the first place and in particular getting to make a second record, because that's what changed my career—getting that second chance. . . . The music I made was always referred to, by record companies who would never sign me, as being too quirky, overly theatrical and overly "cerebral" (Lawrence laughing), which I had to go and look up. There was nothing cerebral about it; it was basically a lot of science fiction gobbledygook. I think Freddie Mercury was my patron saint of the '70s. When I finally got a record deal, I decided on my first record to really tone it down to such a degree that I thought. "Oh, don't be that flamboyant." . . . We did a video . . . I had no input at all, relying entirely on CBS records to push that record, because they'd just had the success of Loverboy, and it fell completely on its face.

The lucky thing is, when I got a second chance in 1984, I thought, "If I'm going to fail I will do it the way I would like to have it done." So when it came time to do "Criminal Mind," it was like this was my one and only shot at doing something that I think is kind of fun. When it came out in 1984, there were people in the record company who said, "The subject matter—you gotta be really careful, this song, 'A Criminal Mind,' it could be too dark." Already they were thinking about the barriers . . . you had these people wringing their hands because there was a lot of money at stake. Either you made a ton of money or you made zero.

I DON'T THINK THERE WAS ONE THING I WORE IN THE 1980S THAT WAS NOT A CRIME.

Gowan

Second guessing is endemic to the record business, perhaps because it gives people cover in case something they were involved with flops. Any opportunity to let someone else put themselves on the line is taken; just as any chance to take credit for a hit is grabbed. As an artist, you need a hero, and Gowan had the right one.

GOWAN **The president of CBS at that time, Bernie DiMatteo, was very enthusiastic about "A Criminal Mind," mainly because his two sons kept playing the song over and over when they got the record, before the album came out. He said to me, "I think this is a great single. What are you thinking about for a video?" When I began to describe it to him, he said, "Yeah, I think that's going to be too dark for them to play on TV." I was talking about the electric chair and stuff like that. Bernie said, "Did you ever watch *Batman*?" "Oh god, I'd love to make it like that! Can we have animation in it?" He said, "Why don't you start working on it and we'll see what we can spend money on and what we won't."**

I went home and started working on the storyboard . . . They got Rob Quartly to make the video and he was the hot guy at the time. They gave him a budget for the animation so basically I was able to turn myself into a cartoon character, which was my life-long dream anyway!

The video for "A Criminal Mind" won the Juno for Video of the Year. Director Rob Quartly recalls the making of the video.

ROB QUARTLY **I think it was Larry's idea to do the comic book feel, so we blended his performance into the comic. There was always a rush to get things done in time for the single release and with animation, that was a challenge. Cel animation [which is hand-drawn] is painstaking work.**

Like most artists, Rob looks back and sees the flaws in a hugely successful video that put Gowan on the map.

ROB QUARTLY **There's a section where Larry is on a conveyer belt and he gets pancake mix poured all over him. I remember looking at it and thinking, "That looks like pancake mix. That's really stupid." We did some video effect to put a bandage over it.**

Lawrence testified to the instantaneous power of video.

GOWAN **We shot that video in November of 1984 when I was playing piano with Ronnie Hawkins. The week the video was released, MuchMusic started playing it immediately. We were playing an auto show in Montreal and at the end of the first set,** there was a bunch of people asking, "Hey, are you that guy with the criminal song?" That's how instant the impact of television was. It was the power of television and the power of the mullet!

I asked if Lawrence had any mullet regret.

GOWAN **No, I'm convinced that decade needed a haircut like that, like the '50s needed the ducktail.**

And as for criminal activity in the fashion department . . .

GOWAN **I don't think there was one thing I wore in the 1980s that was not a crime.**

The video for "A Criminal Mind" won Quartly his second consecutive Juno for Video of the Year.
    Great Dirty World, the follow-up album to *Strange Animal*, featured a classic ballad called "Moonlight Desires." Sony's commitment to Gowan was evident in the budget for the beautiful and grandiose video that accompanied the song. When the crew headed to Mexico, there were some payments that had not been included in the budget.

GOWAN **When we got to Mexico . . . we had hired a Mexican crew and we went with the specific purpose of shooting on the pyramids [at Teotihuacan, near Mexico City]. We had permission, but when we arrived in Mexico City we found out that things are done very**

Catherine McClenahan and Gowan

differently there [from Canada]. There was a government guy who met us at the airport who handed us a lovely welcoming letter saying, "Please feel free to shoot anywhere in Mexico that you feel is appropriate except for the Mexican pyramids." The first little bit of graft money goes to this guy—it might have been the equivalent of fifty bucks, but he was the first one in a long list. Over the course of the next ten days, everything had to be paid off. By about Day Five I'd convinced Jon Anderson [of the band Yes] to fly from England to Mexico to do that one scene on the Pyramid of the Sun [the largest pyramid of Teotihuacan]. That was the loose concept behind it—I'm on [the Pyramid of the Moon], dressed in blue and black—so there's the night. And Jon Anderson is the bright sunshine of day. I'm pulling away from the daylight into what the moonlight does to people.

The video was shot at a number of archeological sites, but none more awe-inspiring, or historically significant, than Teotihuacan, so it probably shouldn't have been surprising that a Canadian music video crew might have raised some hackles among the locals.

GOWAN **The morning of that scene, a bunch of cops came to the hotel and said, "We're going to confiscate your film," and "if we see you on another pyramid . . . you're going to find out what Mexican jail is all about." So Rob went out to Teotihuacan and met the guards and told them, "We're going to come here in the morning," gave them a few hundred bucks and said, "we're going to film from the helicopter, there'll be no cameras on the ground." The idea being that if the cops arrive, there will be no film on the ground; the helicopter will go and land and Rob will know what to do to get the film out of the country, secure it so it doesn't get confiscated and we'll give them some other footage that he had in the helicopter. He did about three passes with the helicopter. No cops showed up so they were well paid off. When the helicopter landed . . . a lot of dust picked up and the pilot lost his bearings and he set it down roughly. Rob got out shaken up. The helicopter pilot got out . . . and was yelling at the Mexican film crew and he left the helicopter there and left on foot. He said something to do with the gods (in Spanish), "You guys are cursed!"**

Director Rob Quartly adds his recollections of this extraordinary shoot.

ROB QUARTLY **There's a thing called a Tyler mount [for stabilization] for shooting on helicopters and taking all the vibration out. It's mounted on the nose of the helicopter. When we got to the chopper at dawn, they'd taken the side door off and suspended a tire with bungee cords. I said, "What's this for?" and they said, "You asked for a 'tire' mount." We ended up crabbing the helicopter sideways to get all the shots, with the camera in the tire.**

Rob offers this bizarre postscript to the story.

ROB QUARTLY **We did take a grand piano up one of the pyramids, and watching that was a movie unto itself, fifteen guys carrying a piano up the pyramid for a dawn shot. The piano was covered in a great big tarp, which we removed to reveal the word "Steinway" written in great huge gold letters. Larry went white and I said, "What's the matter?" "I'm sponsored by Yamaha."**

Later, in post-production, a guy painted over the word "Steinway," frame-by-frame.

THE PARACHUTE CLUB

The new medium helped Canadian artists avoid the pigeonholing that had dominated the industry for so long. A new era meant that every act didn't have to squeeze through the "Canada's answer to . . ." filter before getting support from the industry. Was the Parachute Club an analogue to anything from the U.K. or the U.S.? Not for a minute. I asked Lorraine Segato, lead singer and songwriter, where their influences came from.

LORRAINE SEGATO We were inspired by the music we heard travelling through Cuba, Trinidad and Jamaica. Africa was brought to us . . . through the lives of many of the scrappy artists who were living on Queen Street West. There, we were surrounded by similar artists who were recent immigrants and politically engaged . . . and it was the late '70s and early '80s and Toronto was morphing from its parochial, small-town conservative beginnings. We hung around a lot of reggae musicians from Trinidad and Jamaica who befriended us and taught us how to play authentic reggae and soca grooves. . . . We wanted the band to be polyrhythmic and we wanted to say something. We became absorbed in what is now called world music. . . . There was a surge of cultural, political and artistic change that was pushing the city to grow up and to grow out and we came out of that.

So, how did a band this ambitious and eclectic deal with the music biz?

LORRAINE SEGATO The music business never liked us. It was the fans, the loyal fans, and other musicians who liked us, because we were political, we were opinionated, non-conforming and didn't really fit in anywhere. None of those things make the corporate mentality comfortable, so in terms of the industry, we never really fit in.

This created some challenges when it came time to make the band's first video.

LORRAINE SEGATO In the early days every time we met with video directors, they wanted to push a kind of sexuality on the women in the band that was so old school, so dated and not really well thought out. Very few people were interested in the storyboard or the concept—they were only interested in the look. They never really got to an interesting storyboard that was reflective of who the band was.

After meeting with the best-known directors of the day, they settled on Bob Fresco who was willing to work with the band from the storyboarding onward, developing the concept for "Rise Up." The result was an incredibly memorable video. Lorraine recalls the shoot with affection.

Dan Gallagher with Lorraine Segato of the Parachute Club

LORRAINE SEGATO It was an amazing day. It was very hot and sunny. We had a permit to be on this flatbed truck and we were travelling around and we were singing and we kind of had our own little carnival going on. Everywhere we travelled people joined us as we went along . . .It was a joyous day and you can see it in the video.

To stand out in this new era an act had to be original and have a unique look, but more than anything, I believe it takes a great song to launch a career. The Parachute Club had one of those, right out of the box, with "Rise Up."

LORRAINE SEGATO I'm still very surprised to see how important that song has been to so many lives. It had so much to do with timing. At that point, Canadian radio was focused on things like Loverboy and Bryan Adams. When "Rise Up" came out it was a summer song, summer '83 with this upbeat soca groove, kind of reminding you of Trinidad, of carnival. It had a singable melody and a celebratory groove. It was partially the song, partially the video. It was identifiably Toronto with the diversity of people. The song became this anthemic call to shared power for any group that felt disenfranchised. If you feel that you're not being heard, not being represented, "Rise Up" is one of those songs that is inclusive of everything you are. It was timing, luck and the convergence of video and a new style of music. Daniel Lanois' production had a lot to do with making the song appealing.

"Rise Up," which won the 1984 Juno for Single of the Year, was the first in a number of hit videos for the Parachute Club. The band collaborated with director Ron Berti for "Love Is Fire," winning the Juno for Video of the Year in 1987.

MARTHA AND THE MUFFINS, A.K.A. M+M

Another era-defining band that Daniel Lanois worked with was Martha and the Muffins, whose 1979 hit "Echo Beach" established them worldwide, before video was considered an important tool in building a career. Martha Johnson talks about that first video experience.

MARTHA JOHNSON **I remember we had pretty much nothing to do with its planning. We shot it in London right around the time "Echo Beach" started climbing the U.K. charts. Video was very new to the record business then and the video crew, including the director, were all probably flying by the seat of their pants.**

"Echo Beach" was directed by Russell Mulcahy, who went on to direct videos for Duran Duran, Rod Stewart, Def Leppard and Elton John, as well as films and TV series. But they found their match creatively working with director Bob Fresco on videos like "Black Stations/White Stations" and "Cooling the Medium." Martha talks about Fresco.

MARTHA JOHNSON **Later on . . . we had a lot of creative input. Bob Fresco was the most inventive director we worked with. He had lots of interesting ideas and liked to experiment like we did.**

Martha's partner, Mark Gane, talked about their work with the director of these two innovative videos.

MARK GANE **Bob had a 1940s Hollywood cameraman's special effects manual from which we got a lot of ideas, like how to use miniature scale models, shooting through water sandwiched between glass panes and so on. The creative process genuinely excited him and his enthusiasm was infectious for everyone involved. As grown-ups doing this kind of thing for a living, it was kind of marvellous!**

Here's Martha's memory of one of the videos they did together.

MARTHA JOHNSON **We got the idea for the upside-down room in "Black Stations/White Stations" from the 1951 Fred Astaire movie *Royal Wedding,* where Fred dances up the walls and across the ceiling. In our video, the poor guy who looks like he's sitting at the table on the floor was actually strapped to a chair that was fastened to the ceiling. We kept asking him if he was okay. He always said "yes" so we would keep shooting.**

When Martha and I decided to become a duo, it seemed like an opportune time to shed the weight of the band's past and for me to escape being called a "muffin" . . . in retrospect changing the name was a foolish thing to have done . . . most fans liked the original name better, and many casual listeners never realized that "Echo Beach" and "Black Stations/ White Stations" were by the same people.

Mark Gane, M + M

I wondered what the wackiest thing they had done to make a video was.

MARTHA JOHNSON To get a shaky camera effect we strapped the camera to a clothes dryer in spin cycle.

Mark recalls the band's relationship with Much, starting in the early days of the network.

MARK GANE Much back then had the feeling of a small family of committed people who genuinely loved music in a non-corporate atmosphere of excitement and innovation. We received a lot of support for several years from MuchMusic and it had a crucial role in our mid-'80s success. Of course the reverse was true as well. If your videos didn't get playlisted, which happened to us during the '90s, it was the kiss of death for your album in Canada. You just got buried. That was when I felt that MuchMusic had become too corporate, too powerful and there needed to be alternatives. Then the internet came along.

THE PURSUIT OF HAPPINESS

Proving that you didn't need to have a budget in the tens of thousands to find a home on MuchMusic, a $400 video, shot on the streets of Toronto caught the attention of the programming committee, the group that met weekly to decide what would be aired on Much. We decided to immediately put it into a significant rotation. We were excited to get behind the Pursuit of Happiness, an indie band led by Edmonton singer Moe Berg and their wonderful tongue-in-cheek rock 'n' roll song "I'm an Adult Now."

Manager Jeff Rogers, who had been working with Honeymoon Suite, talked about how he came to manage the band.

JEFF ROGERS **With Honeymoon Suite, it was, "How can I look like a rock star?" With the Pursuit of Happiness, it was, "How can I not look like a rock star, but still do this?" Their first video was them busking on the street and it was the equivalent of a viral video on YouTube. Everyone loved it and everyone talked about it. I was at MuchMusic and editor Joni Daniels asked if I'd consider managing her friend's band and I said, "No, I don't care who they are, I don't want to manage them." I was working on a movie called *Hearts of Fire* with Bob Dylan, and I was the "rock consultant," making $400 a week and I didn't want to blow that. She said, "Please come see them tonight at Larry's Hideaway; Erica [Ehm] will be there to interview them," so I said, "Okay, what are they called?" She said, "The Pursuit of Happiness," and I said, "Are you kidding? I love the Pursuit of Happiness. I can't believe they don't have a manager."**

Steve Anthony with Kris Abbott and Moe Berg of the Pursuit of Happiness

Moe Berg recalls the casual way the video came to be.

MOE BERG **I had an old friend in town named Nelu Ghiran who was a film director. He suggested we shoot a video for one of the songs, more for something to do than anything else . . . We cobbled together some friends as extras but mainly wandered around Toronto looking for cool places for me to "mime" the song.
We set up the main shoot on Queen Street West near the old Bamboo Club. It was all guerrilla film-making, no permits, no makeup. Just a director, producer, cameraman and sound man.**

Moe tells how the street to the screen wasn't such a leap in those days.

MOE BERG **Once the clip was finished, we walked into Much, which you could do at that time, and dropped off the master, hoping it would end up being screened a time or two on *City Limits*, which**

as you well know, was the alternative music show at the time. The next day, someone named Morgen called me to say that not only was it going to be played on *City Limits*, it was going into regular rotation. Again, this was at a time when Much's programming was more open and breaking bands was part of their ambition. That pretty much got the TPOH train onto the tracks and things began to happen very quickly from there. I remember begging the Rivoli to let us do our own show there, really humiliating myself. They finally relented on the condition that we do it with a co-headliner. In the time between that deal and the show, the clip had begun to air. The Rivoli show was completely sold out and getting gigs ceased to be a problem.

After a couple of record deals broke down in the negotiation stage, they finally clicked with an A&R person who got it.

MOE BERG **Kate Hyman [from Chrysalis in New York] came to see the band play in a terrible fern bar in Winnipeg during one of their minus thirty cold snaps. She offered us a deal shortly thereafter, god bless her, and we recorded our debut with Todd Rundgren in the summer of 1988.**

Being able to support bands in their infancy was very satisfying and it fit with Much's self-image at the time. Here's Moe's take on the connection.

MOE BERG **I think the reason a lot of people connect us with MuchMusic is that we both came of age at around the same time . . . This was the start of indie bands being able to make records and videos and get national attention. I think it paved the way for other bands without labels to do the same thing. There are a handful of videos that were unique to MuchMusic that gave it an identity.**

DALBELLO

While Sass Jordan, Colin James, Kim Mitchell and Barenaked Ladies expressed feelings ranging from mild bemusement to complete distaste for their own videos, artists like Jane Siberry and Gowan embraced the opportunity for a new means of expression. Lisa Dal Bello, who performed as Dalbello, was firmly in the latter group, seeing video as more than an advertisement for a record.

LISA DAL BELLO **The idea that you could . . . stretch out your song, I never thought of it as a commercial vehicle at the time, but**

rather an extension of creative expression. You could put into pictures what you saw when you were composing those words and building that sonic landscape. It was open season.

To get to the point where she had the freedom to pursue that artistic vision, Lisa had to go through the record company mill.

LISA DAL BELLO MCA . . . created a new label, one that I was kind of shocked by, they said I was a "dance artist." Years later I remember hearing Alanis [Morissette] say that she'd gone through the same branding without understanding.

Unsurprisingly, the pressure to use sexuality was ever present.

LISA DAL BELLO Right from my first album cover that was often the case. "Why don't you pull that strap down and why don't you bend lower?" . . . I was only seventeen so I was very uncomfortable and without . . . the emotional, experiential vocabulary to express that. You're partially fearful . . . it took a long time for me to be able to draw that line because every time I did, there would be pushback. "Well, you're really hard to deal with," they would say. "Why don't you wear something to show your boobs like Kate Bush?" I was really tiptoeing and didn't have a sense of self yet.

Lisa sang extensively on Alannah Myles' debut album and I remember how effortless her work was and her comfort in the studio.

LISA DAL BELLO My safest place really was in the world of studio session work where there was no tipping of the hat to one's gender at all; you just arrived and did your stuff.

Her first album for MCA resulted in a Juno for Most Promising Female Vocalist of the Year; the unexpected outcome was that she was let go by her label, because of the cost of making the record.

LISA DAL BELLO I went into [legendary movie mogul and chairman of MCA] Lou Wasserman's office and begged, "Please don't drop me," and he said, "Hey sweetheart, it's just business."

Two albums later, Lisa dropped her first name, and as Dalbello, recorded the album *whomanfoursays* for Capitol Records in 1984 with David Bowie guitarist Mick Ronson producing. Musically, the album was a creative leap and the accompanying videos were arresting and highly original. Lisa recalls one idea she had that didn't float with the label.

LISA DAL BELLO For the first video I had gone to Capitol in L.A. and proposed a young up and coming Canadian director, David Cronenberg! They laughed me out of the room.

Once she did make the video for "Gonna Get Close to You," Lisa went for the less obvious.

LISA DAL BELLO While that may have seemed on the surface to be about someone obsessed and following someone else, there was a second layer of meaning which was, it was my own shadow following me. It was a battle of the inner self and the superficial self.

LUBA

I think a lot of people would be surprised to know that the Juno Female Vocalist of the Year for three years running, from 1985 to 1987, was Luba Kowalchyk, a pop singer and songwriter from Montreal with a very soulful voice who had a string of hits through the '80s in Canada. The same month that MuchMusic launched in '84, Luba released "Let it Go," an infectious pop anthem that featured her powerful vocals. The video was a playful Bob Fresco–directed piece that was set, via chroma key, in a blimp. Luba still shakes her head at that video.

LUBA All those strange-looking people on some sort of blimp. It wasn't my idea. My mother still thought—"How did you get up in the balloon?" Those little girls with the weird hats, the spaceship hats. I have no idea [who they were]. I came and they were there. Do you remember those hats? Those girls kept twisting and turning their heads . . . there was a rotor blade . . . I swore somebody was going to have their head chopped off. There wasn't much room on that so-called blimp. It was so bloody hot. We were on a sound stage; it was the middle of summer in Toronto and it was brutal . . . but it was fun in its own bizarre way.

Looking back at the video, I can see what Luba is saying. Odd, inexplicable characters were fairly common in music videos, but the one thing a label and a director usually made sure they got right was the artist's name.

LUBA What struck me was on the blimp . . . I have this logo with a long 'L' and the 'uba' came on top. For some reason they painted the L the same colour as the balloon so it looks like 'UBA.' I mean, can you at least get that right? It was a comedy of errors.

Luba was in a stronger position when it came to choosing who she'd work with for subsequent videos, including the one for "How Many (Rivers to Cross)." Like any good relationship, a lot comes down to chemistry.

LUBA **The label kept pressing me to work with this one director but I found all the videos were very similar and I wanted to do something different so they sent me to London. I met a few different directors but one I really hit it off with—he was born in Canada, lived in Australia and ended up in London . . . from the moment I sat down it was like I knew him; we hit it off.**

The director was Gregg Masuak. Luba talks about how they clicked.

LUBA **Gregg is always laughing. Everything is positive and bright. I kind of feed off that; I can get a little dark and depressive, especially in my music.**

I was curious about the origins of some of the style choices Luba made for the "How Many" video and for her stage performances.

LUBA **The braid was my sister's; my mother got sick of brushing her hair all the time . . . I used to dance in a Ukrainian dance group so**

Luba and J.D. Roberts

we would have to wear a braid . . . gloves, probably because I used to bite my nails . . . I'd go to these vintage stores, collect gloves . . . I always liked the look of gloves, kind of Audrey Hepburn . . . we didn't have stylists back then . . . I'm sure the label would have liked something a little less layered, clothing-wise . . . I loved long coats; I liked the way they flowed, the movement on stage. They would've preferred me in a wet T-shirt.

The video shoot was, as is so often the case, not without unforeseen difficulties.

LUBA It was bloody cold [standing] in that water. There was a day outdoors and a day indoors . . . they had fake rain.

One of the most memorable aspects of the video is the gospel singers on the beach. Surely, that was fairly straightforward to shoot.

LUBA Those choir girls—they were supposed to be a gospel choir but they had no rhythm. They couldn't even clap in time. Gregg was getting aggravated. I was getting aggravated. They staged some sort of walkout; "no, they don't want to come out. They don't want to clap."

Even with the fake rain and dodgy clapping, an arresting performance by Luba helped "How Many" win the Juno for Video of the Year in 1986.

Luba, M+M and the Parachute Club all shared the guiding hand of producer Daniel Lanois, who went on to produce Peter Gabriel, U2, Bob Dylan and Neil Young, among others. Luba spoke of her experience working with Lanois.

I remember him warming up like it was for a soccer match, and he's a big soccer fan, jumping and jumping. I said, "Alan, save some of this." He said, "I'm just getting going!" He's got that thing in his eye. He wanted it.

Rob Quartly (on Alan Frew of Glass Tiger)

LUBA I would consider him a musical genius. He was the first producer I worked with. He just had the strangest things going on in the studio. He'd make a loop with tape and have it going through rooms—it was bizarre . . . but the sounds that he was getting would be super incredible, so different, very experimental. He was really good with vocals—very patient.

Luba talked about visiting MuchMusic, where she was a major star.

LUBA I remember the first day I stepped foot on your premises. I was so nervous I was going to explode. It was new for everybody. It must have been exciting to work there . . . and later, toward the end of the '80s, it was like coming back to family or to very close friends. I just felt very comfortable.

12 Live Aid/ Limits In London

When we see a collection of the world's most famous and beloved pop stars on the same stage, gathered to support something undeniably worthwhile, we're proud of our heroes and savour the individual performances as well as the one-off moments that contribute to making the event unforgettable. What fans don't see is the cajoling, the wheedling, the threats, the favours called, the shaming and strong-arming that made the whole messy affair possible in the first place.

I was lucky enough to bear witness to some of the above, courtesy of Sir Robert Geldof, whose journey from Boomtown Rat-hood to, if not sainthood, then certainly knighthood, was strange and awe-inspiring.

Geldof's band of Irishmen, named after characters in a Woody Guthrie book, had made a handful of hits in the U.K. and elsewhere in Europe, but had been limited to an odd one-off in 1979 in North America with "I Don't Like Mondays," inspired by a shooting incident at a California high school, the title coming from the twisted rationale provided by the shooter. Their latest album had stalled at home and the band was at a low point in the winter of '84 when Geldof saw a story on TV about the Ethiopian famine. Powerfully moved by what he saw, he called his friend Midge Ure from the band Ultravox, and together they wrote "Do They Know It's Christmas?"

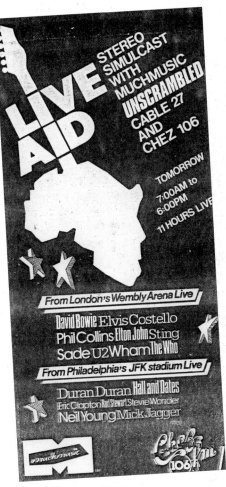

Live Aid poster, 1985

Although the concert that followed was suggested initially by Boy George of Culture Club, the recording by the all-star group known as Band Aid was organized by Geldof and Ure. Neither was a superstar, but they had the connections and the moxie to corral the cream of the British and Irish pop scene. Sting, Paul Weller, Boy George, and members of Duran Duran, Spandau Ballet, U2, Bananarama and others took part and the song, released on December 3, 1984, debuted at #1 in the U.K.

Under the name U.S.A. for Africa, the American contribution to the cause, "We Are the World," written by Michael Jackson and Lionel Richie, featured an all-star cast including Stevie Wonder, Bob Dylan, Tina Turner, Cyndi Lauper, Paul Simon, Ray Charles, Bruce Springsteen and Diana Ross. Quincy Jones, who had produced the U.S.A. for Africa recording, got the ball rolling on the Canadian part of the story when he called David Foster.

DAVID FOSTER I was sitting in my den in West Van, and Quincy Jones called and said, "I'm doing this crazy thing down here next week." He went on to explain "We Are the World" to me. He said we've got the A-plus-plus-plus list; they're going to come right after the American Music Awards and I'm electing you to do the same thing in Canada. Those are the words he used, "I'm electing you." My first response was, "Thanks for thinking of me, but you've got the American Music Awards and everybody's in L.A. We've got no awards show going on in the near future, so how could we pull people from a country that's half as big again as America?" He said, "Foz, you'll figure it out."

In the documentary of the Northern Lights recording session for the Canadian fundraiser, "Tears Are Not Enough," there's a re-enactment of David writing and recording the melody on a portable recorder while driving across the Lions Gate Bridge in Vancouver. To my surprise he revealed that the song wasn't written for the Northern Lights recording. I asked him if he really wrote the song that way.

DAVID FOSTER I really did. I was scoring the film _St. Elmo's Fire_ at the time . . . and I was inspired just by driving over the Lions Gate Bridge. It was one of those crisp winter days and I wrote the basis for [what became] "Tears Are Not Enough," and I sent it to the director of _St. Elmo's Fire_, thinking that he would love it. He called me back and said, "I hate it; it's not right for my movie at all." A day or two later, I got the call from Quincy . . . I called Adams; he called Jim Vallance. I said, "Look I've got this melody that's a whole song. Director hates it. Bryan said, "Yeah, we can work with that." And that became "Tears Are Not Enough." Bryan Adams and Jim spent all night working on the lyrics to my song and at six or seven in the morning, Bryan Adams dropped off a cassette at my house and left it on the doorstep and I played it and I just fucking loved it. They just killed it with the lyric and the additions they'd made to the melody . . . So now we were up and running. And then the director of _St. Elmo's Fire_ called me—this is the punchline. He said, "Oh my god, I made such a mistake. I put the music up against the film and it's . . . brilliant, it's beautiful, I'm so excited." I said, "Dude, you snooze you lose, that melody is gone." He was very upset and then I ended up writing what became the "Love Theme from St. Elmo's Fire" so it kinda worked out good.

If you check the songwriting credits for "Tears Are Not Enough," you'll see that Payolas members Paul Hyde and Bob Rock are included. Paul detailed their contribution.

PAUL HYDE **Foster was producing our album at the time and he gets a phone call from Quincy Jones . . . and he says to us, "He wants me to do a Canadian 'We Are the World' " for famine relief. So we said, "Wow, we've got a song about that." He says, "Great, what's it called?" " 'Tears Are Not Enough.' " He says, "Let's hear it." So we played it and the lyrics were, "Help save the children/ the hungry pleading eyes/ the bony ribs that stick out/ the faces full of flies/ switch off the TV/ I can't stand to watch this stuff/ Tears are not enough." He paused briefly and went, "I love the title," and that was it! He took the title to Adams and Vallance who wrote the song as you know it.**

Jim Vallance recalls the writing and recording process.

JIM VALLANCE **I've been writing songs for forty years. If I've learned anything it's this: there's nothing like a deadline to get the creative juices flowing.**

We wrote "Tears Are Not Enough" in my home studio in a single sixteen-hour session, including the demo track. David had a chord progression and a sketch for the melody. That was enough to get us started. As a reference we recorded a basic track with me on drums and David on keyboards. We did it quickly because it was "just a "demo," when in fact we ended up using it later for the master.

David had to leave because he had another session that day. I got started on the English lyrics while my wife [musician Rachel Paiement] worked on the French lyrics. As luck would have it, Bryan Adams arrived home that day from touring. He rushed over to help.

We worked the rest of the day and into the night. When the lyric was finished Bryan recorded a vocal, and Rachel sang the French verse. The three of us multi-tracked the chorus sections. David arrived and gave the song his stamp of approval. We finished mixing the demo at 4:00 a.m."

Combining the Rolodex (yes, that's what we used to store phone numbers at the time) power of Adams, Foster and manager Bruce Allen, an all-star lineup was pulled together with representatives of a couple of generations of Canadian stars, including Anne Murray, Gordon Lightfoot, Corey Hart, Dan Hill, Burton Cummings, Geddy Lee, Mike Reno from Loverboy, Mark Holmes from Platinum Blonde, Jane Siberry, Lorraine Segato and others. Nine days after writing the song, they were in the studio. I asked David if anyone was particularly hard to get.

DAVID FOSTER I was shocked when Joni Mitchell and Neil Young decided to be part of it. Shocking only because they're so elusive and unreachable. It was one of my favourite moments of the recording when I told Neil Young he was out of tune and he said, "Hey man, that's my sound." I loved that line; it was like, "Shut the fuck up and let me sing."

Released on February 10, 1985, "Tears Are Not Enough" was the biggest Canadian song of the year and the video probably the most played in Much's history. A lot of money was raised for famine relief. Although charity videos with stars wearing headphones, holding hands and swaying together became an oft-parodied cliché (see *In Living Color*'s "Career Aid" sketch), to this day, it's thrilling to see that once-in-a-lifetime assemblage of Canadian stars.

Within a matter of months, buoyed by the fundraising success of the ensemble recordings, talk began about an all-star concert that would take the relief movement to another level. History may be capricious at choosing its unlikely heroes, but Bob Geldof turned out to be the one who had the fire and the tenacity to see this moment through.

Prior to the official announcement of the Live Aid concerts, MuchMusic planned to send me to London in the summer of 1985 with cameraman Dave Russell and producer Michael Heydon, along with winners of a Maxell-sponsored contest that gave them tickets for the Prince's Trust show at Wembley Arena featuring Dire Straits, who were on top of the pop world with their hit "Money for Nothing." As always with Much, we tried to leverage our trip into a series of interviews and get-togethers with whoever would take tea with us, with a one-hour special being the least we would expect to come home with. This one was known as *Limits in London*. Just prior to our departure, one of the most highly anticipated events in the history of pop music, Live Aid, was announced, so of course, we stayed on to cover that. The fact that we had no press credentials was a mere trifling. We did, at the eleventh hour, secure a camera box above one of the stadium's ramps, and my recollection is that it was Bryan Ferry's manager, Martin Kirkup, who we'd met when Ferry came to Much, who helped us with that.

When I arrived there, I was told that I was the first one from Philadelphia that was going to be broadcast *live* to the world. Then Jack Nicholson introduced me, and I walked out. The rest is a blur . . .

Bryan Adams (on appearing at Live Aid)

The entire music community was buzzing with the approach of the Live Aid concert. Rumours circulated as to who was being asked, who was being ignored and who had accepted Geldof's entreaties. Would there be a reunion of the remaining Beatles? Was Phil Collins really going to do the London show and then fly to Philly on the Concorde to play in the U.S.? The answers turned out to be "no" and "yes" respectively.

Upon arriving in London, our first interview was with Ferry's old Roxy Music bandmates, Andy Mackay and Phil Manzanera, who had released a record as the Explorers. Ferry performed as a solo artist at Live Aid with David Gilmour of Pink Floyd on guitar and despite some off-camera expressions of rancour toward their erstwhile leader, Mackay and Manzanera along with drummer Paul Thompson did reunite with Bryan Ferry for a Roxy Music thirtieth anniversary tour in 2001.

We bounced from one encounter to the next, arranged by Michael Heydon on the fly. Breakfast with Adam Ant gave way to a very entertaining interview with Alison Moyet, at her self-effacing wittiest. And Adam, in his own way, took the piss out of his own reputation when I asked about the reaction he'd received from his fellow actors in the Joe Orton play he was doing.

ADAM ANT I think the first day they expected a pink Cadillac to come up, twenty fluffy poodles to run out and this guy carried in on a stretcher with free bottles of tequila, an entourage of fifty people saying, "No photos!" I actually turned up on the train.

We received a surprise invitation to visit Rolling Stones bassist Bill Wyman at his flat on King's Road. He buzzed us in and even though he was widely known as the band's official chronicler, I was still amazed to see the stairway walls covered in original posters for the Stones at the Marquis Club and other legendary venues from their beginnings. Bill greeted us on his own and was relaxed, cordial and voluble, initially about one of his great loves, cricket. England and Australia were playing a match that day and we chatted and watched for sometime before starting the sit-down portion of the interview. He was promoting his side-project, Willie and the Poorboys, but inevitably the conversation turned to the Rolling Stones. He rambled through various Stones-related topics until I asked the question that many had wanted to pose, "Did the Stones consider doing Live Aid?"—a question somewhat loaded by virtue of the fact that while the band was not on the bill, Mick Jagger was scheduled to do a dramatic transatlantic duet with David Bowie on "Dancing in the Street," the Martha and the Vandellas Motown classic. Perhaps coincidentally, Jagger had stepped out on his own in February of that year with his solo debut, *She's the Boss*.

> It's okay, the birds don't read music.
> Joni Mitchell (on not reading music)

BILL WYMAN We were asked; I know Bob [Geldof] very well. We sympathize with the cause but we were in the middle of recording in the studio in Paris . . . we had a meeting in the studio and we decided that we would not do it because of commitments and where we would be in different parts of the country, and it would've meant everybody getting somewhere and rehearsing for a week . . . we thought there was enough people on it anyway. So we sent a letter and said, "We apologize but we can't make it." And then two weeks later, Mick says, "I'm doing it." So we had a big row with him because, you know . . . [turns to the camera] . . . you better not use that . . . [back to me] if you use it it's going to get exaggerated in the press all over the world. But suddenly it came out that he was doing it, and we were all a bit disappointed because we had said, "We are not doing it." And it looks like the rest of the band don't want to and he does.

We didn't use that clip, but surely there's a statute of limitations on reporting inter-band sniping thirty years after the fact. Keith ended up accompanying Bob Dylan at the Live Aid concert in Philadelphia. The Mick and Bowie duet turned out to be too difficult to pull off technologically, so they shot a video before the concert and it was played back during the show without nearly the fanfare it would have gotten had the original plan held up. And after thirty-one years, Bill hung up his Vox Teardrop bass and left the band after the hugely successful 1989 to '90 Steel Wheels and Urban Jungle tours. Those tours were booked by Michael Cohl, Toronto owner of CPI (Concert Productions International). It vaulted Cohl to the bigtime as a promoter and made a boatload of cash for the Stones. Wyman has acknowledged that he, Charlie and Woody really needed the money that the tours generated, pointing out that, in contrast, Mick and Keith, as writers of the band's songs, had a substantial royalty flow that kept the wolf from the door.

We made a side-trip to Bath to spend a day with Martha Johnson and Mark Gane of M+M (formerly Martha and the Muffins), who were doing an album with Peter Gabriel's producer, David Lord. They gave us an excellent tour of Bath, with obvious affection for the history and Roman architecture. Some of their most adventurous music came from that period and their love of Bath saw them move back to live for a few years, during which time they recorded the album *Modern Lullaby* in the bedroom of their flat.

One of our favourite artist encounters was with a young band, Prefab Sprout, whose album *Steve McQueen* had just been released. Their front man and songwriter, Paddy McAloon, remains, to this day, one of the most engaging creative people I've ever met. He was gracious, witty and curious. On that trip we were asking people to name a famous Canadian. Most couldn't name anyone and Paddy immediately cited Glenn Gould. We recorded them rehearsing in a derelict-looking building by the shores of the Thames. They were a buzz band at that moment, but that album, renamed *Two Wheels Good* in North America to appease the family of Steve McQueen,

Bill Wyman of the Rolling
Stones and Christopher Ward

was as much success as they
would ever see on the charts.

We met up with my friend Mike
Myers, who had been such an
integral part of *City Limits* a year
earlier. After a stint at Toronto's
Second City comedy club, Mike
had relocated to London and
hooked up with Neil Mullarkey from
the Cambridge Footlights. We
recorded a Mullarkey and Myers
show upstairs at a tiny pub during
which cameraman Dave Russell was
laughing so uncontrollably, some-
thing I'd never seen before, that the shot got very shaky at times.

And we went to Stonehenge!

We'd been trying to get a few minutes with Geldof since we arrived in
England and one day when we were in the Polygram building to speak with
Alison Moyet, the approval came to go up a couple of flights to a large
office where Geldof and the Polygram staff were coordinating the event that
would be billed as the 'Global Jukebox.' We went up and waited quietly on
the sidelines, watching as Bob Geldof, in the midst of seeming chaos,
worked the phones, all the while receiving whispered updates from staffers
on duty. He looked like a man possessed, his eyes, intense at the best of
times, projecting a blend of raw fatigue and fury, such as I had never seen.
On one phone line he forcefully pressed a Saudi prince to make arrangements to collect donations and on another, he shouted at Huey Lewis, "I
don't care how pregnant your wife is, you will be on that fucking stage in
Philadelphia!" In the end Huey did not appear.

We were ushered onto a small balcony and Dave had no sooner gotten
his camera hoisted onto his shoulder when Bob arrived with an all-business
expression. He delivered his manifesto.

**BOB GELDOF As long as we get money, I would shake hands with the
devil on the left and the devil on my right for the sake of expediency.
Famine demands expedient measures and whatever it takes to keep
those people alive, I'll do it.**

The only relief from his mission came when I asked what felt like a stupid
question at the time, but now I'm not sure. I'd seen the Boomtown Rats at the
El Mocambo in Toronto and I asked if he was looking forward to getting back
together with the band. His face relaxed momentarily and he said how glad he

(Above) Live Aid crowd at Wembley Stadium, July 13, 1985
(Opposite) U2 on stage

would be when he could go back to being the musician that he was prior to this head-on with destiny. Before leaving, he asked what arrangements MuchMusic had made regarding collecting donations. We said that we knew only that the concert was being broadcast on the network and he asked us our boss's name. And phone number. With that he rushed back into the office, called the number and asked for John Martin. When informed that he wasn't there and learning that John was in "the other office" at Emilio's down the street, he got that number and called. The bartender picked up and turned to John.

"It's Bob Geldof for you."

Reportedly John sat up straight and got on the line, received his marching orders and then began the organizing required to enable would-be donors to contribute by cheque or pledge during the broadcast. The team that handled the Canadian Jerry Lewis telethon gave valuable advice on setting up phone lines and taking donations. Much raised a lot of money thanks to that call.

On the morning of July 13, 1985, in the predawn darkness of my hotel room, I managed to shave a small corner of my nose off. Once we found a pharmacy that was open, it was time to head to Wembley Stadium. We had strict instructions to arrive before the gates were opened to the crowd at 10:00 a.m., take our camera position and get ready to shoot. Did people take the prominently displayed Band-Aid on my face as some reference to the group that recorded "Do They Know it's Christmas?"? Maybe. Ouch.

We did arrive on time, walking past the buzzing crowds waiting outside the stadium. We were assigned a small camera well, located about one third of the way back from the stage, above one of the ramps leading onto the field. It was tight quarters with Dave and his camera, Michael Heydon and myself, but we were grateful, given how late-arriving our press credentials had been. It was a gorgeous summer day and we had a clear view of the show. Watching eighty thousand people stream into Wembley was an exhilarating and joyful experience.

Between acts in London the video screen showed performances from JFK Stadium in Philadelphia, including Bryan Adams and Madonna, but it was the original geezer pleasers the Beach Boys who got the crowd in London engaged. When they hit "Help Me Rhonda," I remember rows of Londoners doing coordinated dancing and singing along.

Another group of old timers, Status Quo, opened the Wembley show with "Rockin' All Over the World." My personal favourites were Queen, who unleashed a commanding five-song set, Elvis Costello's lilting solo performance of "All You Need Is Love," and U2, who attempted to compress all the tension and release of one of their two-hour shows into about twenty minutes.

An odd side note—Mike Peters, the lead singer from Irish band the Alarm, after watching his old friend Bono and bandmates from the audience, jumped into our little concrete sanctuary to get away from the crowd. We'd made friends with the band when they came by Much earlier in the year and Mike hung out for much of the show.

Seeing Paul McCartney take the stage and play the opening chords of "Let It Be" was thrilling, so the failure of his microphone for most of his performance was very disappointing. A powerful moment came at the end of the show when McCartney and Pete Townsend lifted Geldof on their shoulders. Almost two billion people around the world watched on television. I knew how privileged we were to have witnessed this event in person.

Live Aid turned out to be not only an artistic and fundraising success, it also gave way to many other similar shows. Bob Dylan is reputed to have said, 'Wouldn't it be great if we did something for our own farmers right here in America?' while on stage at Live Aid. Two months later the first Farm Aid concert was organized by Willie Nelson, Neil Young, John Mellencamp and others, raising over nine million dollars for farmers in America.

Later that year Steve Van Zandt, a.k.a. "Miami Steve" from Springsteen's band, organized a protest against the racist policies of the South African government with the group Artists Against Apartheid and the song "Sun City." In June of 1988, a seventieth birthday tribute was held at Wembley Stadium, the site of Live Aid three years earlier, for the still-imprisoned Nelson Mandela. Two years later, another concert was held at Wembley to celebrate Mandela's release from prison.

13 Oh, the Nuttiness

So many things we did, looking back, seem unapologetically puerile, but among all the loony goings-on, there are a couple of seasonal favourites that still get mentioned regularly—the Christmas tree toss, and *Fromage!*

Is it sad that after all the artist interviews and hours spent on air talking meaningfully about music, the thing people most often recall to me is the *Fromage!* show, featuring Charles de Camembert, in a blue and white striped shirt, a red scarf, a penciled in Salvador Dali moustache and of course, a beret? A raspberry-coloured beret, I might add.

I've always disliked year-end lists; they seemed like a lazy way to fill magazines and airtime with stuff we've seen a lot of. It's too soon to be nostalgic, for goodness' sake. But with *Fromage!* we dug through the videos that had come during the past year that for the most part had been too dreadful to air, and combined with a few choice tacky missteps by the terminally famous, we put together a list of candidates ripe for mockery. In years to come, we would wisely flag the offenders and contenders as we screened them in the weekly programming meetings, building a mighty smorgasbord of tasteless delights, slowly fermenting in time for the year-end show. And those meetings, interminable at times, needed a cheese course. We soon bored of shooting the show in the studio and ventured out to various downtown cheese shops, in particular one at the St. Lawrence Market that had walls of the stuff and just the right "odeur" for the event. The staff, likely not Much viewers, would look on in wonderment as we rhapsodized over a wheel of havarti. A couple of years in, we decided that Charles needed a co-host. Quebec pop star Mitsou took part at a cheese factory in the suburbs, happily joining in on the silliness. Then Natalie Richard from MusiquePlus, the French-language network that paralleled MuchMusic in English Canada, later a VJ on Much, came on as a regular co-host. Natalie was perfect. She's French. She's beautiful. Charles was not French and was ridiculous.

As to who we played, I remember *Miami Vice* star Philip Michael Thomas being given the Mall of Shame Award one year and Huey Lewis receiving the ultimate honour, the Lifetime Acheesement Award. My one rule was no Canucks—not that there was a shortage of Northern video cheddar, but I just felt that there were enough challenges to sustaining a career here without us piling on. We did make one exception and featured Celine Dion, but, hey, she was a huge international star and if you saw the video, you'd understand!

Seeing artists you admire in dire video circumstances was disappointing and yet sometimes it had to be admitted as we sifted through the 'videos

Steve Anthony doing the annual Christmas tree toss with Reg Simard, Dennis Saunders and Mike the Cleaner

and hideos' of the year. To this day I still want to ask whose idea it was to include the floating pieces of toast in Stevie Wonder's "I Just Called to Say I Love You" video.

After I left Much at the end of '89, they continued to send a crew to L.A., where I was living, to shoot *Fromage!* I remember we went to Olivera Street, a Mexican market in the oldest part of the city to shoot one year.

JIM SHUTSA, director I remember us shooting in the Mexican market surreptitiously with a small industrial video camera instead of Betacam and acting like tourists shooting home movies in the market [so we wouldn't be hit for filming without a permit or accosted for performance monies].

My then-one-year-old daughter, Rachel, marched a giant, orange plastic cheese down our street to the strains of "La Marseillaise" for the lifetime award. It's never too early.

In a highly appropriate handing off of the cheese stick, gravelly voiced puppet Ed the Sock stepped into Charles de Camembert's chaussettes for the next generation of *Fromage!*

A grand holiday tradition was the tossing of the MuchMusic Christmas tree from the roof of the building. Michael Williams was the VJ on the original tree toss, but eventually it came to be associated with Steve Anthony. Dennis Saunders remembers the humble origins of the event in 1985.

DENNIS SAUNDERS, director Why? Because it was there, there was a garbage can and a fire escape.

It soon became more complicated.

DENNIS SAUNDERS It started at the old building and then at the new building, we had a big flat roof. It started there on the second floor balcony and I brought my brother-in-law, a pilot who had been working with the NASA program, to do flight analysis. And I had another guy who was a pyro specialist. We had a weather report and a countdown.

CHAD KROEGER, NICKELBACK I remember every year it's like, "What are they gonna do?" They fastened rockets to the tree, tried to hit the dumpster. Did it ever make it into the dumpster?

Steve took it to a whole other level.

STEVE ANTHONY It started very simply but eventually became this four-hour thing stretched over a full shift. We'd do things like speculate what it's like to be a Christmas tree and have a camera inside the tree, knowing it's going to be thrown out. We would

spend hours in the carpentry department, giving it wings, trying to make it aerodynamic, with fins on the back.

We had a non-denominational minister come in to bless the Christmas tree. Then we brought in a couple of engineers from NASA who would go through the footage of the previous years, analyzing what we did wrong, drawing diagrams and so on. We treated it excessively seriously.

I had plans to throw it off the CN Tower, where we would run it on a wire down the tower, where it would break through the camouflage into a pit that we would dig at the base, accompanied by fireworks and ending in a giant explosion. Never happened.

There was one tree toss that lives on poignantly in Steve's memory.

STEVE ANTHONY The best one of all, and it made for great TV and fodder for conversation, was—I was at the front of the tree and Mike the Cleaner was at the back of the tree and as we were running to throw it, my thigh hit the railing full force and I started flipping over the railing as the tree left my hands and as I'm about to fall to my death, Mike the Cleaner grabs my feet and pushes me back down. After "Steve's near death incident" we had to wear safety harnesses.

Mike Myers spent a lot of time hanging out at Much in the early years and he put what he observed to good use. In a Second City show called "Bob Has Seen the Wind" at the Old Fire Hall theatre, the company did a parody of MuchMusic, called "Much Religion." Mike played me and I recall that the two main identifiers he used were a major cowlick and lots of blinking. Did I really blink that much? Deborah Theaker played Erica and recalls this of the scene.

DEBORAH THEAKER It was called Much Religion and we were counting down the Top Ten Commandments. I was Erica Ehm in a wig and . . . Mike was St. Christopher Ward and wore a choir robe and a large cross. I kept an assortment of huge, exaggerated floppy hats backstage to throw over my Erica Ehm wig to suggest extreme hipness. The hats got bigger and more over-the-top as the run progressed, culminating with a huge, droopy Cat in the Hat velvet number that was ridiculous. I tried to make my eyes huge, startled, and unblinking as Erica. I decided she would have that startled, stiff, rabbit-in-the-headlights look to counter Mike's blinking version of you. The night Erica herself came to the show, I felt sick with nerves and gave a terrible, lacklustre performance because I felt bad mocking her right to her face . . . I remember Mike making references to Moses, which had the audience howling because he was referencing Moses Znaimer with religious reverence.

Mike Myers as St.
Christopher Ward
at Second City

MIKE MYERS Welcome back to Much Religion, the nation's religious station. I'm your host, St. Christopher Ward. The last video you saw was a Jerry Falwell video, "Great Balls of Hell Fire and Damnation." I liked it very, very much indeed. Now we've got some tour news. The Pope's coming to town, Pope John Paul George and Ringo. He'll be at Varsity Stadium. So will I, frankly. Mother Teresa will be in town promoting her new album, *Stigmata Attack*. Now I can see by the Pepsi Cola Second Coming Countdown Clock we've only got eight minutes. Erica's gonna come by and give us an update.

DEBORAH THEAKER Welcome to the Power Hour from the Prayer Tower. Okay. The Top Ten Commandments Countdown this week is as follows: Avarice is holding tough at number one and it's up from number three, so that's good. What? Oh my god, they're making me laugh. A little later on we're going to take a look at the new Tammy Bakker video, "Tracks of my Tears," and that should be good. As for the Pepsi Cola Second Coming Countdown, a very cute, shaggy-haired Hebrewite who we all know and love is going to be appearing.

Inevitably perhaps, the labels got in on the act. Promo rep Peter Diemer recalls his desperation to get Blind Melon, a new priority act for his label, into rotation on Much. In their video for "No Rain," a young girl is wearing a bee outfit.

PETER DIEMER It might have been Simon [Evans] saying, "Peter, if you dressed up in that bee suit and just hung around here in the studio for awhile maybe we will add it next week." I called my counterpart in L.A. and said, "I need the bee suit here immediately." I put the stupid thing on and showed up in the bee suit and everybody laughed of course and put me through it, and I said, "Here I am," and they said, "No, [wear the suit until] the next music meeting." So I spent a number of days in the "environment" with my laptop, every so often waving at the camera.

(Opposite) Peter Diemer in the "Blind Melon" bee suit

I need the bee suit here immediately.

Peter Diemer

14 The Specialty Shows

The programming committee met every Tuesday in a small boardroom to screen new videos, yea or nay them for that week's rotation, but mainly to argue. To the extent that there was an order to what we played, the all-night show *City Limits* had been programmed by senior producers Michael Heydon, Anne Howard and me. Associate producers Morgen Flury, Terri Walsh and Simon Evans joined us once Much launched. John Martin passed through the room occasionally when there was something he championed, like Blue Rodeo's "Try" video.

When it came to Much, we figured it was time for a format, a kind of bad word at the time because of the corporate ring to it, but we needed something that would ensure that the most popular videos got their proper exposure and that what went to air wasn't left to the whim of the VJ and producer du jour. When I was in university, I had done the all-night show at CKPT radio, a CHUM affiliate in Peterborough, Ontario (you can imagine the deleterious effect this had on my grades), so I knew what a format looked like and we agreed on a simple A-B-C approach that represented high, medium and low rotation. There was also an "option" slot as part of the grid that left the door open for improvising on the fly if there was a theme that presented itself based on what was happening in the studio, or when an artist came in. Sometimes, I would ask the interview subject if there's anything they wanted to see; often they would choose a video by one of their friends, or something that may not have been released in their homeland, and you became viewers together watching on the studio monitor.

As time went by, the trickle of videos grew to a weekly flood and the length of the meetings expanded accordingly, as did the duration and intensity of the "discussions" about the relative merits of what we were screening. We mocked the videos and each others' tastes relentlessly and hastened to point out the absurdity of those white-faced people marching stoically in the background of the shot, or the bass player who looked like he would rather be anywhere else in the world and not have to be wearing that stupid hat, or sloppy synch (the synchronizing of the singing with the audio), known affectionately as "lipflap."

MORGEN FLURY, producer We argued, sometimes heatedly. We all had our different causes we would fight for and against. You always liked singer/songwriters. I hated metal but couldn't deny it.

Of course anything with animals got a higher mark. Simon, being the anti-VJ was also the anti-programmer and liked anything weird.

I had a reputation for standing up for Canadian videos, literally, on my chair. The recollection of life as a Canuck recording artist was all-too-fresh in my memory and the way our country's weather—wind and snow and icy roads—and all that glorious distance work against establishing a musician's career, made me feel like we northern folk had a couple of strikes against us going into the process of career-building. And, let's face it, budgets weren't as big as they were for American acts for recording, touring and, of course, for videos.

That said, we were witness to the rapid growth of the music video industry in Canada, and it's not blowing the Much horn too loudly to say that we were a major reason this boom happened. The only downside, at least from the point of view of the artists, their managers and labels, was that there was a finite amount of airtime. We easily exceeded our Canadian content requirements, and because the day was a six-hour block, which then became an eight-hour-long block that was repeated over twenty-four hours, there was no burying of the Canadian videos in low-viewing slots, like radio had been doing for years. If you got a rotation it meant something. Record company promo reps were regular visitors to the building, either accompanying visiting or local artists coming in for interviews, or dropping by to get their videos into consideration for the Tuesday meeting.

We listened to their pitches and when it made sense to us, brought their thoughts to the programming meeting. The individual reps and a rotating cast of other characters were welcome faces at Much, but I can only imagine what a challenge it would have been to get our attention when so many voices were vying for it. And, we were notoriously iconoclastic in our approach to the job. Moses and John shielded us from the programmers at CHUM, and I don't think I really knew until later how very interested in taking our place the programmers at CHUM were at the time. The labels had their own priorities but that mattered little to us. If a video looked good and sounded good and had enough champions in the room, it went to air. This approach could both delight and dismay a surprised promo rep. Unlike MTV we didn't get in bed with the labels and trade an exclusive for putting a shitty band into rotation.

After the marathon meeting was over and the programming decisions had been made, their end of the call might sound like—"You added *what*? In *what* rotation? No, that's amazing, I just didn't think . . . by the way, how about . . . oh, you didn't like it, well what about next week when something opens up . . . it sucks you're saying . . . yeah I know, but it's the company's priority this week and they're putting a big push behind it at radio . . . yes, I know you guys don't give a shit about radio, but maybe . . . oh, okay, thanks." Simon and Morgen had to be on the receiving end of all this importuning from the labels; I believe the feeling being that because I was on-air, we would downplay my role in the committee process. And Michael and Anne, as senior producers, could quite rightfully bypass most of the pleading and moaning. And Simon and Morgen were tough!

Promo rep Peter Diemer recalls the label's impression of what was going on in the meetings that determined the fate of their acts.

PETER DIEMER **It was pretty unscientific . . . it was before call-out research and "our focus group says," or "this is blowing up on the telephones." If you guys took a flier on something it would be before radio was telling you this might be a hit. And you enjoyed that because you wanted to be the leader. Then we'd get [a video added to the playlist] and the marketing department would kick into gear and say, "Much just added this into heavy rotation, what are we going to do now? We gotta go and sell it."**

Having video as a promotional tool also changed the way labels did business with radio, according to Peter.

PETER DIEMER **There was a certain point in time where we would bring a machine [to the radio station] . . . a VHS . . . you'd lug it in and plug it in and say, "We're going to show you this video."**

It soon reached a point where there were more quality videos that we genuinely wanted to play then we had time for.

SIMON EVANS **We could have gone live for twenty-four hours and played completely different material all the time. There was way too much stuff for the eight hours a day we had to program.**

Ta da! Enter the era of the specialty show, where videos could be ghettoized, I mean *programmed* for a dedicated audience, in anything from an occasional to a "lunar" rotation as it was known. *City Limits* had made the move to Much from the start, shedding the mainstream videos we included on the all-night show, to become the home for the beloved left-of-centre indie artists' work. It had a core following and a sense of identity that made it a meaningful destination for those videos. Simon and I worked well together, going back to the old *Limits* days, so it made sense for us to continue to do so on Much. Producing *Limits* also suited his musical taste. Interestingly, as the term "indie" came to represent a musical genre, rather than being a descriptor for music made outside the major labels, the identity of *Limits* changed. Bands like Echo and the Bunnymen, the Cure, and the Red Hot Chili Peppers were getting big-label support and primetime play, so did they belong on the *Limits* playlist anymore? I didn't think so, reasoning that there were so many acts desperate for that odd but not insignificant bit of exposure that the show offered. And didn't we have this glorious rep as the haven for the weird and unwanted? ("Fish Heads," anyone?) Simon countered with the fact that these now big acts were the bands that the

Christopher Ward with Flea and Anthony Kiedis of the Red Hot Chili Peppers

Limitoids loved and had followed from the artists' humbler days and that this was our constituency. He maintained that "indie" was a full-fledged genre now and that's what *City Limits* was. Many arguments ensued as I gamely fought for the lonely and the dispossessed that haunted the video fringe. Simon won.

He was right. Once *Limits* slipped into video memory, Simon went on to produce and host the hugely popular *The Wedge*, the new daily one-hour "alternative" show that launched in '92 and replaced *Limits*. Sook-Yin Lee took over in 1995.

JAY FERGUSON, SLOAN *City Limits* **was the show that all my friends liked the most because you would play American underground videos or stuff from England . . . like the Smiths or The The, or Hüsker Dü or the Replacements. We never got to see these bands in Nova Scotia, hardly any underground bands would come.**

When Much launched in '84, *City Limits* and the *Coca-Cola Countdown* were the only so-called specialty shows. Naming rights on the generic countdown show was the least we could do for a major early benefactor. Then director of publicity, Sarah Crawford, explains.

SARAH CRAWFORD **There was one deal that was signed before MuchMusic started and that was with Coca-Cola for one million dollars per year for three years, and that gave us enough money to put the network on the air.**

ROCKFLASH

And then there was the little-news-segment-that-could, called *Rockflash*, originally hosted by *The NewMusic* co-host Jeanne Beker.

JEANNE BEKER I was at a point in my career where it was, "If I have to interview Rod Stewart one more time, I'll kill myself. Enough with Sting already." We were working on *MovieTelevision* and the following year we launched *FashionTelevision*. I was looking for ways out of that rock 'n' roll madness. They gave me *Rockflash* with the idea that "the kids will be out there throwing to videos, but you've been on the scene a long time, you've got the cred to do the news."

When *FashionTelevision* did launch a year later, John did the unexpected again, and contacted Denise Donlon, who was working at the Sam Feldman Agency at the time.

DENISE DONLON John offered me the job replacing Jeanne Becker on *Rockflash*. I didn't understand how he could put someone like me with big rock hair and a lisp on television.

Denise got heat from the top from day one.

DENISE DONLON Moses didn't think I would work and told me so. You know Moses—he likes to push your buttons right away to see what you're made of. He said, "What will you do *when* it doesn't work out?" Not "if."

And Moses wasn't the only challenge that went with the gig.

DENISE DONLON The problem with *Rockflash* was that J.D. was very territorial about the information. I did eight *Rockflash*es and I couldn't repeat anything. There was no Google, no internet. The magazines came in but the news was two months old. We had a daily entertainment news tipsheet called "The Daily Double" and it would arrive on the fax machine. I relied on that heavily, except that J.D. would stand beside the fax machine waiting for it to come out and he would write his name, J.D., and the date, so that you knew that he'd already used that piece of information and you couldn't use it.

Denise's experience and knowledge of, in particular, the Canadian music business and her passion for the music made her a natural for the *Rockflash* segments. She had a great sense of humour and was game for anything. Well, almost anything.

DENISE DONLON You [Christopher] were a joy to work with . . . except that time you covered me in toilet paper. I have the tape— I'm sitting on the phone and you were running 'round the environment with a roll of toilet paper covering everybody. You rolled it around my head, and then the phone and then you'd be off to do somebody else's desk and you'd wrap it around a cameraman and you were live on-air the whole time. Another time, you outed how tall I was on the side of the road [on Queen Street]. I was standing on the ground and you were standing on the curb so that our heads were equal on camera. At one point, you stopped the interview and asked the camera to shoot our feet. There were your perfect shoes on the curb and I was wearing socks with sandals. So thank-you for that.

I remember you bringing Mike Myers over as "Wayne from Bloodjun," wearing a Kenora dinner jacket [a classic red plaid shirt]. He had a fake wig and a baseball hat with horns coming out of it. I'd just done an item on the band Kick Axe and they were going on a cross-Canada tour and the guitar player had just quit. "Wayne" asked me if I could call Kick Axe back and tell them that he was ready and he would fly in anywhere.

When Denise moved to *The NewMusic*, her replacement, Kim Clarke Champniss, had his own tart introduction to life with Moses.

KIM CLARKE CHAMPNISS I'd originally gone on the air as Kim Clarke and then two weeks later [Moses] said, "What happened to the Champniss, I hired a Champniss." . . . I said John Martin said it was okay. You know, Clarke is my middle name, Kim Clarke works well on TV. "No, I like Champniss—if you don't change it you're fired on Monday morning," and it's Friday . . . so it became Kim Clarke Champniss and it changed my life—weird.

When we made the move from 99 Queen Street East to our new and permanent home at 299 Queen Street West, construction was a little behind schedule . . . and it was less than bare bones, with wires hanging everywhere. Maybe it's like when you meet a guy who operates a pneumatic drill on the street for a living, and you ask, "How do you work under those conditions?" and he shrugs and says, "After a while you don't notice." I had completely forgotten that, but Kim recalls the chaos.

KIM CLARKE CHAMPNISS The set was not built and so in typical Much low-budget fashion the [*Rockflash*] segment would come from somewhere in the basement. They found an old brown steel tea tray [with legs] and [Mike Rhodes] would sit behind it while the VJ sat to one side.

Apparently, there was a little handwritten "Rockflash" sign that was taped to the front of the tray. Even after the rubble was cleared, the news segments ended up being a testimonial to the low-tech approach that governed early Much.

DENNIS SAUNDERS, technical director We had this thing called "Rapid Fax" where we would have Kim on a sort of news desk on wheels, and we'd roll him careening across the studio for a bumper and then try to "dock" him.

MIKE & MIKE'S EXCELLENT X-CANADA ADVENTURES

I'd done a trip dubbed "Chris-Cross-Canada" with Mike Campbell in the late spring and summer of 1987. Ten provinces, the Yukon, forty days and twenty-five flights. We went through a couple of cameramen and saw a lot of this country. For the first time, I witnessed in person the impact that Much was having, and it was inspiring. It took weeks to recover from this intense tour.

Campbell was a road dog extraordinaire. Checking into the hotel, he'd have his ultra-cool mini audio set-up in place and the first spin of John Hiatt's *Bring the Family* CD happening before the rest of us had inserted the hotel key in the door. He had that total confidence, "get 'er done" mentality that people loved. He was efficient, business-like and completely rock 'n' roll. His purview was connecting with the cable affiliates across the country, but his role soon expanded.

MIKE CAMPBELL It was decided that I should become the station's National Field Reporter and would report on newsworthy events to feed our *Rockflash* segments. I'd been field-producing items like these on our VJ tours, so I already knew my way around a shoot, but Mike Rhodes in the news department desperately wanted to get out of the building to travel, so I convinced everyone that I needed my own field producer, and off we went for the better part of a year.

When the boys finally found themselves back in the building, they got a surprise from management.

MIKE CAMPBELL One day we were summoned to general manager Dennis Fitzgerald's office. Both of us knew (a) we were having too much fun on the road, (b) it was costing a fortune, and (c) before

satellite uplinks and such were normal, that by the time the tape we were shooting was couriered to Toronto and edited—when it finally hit the air—it was hardly news anymore. We figured we were there to be fired. Dennis told us they were going to give us a weekly show instead.

Rhodes had been producing *Toronto Rocks*, a local Citytv after-school video show, and *Rockflash*, where he appeared as a host as well, but once he hit the highway he found his calling at Much.

MIKE RHODES Mike and I had both seen a lot of Canada in our youth and shared an unbridled love for the country. We celebrated the land, the people and the music. We were able to borrow a camera (and cameraman) from a cable company in Edmonton in 1988 and we set off on what would become *Mike and Mike's Excellent X-Canada Adventures*.

Campbell explains where the *M&M* wanderlust originated.

MIKE CAMPBELL We hardly ever did anything music-related, which was ironic given the network we were working for, but both of us came from families that moved a lot (my father was a search-and-rescue helicopter pilot and Mike's dad started out in the Navy and then worked for the CBC). Subsequently, we'd already seen most of the country and loved the same things about it: the unbelievable geography, the goofy tourist "attractions," the sports teams, regional idiosyncrasies/rivalries and, of course, the characters such a country produces.

The Wawa Goose and the Giant Lobster in Shediac aside, these guys were remarkably serious about their love of country.

MIKE CAMPBELL We used to end our show with our backs to the camera, facing into the sunset (when we were lucky enough to get one) and generally spent those few moments yammering on about how beautiful the place we were visiting was. I loved that part of the show.

I asked Campbell about some highlights and he came back with a staggering list.

MIKE CAMPBELL I was given the opportunity to: travel to Europe and the Middle East with a Canadian entertainment troupe led by John Allan Cameron; take a private train across Canada; fly in an F/A-18, a T-33, a Kiowa helicopter, a Tutor jet with the Snowbirds over Niagara Falls on Canada Day, aerobatics over southern

Alberta; do the four-man
bobsleigh and the luge and the skeleton bob
at Olympic Park in Calgary on the same day;
throw a pass from the fifty-five-yard line at
Taylor Field in Regina (complete to Rhodes
at the goal line, I might add) and watch
several Roughriders games from their bench; skydive in Salmon
Arm; bungee jump in Nanaimo; fly around the peak of Mt. Logan;
build an igloo in Iqaluit; become mayor of Nackawic, New Brunswick,
for a few minutes; be on a bus that Jeff Healey was driving [!];
rappel down the inside of the Science Centre in Regina; ski a
freshly groomed Blackcomb Mountain at the end of a day during
SnowJob; ski the Whistler glacier in August via helicopter and then
bike down the mountain to ride horses and golf; dogsled in the
Northwest Territories; get screeched-in in Newfoundland more
times than I can count—I've kissed an actual cod, frozen cod,
salted cod, a lobster, a wooden puffin, a stuffed puffin and several
Newfie dogs; race miniature motorcycles in Moncton and F1-replica
go-karts in Kelowna; sing onstage with Tom Cochrane and Jim
Cuddy, and way more stuff than that.

Dan Gallagher and Mike Rhodes and
Mike Campbell with Bryan Potvin,
Jay Semko, Don Schmid and Merl
Bryck of the Northern Pikes

Whew! As to who was the cooler of the dynamic duo, Campbell shared
this insight.

MIKE CAMPBELL Technically I was, but Rhodes had a particular
"personal" cool that was fairly powerful to what I liked to call
"off-planet" citizens.

MUCH WEST AND TERRY DAVID MULLIGAN

Terry David Mulligan has worn a few hats, including those of actor, radio host and author, as well as the muskrat headgear favoured by the RCMP. Terry joined the Mounties at age eighteen and lasted four years before moving to the entertainment business for good. He'd been hosting a video show based in Vancouver on CBC called *Good Rockin' Tonite* when the Much opportunity came along.

TERRY DAVID MULLIGAN I decided to phone Moses. At the CBC there was no job security. We had a hit show and they were only willing to negotiate [my] contract every twenty-six weeks. I had kids, a family to look after, and I asked for a year's contract and they said, "We don't do that," and I said, "Yes, you do, for the right people you do." I called Moses and he said, "Who are you?" I said, "I'm your competition and I'm kicking your ass in Vancouver. And secondly, you call yourself 'the nation's music station' but you're nowhere to be in found in Vancouver or the West, for that matter. And if you haven't noticed, we've been hauling away most of the hardware at the Junos the last couple of years." This was Adams, Loverboy, etc.

The casual Much approach to making television would have been new to Terry when he and the management got down to working out the details.

TERRY DAVID MULLIGAN The next thing I remember is having a beer with John [Martin] and Nancy [Oliver] in Gastown, and saying, "How do we do this?" John said, "Go out to BCIT [the British Columbia Institute of Technology] and find yourself a cameraman and a camera and a three-quarter-inch machine and shoot." I had a rotating cast of cameramen for the first few years, many of whom were embarrassed to be shooting MuchMusic, because it wasn't news, it wasn't CBC.

Terry was grateful for one aspect of our erstwhile fearless leader, John Martin.

TERRY DAVID MULLIGAN He had to deal with Moses every day of his life.

Ah, yes, dealing with Moses, that challenge that each one of us had to figure out for ourselves. Here's how Terry worked it out.

TERRY DAVID MULLIGAN I decided early on that the only way I was going to survive Moses and his system was to stay as far away from

him as possible, and I had time and distance working for me. After that decision was made, we got along very well. He was considerate, kind, but I only ever had to deal with him once or twice a year.

Terry adapted seamlessly to the seat-of-the-pants ethos that prevailed at Much.

TERRY DAVID MULLIGAN I used to wait for the first break in the rainy weather and then shoot the whole week in one day. I'd change so [many times], that one time I was in a lane on Robson with my ass hanging out, reaching for my clothing, and somebody comes by and says, "Hey, Terry, how are you doing?" And all he can see is my ass.

I don't think the launch of *Much West* was a reaction to westerners feeling left out, as much as it was a natural growth spurt for Much. As Terry has pointed out, artists from the west were experiencing unprecedented success and they were receiving significant exposure on the network before *Much West* went to air. Terry was uniquely positioned to give us the flavour of that part of the country and to promote the careers of the next wave of local artists that followed Adams and Loverboy—acts like Spirit of the West, Grapes of Wrath and Colin James.

I asked Terry about the east/west divide in those days.

TERRY DAVID MULLIGAN One of the problems is that the political decisions that affect us in the West, are made in the East, and so there's almost immediate resentment of things coming out of the east, telling us what to do, how we will live our lives, what is law, what is not law . . . So, anyone coming out of that east was tarred with the same brush. So, for example . . . it wasn't the "nation's music station," it was *Toronto's* music station with some other areas. It's different now—we became aware of ourselves and our community . . . and what a great life we had and how self-sustaining we were. We didn't need the approval of the east in order to do the things that we wanted to do.

Neil Osborne, lead singer of 54-40, expands on this from the point of view of a band.

NEIL OSBORNE It's a long way to go to get to Toronto [from Vancouver]. We'd already been to L.A. six times. When we got there, we realized we were guests, this isn't our home . . . The record label tells us—you're doing this, you're doing that . . . it's so media intense. We are the poorer cousins but we live in the nicer place. It goes deeper than that. It's a hockey thing, too . . . when the Leafs come to town, half the place is filled with Leafs jerseys.

Bryan Adams and Keith Scott performing for the 1992 MMVAs in Vancouver

Mulligan was paying close attention to what was happening on Much, even before he worked there.

TERRY DAVID MULLIGAN When I first saw Much I thought it was pretty damn cool. A tad pompous, but they had the game to themselves. You could see the creative freedom.

Occasionally, Terry exercised his own sense of freedom.

SHERRY GREENGRASS, producer I got the Mulligan gig. He was notorious for introducing videos we didn't have. He'd give me cutaways of seagulls.

Mulligan's feelings about the network's lack of a national identity applied to the east coast as well.

TERRY DAVID MULLIGAN I remember hearing VJs saying, "This band is touring from coast-to-coast, from Vancouver to Toronto." And I thought, "What the fuck—what about the Maritimes?"

Terry is a fervent supporter of the west coast music scene and is unquestionably one of the most important people to cover it and participate in it. He's got the awards and the respect that few will ever receive. He's also a realist.

TERRY DAVID MULLIGAN You can be a hero in your hometown, you can be top of the heap in Vancouver, but it doesn't mean a thing if you can't sell records in Toronto, Montreal, the rest of the country, or down south.

There's one hometown hero who conquered the world.

TERRY DAVID MULLIGAN The thing about [Bryan] Adams is he proved you could have a career and be on the west coast. . . . Bruce [Allen—longtime Adams manager] said, "We're not going to Toronto, L.A., New York, we're going to do it from here." And they said, "We're going to do it on a handshake." Adams said, "We're going to out-work everybody else, write great hooks, and make history."

TERRY DAVID MULLIGAN Bryan had a sense of who he was—he wasn't trying to figure it out—he's just a kid from North Vancouver . . . He was never manufactured; he was exactly the guy that we knew when we first saw him. One of the first times I ever saw him play was in North Vancouver. The DJ made the mistake of playing Bryan's dance hit ["Let Me Take You Dancing," Bryan's first solo recording at age eighteen] as he walked in, and he walked up to

the guy, took the record and broke it.

Terry has witnessed the history of rock 'n' roll and has the interview list to go with it—Hendrix, Bowie, Roger McGuinn of the Byrds . . . I asked him for a favourite from his Much days.

Tom Cochrane and Terry David Mulligan

TERRY DAVID MULLIGAN Giant Stadium, just after the second Woodstock, Denise [Donlon] sends me to interview the Rolling Stones. We're set up backstage and Ronnie Wood comes out. The deal with the Stones is Ronnie will go out to meet the interviewer and then go back to the dressing room and say, "Don't waste your time, he's a wank." Ronnie was the litmus test. He came out with a huge draft of fresh Guinness, and I said, "Where the hell did you get that?" He said, "We carry our own cask. Would you like some?" We had a great time, finished the draft and he went back in the dressing room and said, "He's all right." And they all came out to talk to me.

JIM SHUTSA, technical director TDM was the ambassador for the west. He'd take us to a bar and spend all of our per diems ordering wine.

SOUL IN THE CITY

Mike Williams lobbied long and hard to get *Soul in the City* on air. He had help from Michele Geister, initially as a volunteer then as an editor for *SITC* and two features Erica Ehm was doing called *Indie Street* and *Fashion Notes*. Michele talks about what brought her to the music and the show.

MICHELE GEISTER It was truly for the love, call it intense passion, of the music . . . and exploration of television production. [I lived] a few blocks from Much where we would mix rock and rap effortlessly at legendary house parties. . . . As my roommates began working on

Michael Williams with Stephen "Cat" Coore and Michael "Ibo" Cooper of Third World

There's a place I know. A television show. They interviewed me and Cut Creator 'cause we're pros. Up in Canada where it snows.

LL Cool J (improvising a rap for MuchMusic with his first band)

radio shows at CKLN, Ryerson's community station, I became aware of underground shows featuring hip hop, reggae and dance music that then became the soundtrack to my life.

At the same time I became even more aware of the music's significance as a powerful youth culture movement and . . . [I] began absorbing everything I could about the history of black power, culture and music so I could responsibly do it justice.

My impression was that, at the time, black music as a whole wasn't getting the support from the business side. Michele concurred.

MICHELE GEISTER Before *RapCity* got its first weekly hour slot, *SITC* was one hour a week trying to program multiple genres of R&B, reggae, dance, funk and blues. There was no mainstream black radio, just these two hours of national video play and intermittent college radio plus the clubs. So even though the play on Much was limited, it still was visionary for the industry and country.

Michele describes how she and Michael Williams worked together to ensure the legitimacy of their show.

MICHELE GEISTER Both of us spent a huge amount of time on the phone to the U.S. trying to get the hottest videos, quite often material that wasn't released in Canada and going after artist interviews, local and otherwise.

I felt strongly that this urban music was more than entertainment, it was an essential cultural expression for a community whose voice and expression was limited in the mainstream and I took it as my duty to ensure its authentic voice and other visual extensions were seen and heard against the commercial hype.

Michael has his own succinct take on what the show was about.

MICHAEL WILLIAMS It was music with soul, not just soul music.

He recalls an amusing moment around the time the show was being conceived.

MICHAEL WILLIAMS [Producer Michael] Heydon played a joke on me. He said, "We've done an intro for you [for *SITC*]. He put the tape in the machine and he and Anne [Howard, producer] and John were all around and it was a cornball intro done to the Partland Brothers' "Soul City" [a very white country rock song]. That was cruel and unusual punishment . . . I didn't react . . . I think they thought that I would go apeshit and I went, "Well, that's one way to do it."

Much celebrated diversity in a way that MTV celebrated some heartland notion of what it meant to be American . . . Much early on was on the game with hip hop . . . and dance music. There was aboriginial music programmed. Much tended to integrate things more—a greater number of different videos at any given moment, a greater range of genres, greater diversity in terms of ethnic or racial background of the artists.

Rob Bowman, author, professor of ethnomusicology

EVERYBODY WANTS TO THINK THEY CAN STILL SELL CHOCOLATE BARS.

15 The Young Rockers

Having lived and worked in Los Angeles, I've seen the starkly different approaches to getting an act off the ground there, compared to how it's done in Canada. It's not unusual for a young band to be bankrolled by a family member, spend some time in the garage practising and writing songs and then find that one of their first gigs is a showcase on the Sunset strip at the Rainbow, the Roxy or the Viper Room for label A&R people. It's often pay-to-play, so bands paper the room with friends and family members. They may be talented, might look great and could be the next Guns N' Roses, but without time to develop their skills, it's far more likely that they'll burn out quickly. In the past, labels could sign an act, give them some money for development and recording demos and wait for the process to play out, but when the 1980s arrived and the competition to sign an act became ferocious, big advances and premature opportunities abounded.

Not so north of the border. Slogging it out in the bars was the norm, often playing cover songs to please the crowd and the bar owner. Loverboy's Mike Reno reflected on what it was like when he started out in the 1970s.

MIKE RENO The Canadian music scene in the early '70s was so insane. You had to be good—so people practised and they wrote songs; they had backdrops, sparkly drums, good light shows. It was very competitive. When there's lots of people around all doing the same thing, you've got to stand out.

I'm reminded of the Marx Brothers who would take their show on the road all over America for a year, honing it as they went along, until they felt they were ready to make a movie of it. If the line didn't get a laugh, it was gone!

I have no doubt there are countless very talented people who got left by the roadside, who never made it out of those grungy rooms where no one listened, who had a family to feed or just ran out of ambition before the magic break arrived. But sometimes, an artist found what it takes to survive the rock 'n' roll wars. Here's Barney Bentall's take on that crossroads in his life and career.

BARNEY BENTALL

BARNEY BENTALL I was very close [to giving up]. We had four kids . . . I was doing odd jobs and playing a lot in the clubs in and around Vancouver and Victoria but it was lean times and we were living in a basement suite and didn't have a proper car. My relatives were involved in a construction company and I had an offer to go work there and I thought I should probably hang it up . . . I didn't have any management and I was broke and I thought, "What am I going to do? Maybe it's time to quit; I've given this a . . . ten-year run." My biggest accomplishment is keeping my family together through all of this . . . it seemed bleak but we had this big following in Vancouver and I said, "We've got to try one more time."

How's that for a backstory? Barney Bentall and his band, the Legendary Hearts, were local favourites, but that can only sustain you for so long.

BARNEY BENTALL We demo'd "Something to Live For" on an eight-track tape machine. We worked one weekend to raise funds; nobody got paid, and we made a $3,000 video. We sent that to MuchMusic . . . and you guys starting playing it in significant rotation. So armed with that, we thought, "Who can represent us in this last-ditch attempt to get a record deal before getting a real job?" We came to the conclusion that I was the best person because I was so desperate at that point. I flew out to Toronto and booked a scuzzy little motel near Maple Leaf Gardens and I was able to

Erica Ehm with
Barney Bentall

see every record company because of the video. I was eating in a restaurant; I have two caps on my front teeth and something happened with a fork and I broke those so all I had were these two little stubs. It made for kind of a comical week because I would go to all these record companies . . . and say, "I lost my front teeth, how do you like me so far?" . . . It's such a visual industry and they're looking to see if this guy's going to be able to sell records and be attractive to the public . . . and I looked like a hillbilly.

You can't make this stuff up, as the saying goes. Through sheer persistence Barney did get the record deal with Sony, through True North Records, home to Bruce Cockburn and Murray McLauchlan. A second ten-year run gave the band radio and video hits with "Crime Against Love," "Livin' in the '90s" and a couple of songs that Juno–winning director Jeth Weinrich did videos for: "Gin Palace" and "Do Ya." But it was the first one that remained Barney's favourite.

BARNEY BENTALL We made another video for "Something to Live For" with a big budget . . . I think we spent $30,000 . . . we then embarked on our first cross-country tour and everywhere we went people would come, and I think the fundamental reason was MuchMusic.

So, the run ended, as it always does. And what happened to the Legendary Hearts?

BARNEY BENTALL Our keyboard player is now a highly regarded plastic surgeon and does a lot of sex-change operations and reconstructive surgery. Jack, our drummer, does painting for the movies. Our old bass player, Barry, is a stockbroker. Gary, who I wrote those songs with, is a lawyer. Colin works in management with Elvis Costello, Lyle Lovett and Ry Cooder. I'm the only one who's too dumb to quit at this point. I am a part-time rancher, full-time musician.

COLIN JAMES

One of Canada's most dynamic new artists of the time, Colin James had schooled himself on deep roots music and, at a very young age, could play those styles with authority and authenticity. The fact that he was charismatic and owned the stage only helped propel his career. Much played "Voodoo Thing," Colin's debut video, in high rotation, but Colin was ambivalent about the medium.

COLIN JAMES I've always had a love-hate relationship with it. I've never loved the process, but obviously, when there's a new medium to get out there to a lot of people, you're gonna try to do it, right? "Voodoo Thing" was an example of a good video. I have some I hated and some I liked. I felt, sometimes, with the video-makers, you became a notch on their reel to advertise as opposed to them trying to advertise you . . . they have a new lens or they want to try this cinéma-verité thing, whatever it is that they're pushing, your wishes kind of became secondary.

Colin offered a couple of examples of his experiences making videos.

COLIN JAMES There's a song called "Freedom," which I love, and I still don't understand what's going on in the video. There are spoons and forks hanging from the ceiling and that's all I know.
     We had a chicken brought in from outside Toronto for the "Breakin' up the House" video. We had a chicken wrangler who had to come out to the shoot.

There was another reason for having misgivings about making videos, as Colin found out when they shot the first single from his second album, *Sudden Stop*.

COLIN JAMES "Just Came Back"—That was a $250,000 shoot. We shot it in New York. Of course, if anyone told me I was really paying for them the whole time, I might not have made as many. The church was in Connecticut. We shot around Battery Park in New York, and down in the industrial area. We had a Vietnam vet helicopter guy who was hired for the day, so everyone got rides in the helicopter. I got out "to say goodbye," as the lyric goes, with three female bodyguards . . . as you do!

The song won Single of the Year at the Junos in '91. Colin's videos made good impressions in many places. When we were chatting at his place for this interview, Colin's wife, Heather, added her thoughts.

HEATHER I was working at a retail store in Victoria when "Voodoo Thing" came out and we had two TVs and we played MuchMusic, and "Voodoo Thing" was on every hour. We hadn't met and weren't seeing each other yet, but that's how I knew who he was . . . it was such a huge part of my day.

I asked Colin, despite his doubts about music video, how he felt about Much in those days.

Colin James and Jeff Healey

COLIN JAMES MuchMusic at its best, at the time when it was at its most fresh and unjaded, where it would have a great performance live with Dwight Yoakam, and then right after that Jeff Healey and I would come in with the guitars and play together and the next day you have the Spice Girls, whatever it was, it was fascinating . . . it was covering everybody, it wasn't saying, here's our demographic. You never knew who was going to be on, it could've been anybody . . . and that was truly exciting.

BLUE RODEO

While acts like Corey Hart and the photogenic Glass Tiger were easy to get behind, there were other artists that Much chose to champion who were not as obvious. It was John Martin's passion for a floundering debut act on Warner that convinced us to give their video high rotation. The response to "Try" by Blue Rodeo set them on the road to being an iconic Canadian band.

Jim Cuddy talks about the origins of the band's sound.

Laurie Brown with Jim Cuddy and
Greg Keelor of Blue Rodeo

JIM CUDDY When I finished Queen's [university] in the spring of '78, Greg picked me up . . . and I had decided I was going to devote one year to music, and Greg said, "We should get a band." I said, "Okay, that's a good idea" . . . and we've had a band ever since then without a break. The HiFis that we started in Toronto—we just did fast pop music of the day, Costello influenced. Then we moved to New York and we had a couple of bands . . . we did reggae, we did ska, we did pop. It was great to be in New York where there were so many players, but a terrible place to start a band. Nobody wants to hear a fucking new band; they want to hear Tom Waits who's playing that night, or David Byrne. At the end of that we realized that the most natural style for us was this strumming country rock stuff that was starting to bubble up again. Everybody was looking back again at the Burrito Brothers, Gram Parsons. Coincidentally, we had no idea what was going on in Toronto, but when we came back to Toronto, that really was what was happening.

Looking back at Blue Rodeo's considerable body of work and the videos that helped establish the band, it strikes me that they have next to nothing to live down. I wondered how they avoided the siren call of mid-'80s weirdness in drum sounds, wardrobe, and anything else that causes others shivers of regret now.

JIM CUDDY We had so accepted failure as our route. By the time we came back [from New York] and started Blue Rodeo I was thirty, and we'd already done seven to eight years of not chasing trends, [yet] trying to adapt what we did to what was popular. Not only did we not like ourselves doing that, we didn't like the people we encountered, so when we first came to Warner, we came with no strings attached. We'd had it suggested that we be k.d. lang's backup band for six months. We had no fucking interest in that. I think because we had failed for so long, we just didn't see any point in trying to change anything that we were.

Kevin Shea who was in promotion at Warner at the time tells the story from the label point of view.

KEVIN SHEA Blue Rodeo had a following. They'd play at the Horseshoe and there'd be lineups around the block . . . but no one wanted to step up because their music was so different than what was happening on radio . . .Their first single had gotten one station, CHUM-FM, because [DJ] Ingrid Schumacher was married to Cleave Anderson, their drummer. We knew "Try" was a magic song . . . but you didn't lead with a ballad, especially to establish a new band. It was panic time; there was no sales. So Jim Cuddy . . . and his wife called in all their favours [to make the "Try" video] . . .

We put the single out to radio and nothing . . . crickets . . . we thought this was a magic track. We couldn't get the radio stations we needed. Then MuchMusic added it into a significant rotation.

Jim remembers well the lead-up to shooting the video.

JIM CUDDY We were very lucky because I got a job at a film company called McWaters Vanlint. Derek Vanlint was well-known— he'd been the cinematographer on *Alien*.

People from the company used to come and see the band play in the clubs and offered to shoot the video for "Try." The costs would be mostly covered, but with one condition. "Derek is going to do it, but you'll have no say in what he does." They paid for film, processing, everything, but at the last moment Derek got sick and they brought this guy I'd been working with, Michael Buckley, who was a South African cameraman. Michael loved filming women and with Michelle [McAdorey from Warner band Crash Vegas], the girl in the video, who was [also] Greg's girlfriend at the time, he knew he wanted to do some beautiful, luxurious, slow-motion shots around her. We filmed at the magic hours, dawn and dusk.

The band's respect for their director and appreciation of the resulting video made it easy to embrace the medium.

JIM CUDDY We weren't going to dress up or any of that shit but when we first saw ourselves walking under the Gardiner [Express-way] in slow motion, we couldn't have been more in love with ourselves. We thought we looked awesome! That was very much the filmmaking of the day—really, really macro shots, lots of slow motion—Michael was a very sensual filmmaker.

"Try" was named Video and Single of the Year at the '89 Juno Awards.

JIM CUDDY "Try" cost us maybe $1,000. And it was all done on 35mm. Our next bunch of videos were with Michael. We were so lucky to have the skills and the support of an actual film company that was mostly doing commercials. I worked fifteen hours a day doing commercials as well as doing the band.

Soon, Jim was able to give up his day job but Blue Rodeo found that having a hit record carried some baggage.

JIM CUDDY I remember when we'd go up north and people would look at us and scream, and that's not from radio. That's from imagery, from the impact of seeing something you've seen a big image of. There was a certain period of time, when we had to weed out the audiences we got just from "Try," and just from that video, because they didn't necessarily like everything else we did. So there was this period of adjustment.

For the title track of the album *Outskirts*, the band hired Don Allan to direct a moody performance piece.

DON ALLAN I set up a giant Ferris wheel in High Park [in Toronto] to make it look surreal. I tried to find a barn that was falling apart with lots of holes in it so we could have giant lights shooting out of it with purple gels on them. We had the band set up in front of the barn and we'd been shooting for a while and we took a break. As I'm walking, these cops are coming towards me and they have a look like they've seen a ghost, hands on their holsters, asking what's going on. They'd gotten a report of a UFO. They didn't know anything about the shoot. They'd been driving along in the area and all of a sudden had seen this barn glowing purple. We actually made *Entertainment Tonight* because of what happened.

When the band went to make the video for the title track of their next album, *Diamond Mine*, they returned to working with Michael Buckley, but things didn't go as planned.

JIM CUDDY The funny thing about "Diamond Mine" is that it was shot in colour and there was an error at the processing plant. They ruined the film. We were away and Michael phoned us and said, in his slow laconic way, "They've ruined the film but I think this is good. Watch it in black and white, it's beautiful." And we did see it in black and white and it was absolutely stunning.

Later, when the band was looking for something different, they approached Curtis Wehrfritz about shooting the video for "Hasn't Hit Me Yet." The director relates the first conversation he had with them about the video.

CURTIS WEHRFRITZ They had been doing a lot of performance videos because [Jim and Greg] are both very charismatic. They approached

Erica Ehm with Greg Keelor and Jim Cuddy of Blue Rodeo

me and I said, "Probably not a good idea," in a polite way. I said, "I'm pretty good at portraiture but I . . . don't want to be a literal cartoonist; I don't want to illustrate your lyric." They said, "Well, what would you do?" and I said, "I wouldn't have you play in it; in fact, I would probably have little of you . . ." I said why don't we do a short film, an imagistic thing. The record company would have to be okay with not featuring the lifestyle of the band. The band had enough power to do that. The script was a collaboration with Greg, shot in and around his farm where they were beginning to record . . . we took on the challenge of shooting up there in February. Greg had been going through some things where he fainted and he said, "The sensation of vertigo when you come to and this benevolent look of concern of faces hovering over you was quite an out-of-body strange and beautiful thing." In the video there's this kind of funeral and there's an image of the guys looking over the lens. [Greg] said, "You're between two worlds and you don't really know what this is."

They worked with Wehrfritz on "Bad Timing," which Jim recalls with affection.

JIM CUDDY I thought "Bad Timing" was a great video. It has my kids in it. Mary Margaret O'Hara is in it going crazy on the motorcycle. Often we worked in our own community with friends—that was sort of the whole point of the band.

THE NORTHERN PIKES

Around the time Barney Bentall and the boys were starting out, the Northern Pikes emerged from the indie scene in Saskatoon. Signed to Virgin Records, they had a hit with a song called "Teenland" from their first album, *Big Blue Sky*. The follow-up, *Snow in June* (sounds like a good prairie album title, doesn't it?), featured what became the band's biggest hit, "She Ain't Pretty," written and sung by band member Bryan Potvin. When it came time for the video, they turned to director Ron Berti and Total Eclipse productions, who the band had developed a strong relationship with. Bryan recalls the genesis of the video.

BRYAN POTVIN Our record company president Doug Chappell loved a cold-and-flu remedy commercial that was on TV at the time. It featured old-school claymation that he thought would be cool to incorporate into the "She Ain't Pretty" video. The opening exterior shot of the saloon was a model the size of a Barbie house. I had this in my possession for a long time after the shoot. I did

keep the little steer skull as a keepsake—I glued it onto the headstock of an acoustic guitar I own. Looks pretty badass.

I asked Bryan about Much's support of the Juno-nominated "She Ain't Pretty" video, and their other work.

BRYAN POTVIN I certainly can't speak for other bands of our vintage who were supported by Much the way we were, but my deep appreciation of how fortunate we were to have that support didn't come until later in life. When you are in a band attempting to succeed the way we were, there is a certain amount of confidence you must have to push yourself forward each day. I always thought we were a very good pop/rock band and we were decent looking guys—I couldn't find a reason why Much wouldn't support us.

I mentioned one of my favourite moments in Much history, which featured Bryan leaning out of a moving train car as it pulled into Melville, Saskatchewan, playing guitar while someone held onto his belt from behind.

BRYAN POTVIN Yeah, I did some pretty idiotic shit back then. I always felt pressure, from myself, to deliver a "show." And that didn't simply mean playing and singing our songs competently—it meant performing, leaving the audience with something that they'll really remember . . . We played a gig once where the stage was encircled by a moat so I decided to traipse through knee-deep water with my electric guitar on—a really bad idea. I gave a MuchMusic cameraman a black eye at a show in St. John's, Newfoundland, when I stage dove into the crowd, guitar and all. I did that another time in Sudbury and the audience parted like the Red Sea. I landed violently on the arena's concrete floor with people all around me looking rather astonished. So the Much train thing was a natural extension of that stuff—brave or stupid or some sort of hybrid of both . . . Yes, it could have been a disaster but think of the headlines my death would have created, ha-ha-ha.

SASS JORDAN

Sass Jordan broke the mould for Canadian female artists in the early Much era—she entered singing raucously, laughing lustily and swearing a blue streak—this was no Jane Siberry, Sarah McLachlan or Luba. She was hilarious, charming and knew what she wanted.

Sass Jordan and Natalie Richard

SASS JORDAN I was doing this television show in Montreal in 1982 called *Radio Video*. I interviewed Phil Collins, KISS, Def Leppard, Bryan Ferry, Nina Hagen, INXS. I did it because I wanted to know what [it would be] like to be the rock star that I'm going to be.

When she launched her career six years later in 1988 with "Tell Somebody," she appeared to be bursting out of the screen.

SASS JORDAN I was on a mission. I loved what I was doing and we were having the greatest time ever. Much pretty much made my career. It made me nationally well-known overnight . . . It made a huge impact. It wasn't just a voice but it was an image that you could identify and relate to. That was the beginning of our cultural shift to visual media becoming so predominant.

It will come as no surprise that there's a cautionary tale here.

SASS JORDAN Overnight I couldn't go to the laundromat. That's why I moved to Los Angeles. I was absolutely horrified that this thing that I had wanted so badly, to be well-known, was now happening to me and I fucking hated it.

There's a benefit to having your voice heard and admired, and it resulted in a once-in-a-lifetime hit for Sass in 1992.

SASS JORDAN Kevin Costner, who starred in *The Bodyguard* with Whitney Houston, was a massive Joe Cocker fan and he wanted to use a Joe Cocker song in the soundtrack. They decided on "Trust in Me," which had been recorded several years earlier. Kevin was driving around L.A. and heard one of my songs on the radio and said, "That's the voice for the duet on this Cocker track because we need to update it, make it new and fresh." That was a dramatic turning point in how I sang—to hear how Joe phrased it. It made a massive impact on me. After that recording I went on tour with Joe Cocker for two months and I didn't meet him until the last night of the tour. I said, "Joe, it was such an extraordinary experience getting to sing with you on that song." And he looks at me and goes, "What song?" He had no idea. It sold thirty-two million copies.

In her amusing and self-deprecating way, Sass sums up her music video career.

SASS JORDAN I didn't like most of them. I thought I was a jackass in most of them. I thought some of them were really fucking boring.

54-40

The Vancouver indie scene of the early '80s was fertile ground for new bands like Spirit of the West, Skinny Puppy and 54-40. Lead singer of 54-40, Neil Osborne, tells a now familiar story of how a young band used the opportunity that video offered.

NEIL OSBORNE The video revolution defined us. When we got signed to Warner Brothers, we were kind of out of left field and we put out "Baby Ran." Rock radio didn't pick up "Baby Ran"; MuchMusic did. That was how we took off . . . if you went out to universities or clubs everybody was playing MuchMusic . . . everybody looks back now and says that [song is] classic rock but at the time we weren't getting played, not until it was obvious that they kind of had to. We'd start selling out the Commodore [a premiere concert venue in Vancouver] or something like that . . . Much became the radio.

Neil talked about how they approached making videos in the early days of the band.

NEIL OSBORNE Making videos was fun. We used to use that word that young bands do—"integrity" (laughs). It was a way of protecting our image, as fragile as it seemed. We wanted to make sure it didn't misrepresent us. Tamara Davis did the "Baby Ran" video, part of it was shot at the Commodore. It looked like old Doors footage. Then we had no budget for the "I Go Blind" video, which is basically Phil [guitarist Comparelli] and I in Cowichan sweaters walking through Stanley Park.

As the band's popularity grew, they took on more ambitious themes. Neil explains the origins of the song "One Gun" and how some of the images found their way into the video.

NEIL OSBORNE My wife was doing investigative work for human rights through university and the Catholic Church in Argentina and Chile. She was smuggled, during the Pinochet era, into Argentina to do some research. She brought back a lot of posters and we wanted to use that as a vehicle. That was a time when you could jam stuff [into a video] as a vehicle to have a political conscience, to say something. I wrote the song "One Gun" about her trip there. The idea being that if you're oppressed you can't have the freedom to express yourself, to love somebody.

Steve Anthony with Neil Osborne
of 54-40

For their fourth major label record,
54-40 was signed to Sony, who
showed their support through the
corporate chequebook.

**NEIL OSBORNE These were the
days when your first video was
$150 grand. Can you believe it?
That was our record budget.**

The first video was for "She-la," an
important song for the band, and for
Neil and his family in particular.

**NEIL OSBORNE My wife was
dealing with battered women
and kids and she ran a transition house—that was the theme.**

Sony hooked them up with a hot new director.

**NEIL OSBORNE [Curtis] Wehrfritz was the talk of the town at the
time. I remember having a meeting with him and he talked so
fancy, I had no idea what he was saying. I had faith that I'd be able
to control what I did, at least, and a little bit how we looked. When
we got to the set I was blown away—the triplets, the camera
angles. When you're talking on paper I have no idea—I'm not a
visual thinker, I'm an aural thinker. It was like a playground—like
going in the Ikea ballroom.**

Curtis talked about how he tried to stay true to the song's meaning.

**CURTIS WEHRFRITZ We built a set and lifted it twenty feet in the
air to create all these gravity switch-ups because that was a
metaphor for upheaval . . . my feeling was "it can't just be a
documentary on missing women."**

As for the look of the band . . .

**CURTIS WEHRFRITZ Neil did the old punk rocker [trick] and got a
can of Coke to make his hair stand up.**

54-40 rode the wave for a long time in rock 'n' roll years, but Neil remembers
the day when he realized that the old paradigm was on its way out.

I'VE ATTAINED A SPIRITUAL AWARENESS THROUGH MUCHMUSIC.

Tom Cochrane

NEIL OSBORNE There was a new president at Sony [Canada], Rick Camilleri. I walk into his office and he's got his feet on his desk and he's throwing a Nerf basketball at the hoop on the wall. He says, "It's all going to end and I'm getting out of here." I'm like, "huh," the dumb musician. "I just want to make my records, man. What are you talking about?" "CDs—we blew it." He gave me the lecture . . . "The record industry is going to end." He was basically telling me what the future was. When you give someone a CD you're giving them a master. When it's vinyl—you buy one, it wears out, you buy another one, a cassette—buy one, it wears out, you buy another one, but with CDs you're giving everybody a master. He got out and went to TV.

Osborne did have an agenda that day at Sony.

NEIL OSBORNE [Guitarist] Phil Comparelli used to say, "Why can't we be like Honeymoon Suite, on the beach with a bunch of babes? Why do we have to do all these weird dark videos in cold places?"

He pitched Camilleri on an idea for the band's next videos.

NEIL OSBORNE So I said, "Look, instead of hiring whatever flamboyant weird dude who's the hottest thing to make our video where we're going to stand in a fucking ice bucket stamping on a cold puddle . . . how about we go around the world in two or three weeks? . . . It'll cost the same as you give some fashion-show guy . . ." He went, "What a great idea." We went to Thailand, then Kenya, Morocco . . . we ended up shooting four videos. We had a fantastic time and we didn't have to stand in a puddle in a freezer.

By the late '90s, another template was fading as bands that had been core acts for the first decade of MuchMusic's existence found themselves moved over to the new, adult-oriented channel, MuchMoreMusic.

NEIL OSBORNE There's always those first signs that you're not flavour of the month anymore, they're thinking you're a little long in the tooth . . . "It's not going to be on Much, it's going to be on MuchMoreMusic. Don't worry, Blue Rodeo's on MuchMore, too." How do you take that? When someone says, "Don't take any offence but . . .," the first thing you're going to do is look for where you're going to take offence. They split it. It was the chocolate bar ads versus the car ads. Everybody wants to think they can still sell chocolate bars.

THE TRAGICALLY HIP

The Tragically Hip have carved out a place as one of the most beloved bands in Canada. They got together in their native Kingston, Ontario, in the early '80s and have been touring, releasing records and winning awards (including fourteen Junos) ever since. While they were developing their sound and working to get a foothold in the clubs around Ontario, they were watching Much. Guitarist Rob Baker recalls.

ROB BAKER Everyone was watching . . . it was like when *Saturday Night Live* first came on TV. Saturday night you'd be at a party with forty people and when *SNL* started everyone would go quiet and settle around the TV and watch, and when the commercials came on, you'd break out in conversation, talk about what you saw and then go quiet again. For a while it was like that with MuchMusic— Friday and Saturday nights people gathered around and watched videos. I was starved for music—anytime you could see musicians perform—I used to rush home after school to watch, I think it was a band from Ottawa, some guy named Chris Ward playing guitar, doing R&B standards, like "Under the Boardwalk."

As grateful as I am to have been a part of Rob's misspent youth watching TV, the band picked up more powerful influences watching Much in the early days.

ROB BAKER When we came up we felt we were a year behind the Northern Pikes and 54-40. They were sort of in Grade 12 and we were in Grade 11. There were a lot of bands that we were exposed to through MuchMusic.

The Tragically Hip, whose name was a reference to former Monkee Michael Nesmith's groundbreaking video from 1981, "Elephant Parts," winner of the first Grammy for music video, was part of a wave of reactionary responses to the use of music video as a glitzy image-building device. Like Blue Rodeo, 54-40 and the Cowboy Junkies, the Hip were determined to be seen as musicians, not pop stars, even if the two roads led to the same destination.

ROB BAKER We had all these things we were going to put our foot down about. We're not going to stand on a mountaintop with a wind machine blowing our hair.

Their first video was simple but effective, serving to help develop the band's status on the road, where long-lasting careers are made.

ROB BAKER "Small Town Bringdown" is a pretty straightforward video, but it made a huge impact on our career . . . that song wasn't a big radio hit, but because Much played it, it allowed us to tour the country . . . you'd roll into Crocks N Rolls in Thunder Bay on a Wednesday night and you'd have sixty people out to see you, which otherwise the Tragically Hip would never have had.

The 1989 release *Up to Here* broke the band and featured powerful videos for "New Orleans Is Sinking" and "Blow at High Dough." For the latter, the Hip stayed with presenting themselves as a performing rock band but added another layer to the visuals to make the video stand out.

ROB BAKER "Blow at High Dough" was the first chance we ever got to conceive the video . . . we sat down in a little brainstorm session and I wrote down all these images on the dust sleeve from an LP. We said, "We'll make it as much like the Ed Sullivan Show as we can and we'll have bluescreen behind us. We'll show a bunch of wacky black-and-white images. The video came back and it was exactly what we asked them to do.

For the video for "New Orleans Is Sinking," the band stayed close to home.

ROB BAKER The director was someone who had been coming out to the shows for a year or so. We'd seen a crazy short film that he made about a thirty-year-old guy living at home with his mother with the umbilical cord still attached. He sat down and told us his idea for the video and we said "yeah."

I asked Rob about the collaborative approach to creating videos.

ROB BAKER [The video for] "Locked in the Trunk of a Car" had a lot to do with what we were reading and watching at the time. We liked the whole film noir thriller [genre]. In those early days, there was lots of time sitting around in hotel rooms and books, movies, music—that was the chit chat.

As the Hip's stature grew and more videos were expected, they found new ways to visually support the songs. I mentioned the video for "Bobcaygeon," which features an understated performance from lead singer Gord Downie.

ROB BAKER I think Gord has a good concept of when grand gestures will carry and when they're not necessary. If you have a camera in your face and you're blown up big on the screen, you can do a lot more with a lot less. I think that insinuates itself into live performance as well now that they can capture every little gesture. You're as big as Mount Rushmore on either side of the screen.

Speaking with bands from this era, there's a common theme regarding budgets and the process leading up to shooting videos.

ROB BAKER It's a funny thing how it goes from the first video. "Hey we've got a guy and he's going to do a video for you." Fantastic! We're so excited. Three years down the line, you're sitting in an office in L.A. and you have a whole morning of interviewing video directors. Instead of a fifteen-thousand-dollar budget you've got a hundred thousand to make a video. And [the videos] didn't necessarily get any better.

It was nice to see a small indie band from wherever, Winnipeg—all of a sudden they start getting their video played. It was really cool that [Much] would take chances like that.

Chad Kroeger, Nickelback

ONE
TO
LIFT
THE
LID.

16 Worst Interviews

Often when VJs recall their favourite interview, it's all hearts and flowers and accolades for the subject: "I couldn't believe how nice/sincere/honest they were," "the biggest stars are always the most humble," or "they answered my questions so thoughtfully." Nice, humble, thoughtful, sincere—blah blah blah. They could be talking about your great aunt or Mother Teresa. *Boooow-ring!* Tell me something I don't know. Send me your wretched, self-inflated, obnoxious, whining, pathetic stars—because we all know they are legion. Of course, the person in the interviewer's chair has to share some of the blame for an interview gone sideways.

LAURIE BROWN There were a million awful, awkward moments in interviews where I got something wrong, or they just didn't like me, or they were hungover. I would just feel terror running through my body because the whole thing was falling apart.

In a rare case of an on-air person taking responsibility for screwing up, Master T does just that on reviewing his first ever interview, with the brilliant but irascible John Hiatt.

MASTER T I was ill-prepared, not researched and Hiatt knew I was not into the music. That guy ripped me a new asshole. Afterwards I thought, I will never let that happen again.

We all had our share of rude rock stars. It goes with the territory and often it was harmless. I played in bands and I remember after three months or three years on the road, you'd have your own language, a highly developed sense of mockery and a jaundiced view of your tiny insular world, which consisted of a daily mix of dodgy hotels, crowded vans, funky backstages, bad food and promoters with legendary halitosis. If it's Wednesday, it must be Lethbridge. Now, most of the bands that had gotten to the stage where they'd be on Much, were beyond some of those indignities, but there are certain aspects of touring that remain unsavoury at any level. They travel the world and see next to nothing. As Alannah Myles and I used to say when Alannah toured the world for a year and a half on her debut album, she was a star for an hour and a piece of baggage for the other twenty-three. So, Mister Mister, Frankie Goes to Hollywood, and pompous stars-of-the-moment like the Fine Young Cannibals, all candidates for '80s 'Where are they now?' profiles, could be trying, but largely harmless, and have long ago been forgiven their snotty, pouty trespasses.

I was a big Elvis Costello fan when I went to the Four Seasons to interview him in 1989. I was prepared and looking forward to talking about his latest album, *Spike*, which featured songs Costello had co-written with Paul McCartney. I was collecting interviews for a series I was developing on songwriting, and Costello represented a major contemporary writer. Except, he didn't want to talk about songwriting. Asked about his approach, he growled that this was "like taking a toy apart" and begrudgingly offered up an analysis of a recent song called "Pads, Paws and Claws." Ironically, years later, as the host of *Spectacle*, Costello had to pose similar questions to songwriting luminaries like Sting and Elton John. My recollection was of an uncomfortable conversation with a cranky subject, whose barbed replies sometimes felt directed at me.

ELVIS COSTELLO I said it completely clearly as far as I'm concerned. You just have to think about it.

And when he didn't want to answer something, he narrowed his eyes and challenged me to come up with something else, or dismissed the value of his own answers.

ELVIS COSTELLO It's just the mood I'm in at the moment. I don't have any set opinions. My opinions about things are not set in concrete.

Through the years, I looked back at it as one of my worst interview experiences. But, having screened it again in the final stages of writing this book, I realized I was wrong. What I came away with was vintage Costello, full of spit and snarl, and totally entertaining! Let's start with a seemingly harmless question about the name of the album, *Spike*.

ELVIS COSTELLO That's show business for you. They take an elephant gun, shoot the artist and hang him up on the boardroom wall of the country club or the record company or wherever they keep their trophies these days. Spike, the beloved entertainer—it's an instruction, not a name.

Any thoughts on making videos?

ELVIS COSTELLO Before [MTV], the video clips were made very cheaply with a kind of fun "what we did on our holidays" type of atmosphere . . . now they can backflip you, turn you upside down, inside out, they can put new underwear on you without taking your clothes off with video trickery. None of it's very interesting. You're standing there; they're playing your record . . . coming through a

speaker about this big [gestures with two fingers]. It sounds like [makes unintelligible garbled sounds] and you're supposed to look like you're giving it your all, and the veins are bulging out on the side of your neck with the intensity of the performance. Don't make me laugh. You're lip-synching; you're pretending to sing the song, pretending to play a guitar that isn't plugged in. Or you're pretending to be Humphrey Bogart, with dry ice all around you . . . the minute people got the idea that they could be their favourite movie star in the video—that was a real mistake.

I'm not sure how this topic came up.

ELVIS COSTELLO Heavy metal is boring music for boring people by boring people. I hate Led Zeppelin and everything they've spawned.

And then there was this, in the pet peeve department.

ELVIS COSTELLO The worst thing that ever happened in my opinion, was about 1969 they coined this word "rock." Before it used to be called "rock 'n' roll" . . . the minute they took the "roll" out of it, that's when a lot of the lights went out for me. Rock 'n' roll is a euphemism for sex . . . and a rock is a thing you dig up in the ground. It doesn't move; it doesn't breathe; it doesn't dance around; it doesn't buy you a drink. "Rock" is really responsible for most of the boredom of today.

I thought I'd be on safe ground asking about his recent collaboration with Paul McCartney.

ELVIS COSTELLO He doesn't need any help writing Paul McCartney songs any more than I need any help writing my kind of songs. It was very funny, a very funny kind of business, it wasn't this (mimes *The Thinker*). It was sort of funny. Remember "funny"? Like funny. Like funny, you know. Like (raising his voice) funny, funny, funny! Like that kind of funny. We'd play Ping-Pong with the idea and at the end somebody would get the point, then we'd have a finished song. There was no furrowed brow; there was no dusty manuscript with some big quill pens. It was just writing songs. It's rock 'n' roll songs; it's not difficult.

To deflate the notion that "the biggest stars are the nicest ones," I had a memorably unpleasant interview with Mark Knopfler of Dire Straits in July of 1985 in London, just prior to Live Aid. We had run a big contest with Polygram, the band's label, and one of our advertisers, and the winners were flown to London to meet Dire Straits and attend the Prince's Trust concert at Wembley Arena. Knopfler's people cancelled the interview a

IF *MAD MAX* HAD BEEN SET IN A TV STUDIO, IT WOULD BE THERE.

Ed the Sock
(re his first impression of the Much studio)

number of times and it was on the last possible day, the day of the concert, that they agreed to do it. Cameraman Dave Russell, producer Michael Heydon and I were led to the stage of the arena where Knopfler was waiting. All very well, except that he didn't turn around to greet us . . . for a very long time. And when he finally did, with a Pythonesque condescension, he demanded that we take care of the lighting situation, ignoring the fact that the lights were entirely the domain of his crew. He sighed; he looked away; he shot me all the expressions of ennui in his repertoire and begrudgingly answered my questions. Later that night, they did a brilliant show. Sting joined them for the "I want my MTV" opening on "Money for Nothing" and it was very cool when Prince Charles and Lady Diana were escorted in to a warm welcome just before the lights went down.

MARK KNOPFLER You rehearse in a smallish place and then you move into production rehearsals where you're running light rigs and PA systems and a stage is built and there's lots of people working away. Getting something like this going again is like reawakening a pre-historic monster and then it wakes up and rolls downhill, after a while it becomes pretty much impossible to stop.

Well, that happens until you stop selling records and then the monster is dead.

The members of KISS, collectively and individually, have drawn the ire of many, including two of the women at Much. Erica doesn't pull any punches.

ERICA EHM I interviewed KISS and they were the most disgusting bunch of jerks I remember interviewing. Those bastards—they are such misogynists and were so rude and lascivious to me on camera.

GENE SIMMONS The more I use my brain and the more I use other parts of my body, the better they work.

When I asked Laurie about her worst interview moment, she didn't hesitate.

LAURIE BROWN Gene Simmons from KISS on the *Power Hour*. I wish I could do that one over again . . . bands like that drove me crazy. KISS was terrible. He was such an awful misogynist.

Even worse, Laurie added sarcastically, "His makeup application was very crude!" We've all had that feeling of just missing an opportunity to expose the folly of the terminally tasteless. "I just fell right into his trap. I said, 'What is it that you want from women?' He said, 'I want them to lick the bottom of my boots.'"

The KISS leader's cynicism wasn't limited to his attitude toward women. He didn't express a lot of respect for his fellow musicians either. In this comment, he seems to assume that all players are motivated by one thing.

GENE SIMMONS It's the first reason musicians put guitars around their necks. No matter how politically oriented you are [mimes playing guitar and pretending to sing] "people are starving in Ethiopia," at the end of the night he wants to go back to the hotel and have a beautiful girl. "Everybody's starving. Everybody's poor." But in the back of his mind, "I wonder if I look cool."

LAURIE BROWN Afterwards I thought, "I walked right into it, that's all he wanted to do is to get me." I should have laughed.

Hosting the *Power Hour* gave Laurie access to artists she may have not wanted to get too close to. Artists like Guns N' Roses. During the interview there was lots of belching, sniffling, hot dog consumption and Slash smoking through his hair. They didn't want to do a station ID so we just shot them smoking and eating. And this was the good part of the visit.

LAURIE BROWN Slash was so strung-out, he was sweating and he had the shakes; it was unbelievable, and I was taking them to task for an album cover; I was going for it. He was so hungover, he had no patience for me at all; he could barely form a word and it was awful. We went to video and then he threw up. It was a bad day for both of us.

Simon Evans was on assignment in England and he and his cameraman, Basil Young, had been shooting all night when they found they had the first North

The incompetence here is amazing. You're all flipping useless. Trendy and useless. I deserve an apology. Who runs this place?

Tracey Ullman (after we accidently played the wrong video)

Natalie Richard with Kenney Dale Johnson and Chris Isaak

American interview with Radiohead, who had just broken on the strength of their first single, "Creep." This episode is unfortunate for its own reasons.

SIMON EVANS For the first two minutes of the interview, Thom Yorke is bending over, rubbing his eyes with the palms of his hands and you can't hear him. So I asked Basil to turn the camera off and I asked Thom, "Do you want to get something out of your eye?" And he said, "I'm okay," and we started the interview again and it was the same thing with him bent over rubbing his eyes. The camera never got turned back on, because we [Basil and I] were so sleepy and all we've got is those first two minutes.

Denise Donlon has the unfortunate distinction of having had to sit down with her least favourite interview subject three times!

DENISE DONLON My worst interview was Chris Isaak. On three occasions! The second time, his record had just come out and he had a huge hit, "Wicked Game." I asked him about Elvis and the anniversary of his death coming up. He ripped his microphone off, threw it on the ground, said, "I don't have to take this shit," and stormed off. What I didn't know was that his record had been getting a fair amount of flack in America, saying that he'd been ripping Elvis Presley, so it was a big deal to him. All I was doing was collecting another quote about Elvis for _The NewMusic_ special that we had coming up. He did send me a postcard, which I still have. I think the record company sat him down and held his hand while he wrote it. It said, "Dear Denise, I'm really sorry. The sun was in my eyes, the dog ate my homework and my underwear was too tight. Love, Chris." So I forgave him, but then the next time I had to interview him, he was a jerk again.

Regardless of his serial misbehaviour, we still had him back!

Ziggy shared her feelings about her least favourite interview subject.

ZIGGY LORENC **The Beastie Boys were awful.**

I screened the interview and they were puerile, turning Ziggy's questions around, making stupid plays on words. She listened patiently and then would ask her next question with interest and respect.

ZIGGY LORENC **At the end I got them back—I told them I thought they'd recorded their album in a dumpster behind Burger World with a toaster.**

Steve may lay claim to the worst interview experience of all time, but, arguably, he might only have himself to blame.

STEVE ANTHONY **The Ramones were complete dicks and a great disappointment. We sat down to do the interview and Joey has the hair like a sheepdog. I knew what was going on currently with them but no matter which way I went he just gave me a "yes" or "no" answer. So this was turning out to be not very entertaining television. During the video, I went to makeup and got hair scissors and we came back from video and I got another monosyllabic grunt for an answer, and I said, "Joey if you give me one more monosyllabic answer, I'm going to cut your bangs with these scissors." Deadpan, he replies, "I'll take those scissors and I'll slash your throat." I thought oh my god, he just threatened my life on national television!**

On another occasion Hulk Hogan got Steve in a headlock and lifted him off the ground . . . in the nicest possible way.

Although we can't really refer to her as anyone's worst interview, more than one VJ recalled meeting Mariah Carey with amusement.

ZIGGY LORENC **[She was] completely vacuous. She came in with seventy-two Louis Vuitton suitcases and an entourage of twenty-five people. The makeup artists wouldn't stop making her up and she just sat there looking out into space. I asked about shopping.**

Steve Anthony and Hulk Hogan

Ziggy Lorenc with Mariah Carey

VJ Natalie Richard interviewed Mariah as well.

NATALIE RICHARD I remember Mariah Carey wouldn't stop looking at herself in the monitor. She wouldn't look at me.

Master T had his own unique encounter.

MASTER T I never wanted to sit down with the artist and have small talk. I remember I was forced to do it with Mariah Carey. The longer I was there, the more irritating I found her. They were dusting her cleavage. During the whole commercial break I had to watch the process of her being pampered. She had a shiny cleavage so they dusted her up. She had to go to the washroom and had to turn her mic off and there are four people scurrying around—one for the toilet paper, one to lift the lid.

As a postscript, I'd like to add my interview with the Scottish band, the Jesus and Mary Chain. They never really registered in North America but they'd had a hot minute in the U.K., where they were renowned for twenty-minute concerts with their backs to the audience and for the riots at their shows. So, of course, this made them *City Limits* darlings and we had to have them on.

As I sat down with the Reid brothers, Jim and William, it became apparent to me very quickly that, thanks to their thick Scottish accents, I couldn't understand a word they were saying. I leaned in, I guessed, I said, "Excuse me?," but ultimately, I was forced to just ask a question, wait for their lips to stop moving and then ask another question. I honestly believe that viewers couldn't tell at the time, but if you screened the interview now knowing this, it would be embarrassingly apparent.

It's a time-honoured rock 'n' roll tradition that bands of brothers battle. Like the Everly Brothers and Ray and Dave Davies of the Kinks before them, and Liam and Noel of Oasis later, the Reid brothers stuck to the script. So, I shouldn't have been surprised, years later, when Kevin Shea, then the band's representative at WEA records, told me that when he brought the lads to Much for their interview, it was dicey even before they got to the station.

KEVIN SHEA I had the Jesus and Mary Chain. They were tough. I had to talk them into doing MuchMusic because they didn't want to do it. They'd had a few cocktails before I picked them up. We parked on St. Patrick off Queen and walked past a comic book store. One of the brothers looked in the window and said, "I love comic books," and the other one said, "You love comic books? What a fuckin' jerk." So they got into a fight in the middle of the street and the streetcar had to stop so I could pull them onto the sidewalk.

Kim Clarke Champniss has had some legendary encounters over the years, but probably none more bizarre than the one with John Lydon, a.k.a. Johnny Rotten, on the occasion of the Sex Pistols' return to the stage in 1996. Kim managed one question before John took umbrage, yanked off his microphone and began flinging grapes across the hotel room where the interview took place. It's all on YouTube!

KIM CLARKE CHAMPNISS The magic of the Sex Pistols really lies in the potency of the image you guys created twenty years ago.

JOHN LYDON What an asshole you are. It's nothing to do with the image, you great fool. It's to do with the damn songs. Interview over.

Paul Cook then attempts to gamely continue the exchange while the other band members look on bored or bemused, I can't tell which.

PAUL COOK Like John says, it's not because of the image we created—the songs stand the test of time. Obviously. There's kids there last night singing every word.

At this point, Lydon calls out from across the room.

JOHN LYDON If this had started as an interview, question, answer, that would have been fine but its not—this is all about you, your ego and your preconceptions. (Throwing grapes.) I ain't interested.

Kim recalls, with sympathy, the Virgin Records promo rep, Nancy Yu.

KIM CLARKE CHAMPNISS She was in the room ducking, horrified.

Steven Kerzner, Ed the Sock's right hand man, recalls how Ed was not the first choice to do interviews.

Ed the Sock

STEVE KERZNER They wouldn't let me near celebrities; I don't even think they wanted me near the people who were coming in off the street. I think they wanted to put me in a plastic bubble like John Travolta in that 1976 TV movie . . . I only ever got interviews if there was a bubonic plague that struck every other VJ. Okay, we'll let Ed talk to him. But everyone was ready to "cut!" and go to commercial at a moment's notice.

One unfortunate encounter for Ed was with Brad Roberts of the Crash Test Dummies. At this time, there was a directive to ask the visiting artists what they were reading.

STEVE KERZNER I always thought this was stupid because no one cares what books rock stars read. I didn't assume they read books; I assumed they mostly watched TV and read magazines. I never thought these were people who were deep into Nabokov. So what kind of answers were we ever going to get? We got them saying things that they thought people wanted to hear them say, but they never read the stuff.

With Brad, he said that his favourite magazine was *Shaved Asians*. I'd never read *Shaved Asians* but it wasn't about men's grooming habits in North Korea.

There was a little blowback on this one, but not from the viewers—and not directed at the artist! Ed wasn't a happy sock.

STEVE KERZNER Afterwards, I got blamed because he said that and "you shouldn't have asked him that question." That was the question [management] told me to ask him!

Brad remembers the lead-up to that interview.

BRAD ROBERTS I was so sick of doing fucking interviews by then that I decided I would get super high before I did them . . . and it was horrible . . . I smoked weed. It's not like when you're paranoid and you think everyone's watching you . . . [on TV] they really are watching you . . . Then I decided it would be a good idea . . . to get a double Scotch down my belly and I'd relax. So I did and then I went on MuchMusic. It was the perfect combination—I wasn't freaking-out high, I wasn't out of my mind but I wasn't hammered either; I just had a good warm glow in my belly.

As for the infamous response to the innocuous "what are you reading?" question, Brad has a different memory, but remembers being excited to meet Ed the Sock.

BRAD ROBERTS That was a huge fuckin' highlight. That guy was hilarious. For some reason he asked me if I'd been to Singapore and I said, "No, but I have a subscription to a magazine called *Shaved Asians*," which was a magazine cover I'd seen that day. They didn't play that a second time.

THE NEW
COW WAS
DOOR #3
ON
LET'S
MAKE
A DEAL.

17 Northern Tales

Some stories are so quintessentially, beautifully Canadian that it's hard to imagine them happening anywhere else in the world. The successes of artists like Susan Aglukark, Loreena McKennitt, Ashley MacIsaac and k.d. lang were celebrated at Much and gave us a chance to show our true northern colours. I asked Jimmy Rankin, who was a member of the Rankin Family and who has had a long, successful solo career, what a typical Saturday night was like for him growing up.

> I worry about the globalization of culture and content . . . I still want there to be opportunity for Canadian voices and Canadian music to be heard. I don't want it all to be decided and programmed from Burbank.

Jay Switzer (on the future of Much)

JIMMY RANKIN **I grew up in a little village on the west coast of Cape Breton . . . a place called Mabou, a very musical community, listening to a lot of Celtic music growing up around there. Our place was over the fence, next door to the dance hall. It's still there; it's a great old hall. There was the church and the community hall where they'd have all the weddings and dances and back in those days, growing up, you could open your window on a Saturday night. There were a lot of fiddle dances back then and a lot of bands going through . . . I could lean out the window with my siblings and listen to the music in the hall which was anything from Cape Breton fiddle music to country music to rock 'n' roll. . . . The stage in the hall had two windows that opened out—it was like a perfect speaker right into our backyard . . . then there was all the action in the parking lot and that was entertaining too.**

My family was very musical so there was always a lot of Celtic music . . . and the older siblings in my family formed a band. We

were called the Rankin Family back then. They would play around these community halls for weddings in the summertime and dances . . . eventually I joined the band around twelve and started playing drums. My first gig as a drummer was in that hall in Mabou. I would sit back there and watch my older siblings perform and watch all the adults having a good time and I thought how crazy it was. These people that I saw pretty much every day then seeing them on a Friday or Saturday letting loose and having a good time. I just thought adults were crazy and eventually I became one of them. A Saturday night for me when I was a kid growing up was playing music—we called them "pig and whistles" in those days.

The Rankin Family released independent recordings beginning in 1989 before being signed to EMI in Canada. It was the re-release of one of Jimmy's original songs, "Fare Thee Well Love," that changed the group's career and brought Celtic music to many Canadians for the first time. The casual nature of the song's creation makes the story even more unlikely.

JIMMY RANKIN I wanted to write a Celtic ballad. Out of that came "Fare Thee Well Love," which was close to five minutes long. We tried to feature everybody on the record. We didn't have a song for Cookie or for me so I changed the wording around a little and made it into a duet. Chad Irschick [the producer] had an idea for

Steve Anthony with John Morris, Raylene, Heather, Jimmy and Cookie Rankin of the Rankin Family turning it into a more contemporary sounding song. It was the '80s, early '90s, when everybody was experimenting with synthesizers.

Without the burden of great expectations, Jimmy's story has much in common with others of surprising success coming from humble origins.

JIMMY RANKIN **We made records . . . on a shoestring budget; it was all self-financed. I remember singing the vocal with Cookie; we were just standing around one mic and maybe did two or three takes.**

The languid pace of the video was in stark contrast to the typical fare of the day, with musicians posing or clowning to the rhythm of frantic editing, wind machines and flash pots in full effect.

JIMMY RANKIN **I look back and the video was beautifully shot, we were all young and living. All that was very new to us and I think if you look at the video I'm kind of giggly because it was all silly, lip-synching to this song.**

Label promo rep Peter Diemer reflected on the unlikeliness of the Rankins' success.

PETER DIEMER **There was an Atlantic Canada band that had no right, based on the way radio was at that time, to have national radio coverage. It was beautiful Gaelic music, with beautiful harmonies. The video brought the story to life in a very different way—it was simple; they weren't out shooting on boats at high speed. All of a sudden there were these five people that nobody had really heard of outside of Cape Breton or Halifax . . . and we were allowed to get their voices and their images across the country!**

The video became a favourite on MuchMusic. Jimmy remembers the group's first visit to the studio on Queen Street, when they did a live performance.

JIMMY RANKIN **MuchMusic was very hip and there was a bunch of country bumpkins coming in and singing. It was Valentine's Day and Steve [Anthony] came out with roses for the girls; he was very charming.**

"Fare Thee Well Love" won the 1994 Juno for Single of the Year.

THE COWBOY JUNKIES

Another family saga was being played out in Toronto with Margo, Peter and Michael Timmins and their friend Alan Anton. From the start they had very firm ideas about what they wanted to do . . . and not do. The name of the band, the Cowboy Junkies, caused record companies to flinch. They took a very unconventional approach to recording that paid off spectacularly. And lead singer Margo Timmins had a few reservations about making music videos, to put it mildly.

MARGO TIMMINS **When we started to think about recording our first record, we started to look at studios and do it the traditional way but they were too expensive; we couldn't do it. And the sound we wanted was the sound we had in our garage at the time.**

They chose the Church of the Holy Trinity, a beautiful 165-year-old Anglican church nestled in among office buildings and the Eaton Centre. At the time, the name of the band caused controversy in many places, but the band had a plan to avert any concern the people at the church might have.

MARGO TIMMINS **We told them we were the Timmins Family Singers, something akin to the Von Trapps.**

Margo tells the story behind a magical recording that almost didn't work.

MARGO TIMMINS **For the first seven hours of that day, we were insane—it just was not working. We kept moving the mics around and me around, and the equipment around, throwing blankets over people and things because the room was just too live and the recordings we were getting were too ambient . . . We were about to pack it in; it was seven hours, it was a whole day. We'd rented it for twenty-four hours, so we had time, but we were exhausted and frustrated, and Peter and the boys came up with another plot and moved everything around yet again and that one was the right setup. You look back on things and you wonder if maybe it was the fact that we had been frustrated and had been playing and trying for seven hours that we were now in that place of exhaustion so we were able to lay back and just do it as opposed to being hyper and tentative and nervous.**

The band was offered a dream deal with RCA in New York, one that included complete artistic freedom and the surprising choice to release *The Trinity Sessions* as is, instead of treating the recordings as demos and re-recording it as happens in most situations. This last decision proved brilliant as the 1988 album became platinum in the U.S. and two times platinum in Canada. However, it did mean that the band was expected to make videos. Margo explains that they understood the expectation.

Cowboy Junkies performing on *Intimate and Interactive*

MARGO TIMMINS **It was part of what we had to do for the record company. We had to help them sell records—they were giving us money to make the records.**

But that didn't mean she was going to like it.

MARGO TIMMINS

I hated it! I hated it! I never felt that video and music was a good combination for bands like us. I thought they were great for the Madonna-type bands, big pop and lots of dancing, beautiful girls in small outfits and I . . . loved to look at them. For a band like us, I didn't think it added to the song, I think it took away . . . you sing a song so the listener would bring their life to it. It's like books and movies. As soon as you make a movie out of a book, all the characters take on a certain look and sound and take away from your own imagination. I think with songs, you bring your experience to the song and that becomes intimate to you and specific to you and your life. Once you start to make a . . . visual story, then I think it takes away from that.

Thus the Margo Timmins "Not-To-Do" list.

MARGO TIMMINS **I never wanted to put on the short skirt and the bustier. That was never me and it always made me feel awkward so you'd get the costume people and you'd say, "okay, I'm not going to wear a miniskirt, I'm not walking in the video; I'm not riding a horse; I'm not kissing anybody [laughing] and I'm not going to wear anything too tight." They'd always show up with racks and racks of these really sexy clothes and the boys and I would laugh. In the dressing room, I'd put on these sequined jackets . . . I'd usually end up wearing my own clothes. People see you on the screen with all the lights and your big hair . . . I have two sisters—one's an actress and the other's in fashion and they loved that stuff and would kill to do that.**

Much launched an important new show, the *Intimate and Interactive* concert series, with the Cowboy Junkies. The show featured live performances in the Much studio in front of a small live audience and interview segments that included questions from the viewers delivered by phone and fax. Margo and the band were completely at home in this setting.

MARGO TIMMINS The *Intimate and Interactive*—that was great. Anytime we played live I couldn't care less. Turn on the cameras . . . Denise was great. I always liked her. To me she was real. I didn't do very well with the hyper MuchMusic VJs, the ones that were twelve, loud and over-the-top. Denise always had a calm and an intellect and I always thought she was talking to you as opposed to putting on a show.

Denise tells the story of another debut, the arrival of a son for her and her husband, Murray McLauchlan, on the same occasion.

DENISE DONLON My water broke when I walked into the station. The doctor said, "Keep busy"! So I did, but contractions started during the show. They'd set me up behind the piano because I was huge and didn't have a watch on—again because my wrists were too huge so I timed contractions by the rundown. . . . song—3:45, commercial—2:00, phone call—1:00, and they were six minutes apart by end of show. We went to the hospital and ta da! Duncan.

The papers the next day referred to "the littlest Cowboy Junkies fan" and the fact that "MuchMusic host almost has baby on air."

Graham Henderson, head of Music Canada (formerly CRIA, the Canadian Recording Industry Association), an umbrella organization of Canadian record labels, happens to be married to Margo. He had thoughts on the Junkies' emergence and the industry in the late '80s.

GRAHAM HENDERSON At the time it was pretty obvious that [MuchMusic] held the keys to the kingdom. If you could get into a decent rotation at Much, it was the difference between a hit record and not-a-hit record . . . Much was more open to the Cowboy Junkies . . . that type of band. Much was in its ascendancy in '87 to '88, and that's when that whole alternative scene broke . . . There was a changing of the guard. We're done with Honeymoon Suite and Loverboy and now we're moving into this, and this was the Tragically Hip, Blue Rodeo, k.d. lang, and 54-40. Much played a real role in that because Much was playing those sorts of bands and radio wasn't.

Graham tells a story of the band being in the right place at the right time in the emergence of alternative music as a genuine force.

GRAHAM HENDERSON The Cowboy Junkies held that banner . . . internationally along with Suzanne Vega and all those other artists who were changing the dial—Tracy Chapman. I point to that *Saturday Night Live* show that the Cowboy Junkies did . . . They weren't tapped to do *SNL* as the primary act; they were back-up. They were asked, "Would you step in if the band we've asked can't make it because there were some issues at the border?" There were issues at the border; that band didn't show up and that band was Flock of Seagulls. Talk about a bone-chilling '80s blast from the past. Into their shoes stepped the Cowboy Junkies who were one of the first of that type of act to get on *SNL*. The band sold 350,000 records in the next two weeks as a result of that show.

LEONARD COHEN— "CLOSING TIME"

So, what do you do if you're a director who's been hired to create a music video for a fifty-something artist who's one of the best-loved artists the country has ever produced, one who is accustomed to a stoic approach to performance and doesn't like your idea of how to do the video? Answer: You tread very carefully and respectfully. Curtis Wehrfritz used his diplomatic skills along with his directorial ones in addressing Leonard Cohen about the video for his 1993 song, "Closing Time."

Curtis thought very seriously about the work before taking on the challenge.

CURTIS WEHRFRITZ It's about this dysfunctional moment when people are high or drunk at 2:30 or 3:00 and the metaphor was that your spirit is playing above you even when you . . . can't talk right. There are so many things he touched on with that lyric and to me it was about this strange epiphany when you start to get in between two worlds. Even though the guy's drunk on the table his body is floating above him.

He pitched Cohen on the treatment, but left him a way out if he wasn't happy with the results.

CURTIS WEHRFRITZ I said . . . "You have complete creative control but we will shoot your performance first and . . . as a creative person I would like to have the right to do the video as I see it." He's a very wise and cunning and playful character . . . I said, "I really love your stoicism and I think it's really important how musicians present themselves . . . but you have such a remarkable manner and charisma about you; the other thing I want to try is, I think we should be a little playful." I said, "We'll take it out if it doesn't work but I think it could be a new facet to this beautiful man you've built who's a bit more of a stoic poet. Your turn of words and the sensuality and humour is in you and it's very evident. I really think it's time to let a little of that out of the cage." [This idea] was not

supported by Leonard at all. He was able to let us do it but it was really on a basis of "go hang yourself."

"Closing Time" by Leonard Cohen won Curtis Wehrfritz the Juno for Video of the Year in 1993.

JANE SIBERRY

Can a seven-and-a-half-minute-long song and video launch a career? In Canada, it can and did for Toronto-born artist Jane Siberry. Indie label Duke Street Records released her second album, *No Borders Here*, which featured the arresting "Mimi on the Beach." The creation of the video was second nature to Jane.

JANE SIBERRY I often see songs before I put them into words . . . I've always been very visual and I like the medium of music and moving visuals. I think that's a little bit the ultimate.

The "Mimi" video was shot at Sandbanks Provincial Park. Even though it was an unqualified success, Jane had ideas for the video that didn't end up being captured.

JANE SIBERRY My main interest was in having an androgynous male playing Mimi so it was clear that it's not about girls or women, but nobody really understood that, so we ended up using the cameraman's girlfriend at the last minute and she was not at all what I wanted, but it doesn't matter now. A lot of people thought I was gay from that video so that was a surprise to me.

For one of her best-known songs, "One More Colour," Jane did a video with director Deborah Samuel, who worked with the Parachute Club, Véronique Béliveau, Alannah Myles and others. Deborah understood the challenge.

DEBORAH SAMUEL Jane is a unique and sensitive artist. She has her own very defined style and how she sees the world and that has to be honoured in creating a video.

Later, Jane directed her own videos for "An Angel Stepped Down" and "Temple," but when I asked about her other experiences in video-making and whether she had found a director she connected with who really got what she was trying to do, Jane's answer was blunt.

JANE SIBERRY Nope. It's the same with producing. I see too much what I think, what I think is right so it's probably better, at least for me, if I can take things to the end. I respect everyone but I was disappointed quite a bit. But that's part of all our learning curves—you give the artwork to someone and you thought they would hear what you heard. I really feel sorry for filmmakers, having so much pressure moneywise, and working with so many people. I really like to work alone. It's the only area of my life where I feel like I can really go for it; otherwise, everything else is a compromise.

When she got a U.S. major label deal, one compromise that Jane had to make was to re-do the "One More Colour" video for the American market with Jerry Casale, founding member of Devo, who had directed all of that band's videos as well as pieces for the Cars, Rush and others. The remake video features Jane walking down a road, singing, with a cow. I asked if the choice of the cow was a whimsical thought.

JANE SIBERRY No, a purposeful thought. Something simple like the song, like a counterpoint. Me and a road and a cow. Me and a road is not interesting. Me and a road and a cow I thought made a good counterpoint. And then Jerry Casale got into the act as director and made a cow puppet with huge udders. I asked if he would mind cutting off the udders but he was not into that at all. It was just silly.

Like so many video shoots, this one didn't go according to plan.

Laurie Brown with Jane Siberry

JANE SIBERRY The first cow . . . fell out of the back of the truck and had to be replaced. The makeup artist wondered why I went completely white under all her makeup work but someone had come in and whispered that the cow had fallen out of the truck [while it was moving]. I thought that was really bad karma to use an animal and then have it hurt. But they did find it and it was on the side of the road, grazing . . . They brought a new cow—she was used to Hollywood; she was behind door #3 on *Let's Make a Deal*.

Jane's emergence as a unique artist and the success of 1984's *No Borders Here* coincided perfectly with the launch of Much and helped form the maverick reputation of the young network.

18 Hit the Road, Much

The NewMusic paved the way for Much to take the show on the road. There was a template, an experienced crew and a history of rock 'n' roll wanderlust established by The NewMusic covering events like Reggae Sunsplash, an annual music festival held in Jamaica, Bob Marley's funeral, and various other festivals. Over the early years, Much covered big-time events like the Freddie Mercury AIDS awareness concert, the concert for Nelson Mandela, Woodstock '94 and, the coup de grâce, Live Aid in London.

In January 1985, mere months after Much had launched, J.D. took what he had learned at The NewMusic to Rock in Rio, a mega event that still happens annually. Brazil was emerging from years of political oppression and was ready for the large-scale celebration that became the first of thirty years of shows. Queen, AC/DC, James Taylor and many more showed up for the inaugural event and Much made it, too.

J.D. ROBERTS, Cameraman Dave Russell and I travelled to Rio in 1985 with a Much contest winner. Our goal was to gather enough material to put together an hour-long documentary on the festival. We didn't know anyone—didn't speak Portuguese—or have permission to take any footage of any band. But through sheer determination, and that "anything is possible" attitude, we interviewed all the big bands, including [getting] Ozzy Osbourne's first interview after his time at the Betty Ford clinic. And we talked our way onto to the stage as well. I remember being on a platform right under Rod Stewart's nose as he was belting out "Maggie May." We got some great footage—dollar-ninety-eight TV at its finest!

At home we made regular trips to ski country, to resorts like Whistler, Sun Peaks in Kamloops and Marble Mountain in Newfoundland for the SnowJob specials, as well as spring trips to Florida, called SandJobs. There were Big Ticket concerts shot all across Canada, four years of Kumbaya, the concerts to benefit AIDS charities organized by Molly Johnson, and a monster of an awards show in 1990, never to be duplicated, called the Diet Pepsi Canadian Music Video Awards, nineteen days and nights spent on a train travelling across the country. This ragtag affair eventually became the station's signature event, the MuchMusic Video Awards (MMVAs).

One guy has been on duty for most of these gigs—Doug McClement, the head of Live Wire Remote Recorders and the owner of the Comfort Sound mobile recording truck. In the small world department, I did all my earliest song demos in the '70s at Doug's original basement home studio, called Comfort Sound. Doug's skills as an audio engineer are equalled by his prodigious memory. He has records of every show he's done for Much, personal photos and a collection of laminated backstage passes! Doug talks about the crew he worked with on location shoots going back to the early '80s.

DOUG McCLEMENT [They were] an amazing technical team and almost all of them were musicians. Dave Russell [who's gone on to direct *The Hour* with former Much VJ George Stroumboulopoulos and *Spectacle* with Elvis Costello] . . . Dennis Saunders [a lot of people forget that he directed the Stevie Ray Vaughan show *Live at the El Mocambo*, an extraordinary document] and all those guys could play . . . [Director] Tom O'Neill was a drummer so his cuts were in time . . . we had shows where they lost intercom [and with it the director's ability to communicate what shots he wants], somebody stepped on the cable or drove over it with a forklift and the camera guys were shooting blind and they got the shots because they were musicians.

The John Martin approach to getting things done worked away from the studio as well.

DOUG McCLEMENT We were doing Jammin' in Jamaica and . . . Much wouldn't go in with a game plan; they'd be driving along and see a waterfall and John Martin would go, "Let's shoot the Waltons in the waterfall." There's no "okay, where are we going to get power? . . . but you guys will figure it out." I've got a car battery powering my mixer, and the Waltons [a Juno-winning band from Regina] are standing knee-deep in the action . . . I showed people a video of that and they ask, "How are they lip-synching, what are you playing back?" And I say, "They aren't lip-synching, they're playing, that's a live gig!" John should have had a T-shirt that said: *Forgiveness is easier to obtain than permission*, because that was pretty much his motto.

Doug has found himself in many situations with Much where there wasn't time to question the wisdom, let alone the viability of what they were asked to do.

DOUG McCLEMENT We did Spirit of the West on the gondola going up Blackcomb mountain sitting four abreast on a ski-lift with a wireless mic on each person [plus guitar, tambourine and accordion]. So at the start of the hill we had the band run the song for about thirty seconds; I set the levels and said, "It's fifteen minutes up the hill, you have time to do the song four times and hopefully one of them will be useful." Cameraman Dave Hurlbut is

Doug McClement at SandJob in the hotel/control room

in the ambulance car laying on his stomach . . . on a stretcher for an injured skier and I've got four wireless receivers on the back of the camera, one for each guy.

If the crew were expecting something a little more organized in Florida, it didn't work that way. Director Jim Shutsa recalls.

JIM SHUTSA With SandJob, there was no preplanning. We'd go somewhere for ten days and you'd have to rein everyone, including us in. There was alcohol involved. We'd set up a scenario and Craig [Halkett] would then program around it. What videos go with a bellyflop contest?

Editor Mark Keys remembers the rigour of these party gigs.

MARK KEYS These were great events but actually really hard to work on; we would floor direct shows during the day and then edit the segments at night. I had both of these jobs, so often times they were twenty-hour days. However that didn't stop pretty much everybody from having a ton of sex.

Doug had his own issues to deal with.

DOUG McCLEMENT We didn't have a truck the first year [1991]. We went to Daytona. I was set up in a hotel. We ran the cables out the window of the hotel . . . we rented the gear locally and set up the control room in the hotel room, mattresses up against the wall . . . to make room for the console . . . it was live to air. We did a concert every night. Barney Bentall, Jeff Healey, the Sattalites.

THE BIG TICKET—
PRINCE ALBERT, SASKATCHEWAN

The Big Ticket concert shows were shot at every major centre across the country, with all of the logistical challenges that come with the territory, but there was one in particular that is memorable for many reasons, not the least of which is the fact that it was shot at a maximum security prison in Prince Albert, Saskatchewan. David Kines, former director of operations, recalls.

DAVID KINES **There was an annual concert that the prisoners organized at the penitentiary. We'd heard that D.O.A. and BTO, who were then still talking to each other, were going to perform. So we all fly to Saskatoon, then drive to Prince Albert. The stage is in the middle of the yard, and there are guards with shotguns up above. We set up, sound check and then a torrential rain comes in. Everything, including guitar amps, gets soaked, so we hastily move everything into the gym, but the gear wasn't working, so we put out a call to "the ranges" asking, "Who's got hairdryers?" So we plugged in all the prisoners' hairdryers and we're drying off Joey "Shithead" Keithley's guitar amp.**

Doug McClement, responsible for recording the show, recalls his first sighting of the venue, if we can call this a venue.

DOUG McCLEMENT **I remember driving out there and seeing the prison on the horizon because it's so flat in Saskatchewan, and somebody asked, "Are there escapes from this place?" And they said, "This place is sort of like Alcatraz—we'd see them for hours on the horizon." It's out in the middle of nowhere; it's like a pool table.**

Doug talks about the pre-production meeting.

DOUG McCLEMENT **At the meeting the night before we were in the warden's office sitting around a table, and Kelly, who's doing lights, says to the warden, "So I guess we won't have any problem getting follow spots [a spotlight manned by an operator who follows the performer] for the gig," and everybody is laughing. Someone on the crew said, "Wow, this is a pretty primo hostage situation, a TV crew in prison," and one of the trustees [a prisoner who has earned responsibilities through good behaviour] said, "We've been looking forward to this for a year; if anybody did anything to screw this up he'd be a dead man." He said, "We don't**

get this type of thing ever, so you're probably in the safest place in the country right now."

One of the band members had a surprise for everyone.

DOUG McCLEMENT Joey Shithead, the lead singer from D.O.A., pulls up a chainsaw and holds it up to the mic, and I think the chains had been taken off but it sounds like a chainsaw, and of course the prisoners are like, "YEAHHHH." The guards are looking at each other like somebody is going to lose their job; these guys smuggled a chainsaw into a national prison.

And Doug had to equalize it. Maybe add a little reverb.

KUMBAYA

An event that helped to define the early '90s at Much was the Kumbaya Festival, a massive concert to raise awareness and funds for AIDS charities. Over its four years from 1993 to 1996, Kumbaya featured a long list of Canadian entertainers, raising over a million dollars in that time. Singer Molly Johnson was the fearless force behind these concerts and she credits Much with their success.

MOLLY JOHNSON John Martin and Denise Donlon were the founders of Kumbaya in 1993 with me and June Callwood. That would not have gotten off the ground if I hadn't begged those two to meet me in that pub across the street. They went to fuckin' town with it. They got everybody in the building to donate their day. I was able to use that as a precedent for everybody. I got Ontario Place, I got the cops, I got insurance, I got hotels, I got limos, I got flights— all donated because John and Denise led that. The only thing we couldn't get donated was the satellite feed. It's $10,000. So I walked over to Molson's in spray-painted Doc Martens, torn jeans and a mohawk and they gave me ten grand. . . . MuchMusic was all the leverage I had. It was Denise and John—that was it.

Along with the biggest names in the Canadian music business—Blue Rodeo, Bruce Cockburn, Barenaked Ladies, Jane Siberry, Tom Cochrane, Randy Bachman, Jann Arden and others, Molly secured the involvement of comedians, broadcasters, poets and athletes. In a recent conversation, Molly still has the fire in her voice when speaking about Kumbaya and I told her she reminded me of Bob Geldof, who I interviewed days before Live Aid.

MOLLY JOHNSON I had the shit kicked out of me by the music business so bad I was not going to make another record and I sat there pouting, then I looked in my phone book and said, "Look who I know," and I just started calling people. I took my really pissed off "I'm never going to make another record" attitude and drove it into something. I got evicted. I didn't have a gig. I didn't make any money. I was obsessed.

It takes a unique individual with an indomitable drive to make an event of this scope succeed—someone willing to take risks.

MOLLY JOHNSON Not allowing managers [of the acts] backstage . . . What happened was the artists started jumping into each other's sets. There you have for the first time, Mary Margaret O'Hara playing with Blue Rodeo. That moment with Dougie Gilmour of the Maple Leafs . . . I'm holding, as always, handfuls of condoms that we were throwing into the audience constantly. We sent him out there with hockey sticks and Doug Gilmour showed kids how to put condoms on a hockey stick.

One call to a Canadian icon had an unforeseen outcome.

MOLLY JOHNSON I cold-called Margaret Atwood. I got her assistant who says, "That's a lovely idea but Margaret has rented a van and is driving her daughter to Montreal for university . . . but thanks for calling." A couple days later I get the call, "Molly, is there any room for Margaret? Her daughter doesn't want her to drive her to Montreal" . . . I said, "Yeah, we've got room for Margaret Atwood." Her daughter goes to Montreal and what's the first thing a student does when they get to their dorm?—they turn on MuchMusic. And what does her daughter see but her mother on MuchMusic talking to Geddy Lee and Tom Cochrane and all these superstars. Long and short of it is, I made Margaret Atwood superiorly cool. So I get to call her Peggy now.

THE PEPSI TRAIN—THE CMVAS

It's probably not a stretch to say that the biggest, baddest and boldest bash ever thrown in MuchMusic's history was the 1990 Canadian Music Video Awards, the original MMVAs, sponsored by Diet Pepsi. Likely inspired by the Festival Express train tour of 1970, John Martin and an adventurous Pepsi exec cooked up this extravaganza and against pretty good odds, got the Canadian National Railway to agree to let them take a train across the country for nineteen days, playing shows in cities and towns, often unplanned, and videotape the whole thing.

Like anything different from the usual, or anything John came up with, it was controversial. James Woods, then in publicity, remembers it this way.

JAMES WOODS **The Pepsi train was awful, it was a booze cruise. There was no other reason for that thing to happen. They stopped in cities, handing out awards that no one remembered. It shouldn't have been Pepsi, maybe Labatt.**

But others, and in fact most of the people I spoke with, remember something altogether different.

JIM SHUTSA, technical director **The Pepsi train was the big dream that worked. We thought John was crazy, but 'we're in, because it's a train ride across Canada. How can we possibly turn this down?' It was supposed to be a Pepsi taste challenge and we were supposed to go with them and Much ended up owning that train before we got to province number two. It was phenomenal. The best thing we did and the stupidest thing we did was put the edit bay in the bar car. In the end it was the highlight of my career at Much.**

Audio engineer Doug McClement has very strong memories of the experience, and echoes Jim's residual feelings about it.

DOUG McCLEMENT **The interesting thing for me was how it snowballed as we went across the country. We started in Vancouver [leaving the CN station June 7 at noon], and not too many people knew about it, and then we went to Jasper and there'd be more people, and as we went across, by the time we got to Capreol, outside of Sudbury, they shut down the schools . . . there were two thousand people at the train station when we pulled in. It was like a politician's tour. So the thing just snowballed; we got to Quebec and Celine Dion is singing in the train station . . . to a DAT [digital audio tape] machine, there's no band, it's her first English-language album, it's her and her rapper basically, and I'd never felt more Canadian . . . We got to Sioux Lookout, Ontario, an Indian reservation up north, and they opened the doors . . . and the crowd spontaneously broke into "O Canada." I thought I was going to cry.**

As you might imagine, there were technical issues recording bands live on a rolling train. But they might not be the kind you would expect.

DOUG McCLEMENT **The funny thing was . . . this was one of the few Much gigs where there was ever a production meeting [and]**

On board the Pepsi train

the big concern was, "Doug, what are they going to do? The train noise is going to be so loud, viewers are gonna hear the train noise. Train noise and . . . how are you going to get power? It's going to be all over the map." It turned out they hooked us up to the generator on the engine, had cables running over the roof of the train to our control room and . . . the power was rock solid when the train was in motion . . . In the baggage car we made a frame of two-by-fours and we stapled packing blankets all the way around and we did the first stuff with Jeff Healey and Barney Bentall going through southern B.C. and we satellited the stuff down to Toronto and the comment back was, "Not enough train noise, sounds like a studio," so that night, we hung two mics out the side of the train and recorded train noise for an hour and put it on a loop, so we actually had to *add* train noise.

David Kirkwood in sales recalls John's original vision for the train.

DAVID KIRKWOOD **John Martin said, "This won't look like much this year, but mark my words, this will be the most important thing MuchMusic does in years to come." John imagined this train with Diet Pepsi down the side, musicians coming on and off doing whistle stops and people playing. It was the beginning of a very different kind of awards show. They didn't want the standard Emmys, Grammys format.**

Not much risk of that. I'd heard the conflicting views of the Pepsi Train. John isn't around to explain his idea, and as I contemplated writing about the tour I was beginning to lose sight of what had actually taken place, so I screened the whole thing in the basement of 299 Queen Street West on a little Beta machine in the tape library. It was magnificent. It was a mess, a glorious, sprawling attempt at doing something grand, in a humble, Canadian way. Was it a success? And by what metrics? Who cares? It was Blue Rodeo, the Northern Pikes, Jane Siberry, 54-40, Celine Dion, Lee Aaron, Bruce Cockburn, and others, as you had never seen them. Oh yeah—and Jeff Healey was the house band jamming the whole way on classic songs like "Helpless," "Knockin' on Heaven's Door" and "All Right Now" with various vocalists and musical contributors. And there was table hockey!

Perhaps oddly, the most enduring image for me was that of an artist whose work is an indelible part of the fabric of Canadian music, Bruce Cockburn. An artist, I should add, who largely got left behind by the video era. He wrote great songs, played beautifully and sang with heart and conviction, but we'd entered a time when, sadly, that wasn't enough. But there was a moment, brilliantly captured by director Tom O'Neill, with Bruce walking down the railway tracks doing a solo performance of "Child of the Wind," and a train passes, by good fortune alone, at the end of the song. If you were to watch it, I dare you not to be moved and maybe feel a little teary-eyed and patriotic.

The train and the Canadian Music Video Awards gave way to the MMVAs, held annually at 299 Queen Street, so it was a brilliant one-off, magically pulled together, seat-of-the-pants style, and destined never to be repeated.

And I suppose there were some awards, but by the time the show got to air, they had already been handed out. I don't remember anything about them.

In a glitch-ridden and primitive way, MuchMusic's second annual World Music Video Awards show . . . linked live performances and video presentations in [Toronto], Moscow, London, and Munich. It was a technological triumph, proof our satellite-packed skies are truly open and that national cultural boundaries no longer exist.

Greg Quill

THE
UNPREDIC
TABILITY
IS THE
REASON
PEOPLE
TUNE IN.

19 The VJs—
The Third Wave

ANGELA DOHRMANN

"THE UNPREDICTABILITY IS THE REASON PEOPLE TUNE IN."

When Angela Dohrmann replaced me on air in 1990, Greg Quill wrote a feature piece in the *Toronto Star* that called her "everything a MuchMusic veejay shouldn't be." He listed her attributes, which in retrospect, seem odd as disqualifiers:

"Blonde . . . blue-eyed. Obviously glad to be post-adolescent and comfortable with her relative maturity (she's in her late 20s). Intelligent and witty. Less than self-absorbed. And as far as the music business goes, a self-confessed neophyte."

Okay, maybe the last one was a potential issue. Angela's background was different from that of her predecessors. She wasn't a musician or a radio type.

ANGELA DOHRMANN I'm a trained stage actor. My first job was with a Shakespeare company . . . I fell into comedy. I ended up at the Second City touring company for a nanosecond, and I was temping at this soul-sucking job, training people on WordPerfect.

She was experiencing her own version of the rock 'n' roll lifestyle when the Much opportunity came along.

ANGELA DOHRMANN I was so poor and living illegally under the Kids in the Hall's office in this warehouse loft space . . . there was a constant snow of dust coming down . . . It was $1.00 a square foot. I had 300 square feet . . . Kids in the Hall had a Ping-Pong table which they used while they were writing, which was a joy.

Poverty is one of the common elements in so many entertainment business stories, but this was one very resourceful woman.

ANGELA DOHRMANN I had no training on camera . . . Do you remember when electronics stores, selling video cameras would have one set up so you could see yourself on TV as you walked by? There was a storefront on Yonge Street. I would go down there

with my "sides" [part of a script given to an actor, generally for an audition] on the street and try to see, "What does this angle look like? What choices should I make? . . . How does this transfer to camera?"

(Opposite) Angela
Dohrmann and elephant

Once she got in front of a real camera, Angela was a natural. Greg Quill referred to her as "the least self-conscious of any veejay I've seen on MuchMusic or MTV." She loved the freedom she found at 299 Queen Street West and expressed amazement at "how much rope they gave us."

ANGELA DOHRMANN The great gift of it was that they didn't Svengali the whole thing, that they encouraged an honesty and naturalness about who you were, rather than, "Here's the model, how do we make you conform to it?" Now, looking back, I'm astounded at how little oversight there was as to what was going to come out of our mouths.

There was a sly, subversive quality to her work that sometimes led to some lines being crossed. Angela recalls having to do a live product pitch that went off the rails.

ANGELA DOHRMANN The product was microwaveable shakes, where you get it in your freezer aisle and you put it in the micro-wave and then in three minutes there was a shake. I was on-air pitching this product for the first time and I remember turning to camera and saying, "Well, if it doesn't biodegrade in a landfill, what's it going to do inside of you?" Then the phones [rang] and poor Dennis [Saunders, technical director] was called onto the carpet on Monday. I had to be reminded, "Where's your bread being buttered?" There's comedy and there's "shut the fuck up."

Trust me, "poor Dennis" was okay with it. It was with admiration that he recalled Angela's stint as a VJ.

DENNIS SAUNDERS Angela got me in trouble three Mondays in a row with Ron Waters [vice-president and GM for Citytv and MuchMusic]. One of them she's jerking off on camera, another one the camera comes up and she's going "fuckfuckfuck . . ."

The most legendary Angela moment was recounted by a couple of the participants, including Dennis.

DENNIS SAUNDERS I'm waiting for Gwar [a theatrical, satirical American band whose performances featured bizarre sci-fi costuming and fake blood being sprayed into the audience].

I THINK ART IS THE SPIRITUAL BACKBONE O THE PLANET, SO IF THERE WERE NO MUCHMUSIC, WE'D ALL DIE

Alanis Morissette

They're late but I get a call from the label and they're close by. For the first and only time, I hold off the news, the important rock news of the day. Gwar pull up, jump out of their van, one of them with a prosthetic pecker. One of the local punks had a pet ferret who started noshing on the pecker while the interview was going on. I'm thinking maybe this wasn't such a good idea. Steve shows up with a little plastic mallet while Angela is doing the interview. Before we can do anything, he's got it out and Angela starts whacking the guy's peepee. Denise [Donlon] was not amused.

Angela Dohrmann and Bob Geldof

STEVE ANTHONY Angela hitting the guy from Gwar's penis with a hammer that made the sound effect of breaking glass. The cameraman is being told not to shoot it, but what could they do? So, there was this giant schlong, getting hit by a hammer—that's MuchMusic.

When I asked Angela about this particular event, she didn't remember, but offers up this possible explanation.

ANGELA DOHRMANN I do remember the travesty of Gwar. I mean that's just a walking set-up . . . My own boundaries weren't as mature as they should have been at the time.

As to that "self-confessed neophyte" problem, I think Angela made it work for her through a combination of smarts, improv skills and genuine curiosity.

ANGELA DOHRMANN I didn't know the talk of music, the vernacular. I'd be in awe of the art form because it was pretty new to me. There's no amount of paperwork in the file that can prepare you for some of the brilliance of the musician.

Over the years, we were treated to some extraordinary casual performances in the studio. I remember some glorious moments courtesy of Daniel Lanois, Steve Earle (who agreed to go outside and busk on Queen Street for us!) and Crowded House. Angela talked about the feeling of taking in just such a performance from the unique front-row seat that being a VJ afforded.

ANGELA DOHRMANN [I would be] sitting across from somebody who just stopped playing music and I'm humbled to be in their court and having to ask the question. [Virtuoso American guitarist] Michael Hedges blew me away. If I had time and money, I would have taken music appreciation classes because that part of what I brought to the table was sorely lacking.

Of course, we all had interviews that were memorable for other reasons. Angela talked about her encounter with Sir Bob Geldof.

ANGELA DOHRMANN I was sweating bullets. He had this cuss machine, this little joke thing in his pocket that if you pressed a button would emit profanity, like [in a tiny cartoon voice] "fuck you," "motherfucker," "asshole." He'd be doing that seconds to air, saying, "One wrong question and I've got this in my pocket."

When I asked if that was one of her favourite or worst interviews, she replied, "Favourite, in that, it was scary as hell and I did it."
   Even minus a musical background, Angela had the thing that keeps people watching, the thing that was at the heart of MuchMusic. She sums it up.

ANGELA DOHRMANN The unpredictability is the reason people tune in.

RICK CAMPANELLI

"I WAS GOING TO BE A TEACHER BUT I THOUGHT I'D DO THIS FOR THE TIME BEING."

I think the next generation of Much VJs was ushered in by Rick Campanelli, forever to be known as "Rick the Temp" during his Much days, and to some, for years after. Not an actor, a musician, or a DJ, Rick was a fan who became a fan favourite in a most unusual and very public way. It's quite a story.

RICK CAMPANELLI They came up with the Temp contest in 1993 for a viewer to work at Much for the months of July and August . . . I jumped at the opportunity and sent my entry in . . . Of course, I didn't win the contest that year. A teacher named Ben from Edmonton won . . . I still remember that he sent in photos of himself wearing a cape and flying over the city's skyline! . . . So a year went by and Much announced the Temp contest for 1994 . . . well I brought my A-game to that year's

Sook-Yin Lee (right) with VJ Search winners, including future VJs Rick Campanelli and Diego Fuentes (second and third from left)

entry. I remember working on my entry at the same time as I was studying for my final exams at Brock University—I used my parents' basement . . . That year they only allowed us to use twenty-five words or less to explain why we'd make the perfect MuchMusic Temp! . . . I bought a roll of packing paper—which was about fifty yards long—and I airbrushed my statement on the paper. . . . The original line was "Rather than wasting another summer on my ass just watching you guys on TV I have the power to be there and help!" Pretty lame right? . . . I kept refining and substituting some of my words for MuchMusic . . . shows that were airing at that time. The end result was "Rather than OUTLAWING another summer on my FAX WEDGING you guys I feel obligated to EXTEND my POWER and help BUZZ around your ELECTRIC ENVIRONMENT!" Exactly twenty-five words—seven of which were MuchMusic words . . . I cut out stencilled letters and began spray painting . . . this whole project took me close to two weeks . . . So after I was done creating my banner/ entry, I designed and built the "M" shaped box to ship my entry in. My parents had just bought an appliance, I think it was a new fridge or stove, for the house, so I used the massive box and actually turned it into the letter "M" that would open from the top and helium balloons would lift up my banner in scroll-like fashion . . .

Tony Bennett and
Natalie Richard

Anyway I had it delivered on the very last day that they were
accepting Temp entries that year, and I guess you can say the
rest is history . . . I will never forget tuning into MuchMusic the
day they were about to announce who the winner of the 1994 Temp
contest was. Erica Ehm had just come back from a commercial
break and was sitting behind my "M" shaped box—she had her
arms on top of it and I just knew in that split second my life was
about to change! It did, big-time . . . my creation was picked as
the winner of the Temp contest . . . that was twenty years ago . . .
and THAT just got my foot in the door . . . it was the VJ Search of
1995 that would get me even closer to my dream of becoming a
MuchMusic VJ.

JAKOB DYLAN How'd you end up as a VJ?

RICK CAMPANELLI I won a contest. I was going to be a teacher
but I thought I'd do this for the time being.

JAKOB DYLAN You seem to be doing all right.

Rick was either the first of a new generation or the last of the old guard of
VJs. He was old school in his love for music and dedication to preparation
for the gig. And he stuck with the template, so ingrained by then, that saw
the VJs interacting with the crew.

RICK CAMPANELLI I worked off the crew—the crew was my co-host and I would interact with them as much as I could . . . because they were also a bunch of different personalities . . . I still remember the day when my boss at the time said, "Rick, don't interact with the crew" . . . I said to myself, "Are you kidding me?" From that day forward MuchMusic was never the same to me.

NATALIE RICHARD

"MUCHMUSIC WAS FOR ME LIKE *THE MICKEY MOUSE CLUB*"

Natalie Richard was doing the weather on the French CBC news out of Toronto in 1986 when a colleague suggested she audition for a VJ spot on MusiquePlus, the new French-language network that paralleled MuchMusic in English Canada.

NATALIE RICHARD I took the train to Montreal to give my tape to Pierre Marchand [the boss at MusiquePlus] and I told him, "I'm your next VJ." He said, "We'll see about that. Can you speak English?"

Natalie could speak English and after doing a demo interview with Matt Zimbel of Manteca, she got the gig, even though she had a good job at the time.

NATALIE RICHARD It was very exciting because it was the beginning of a new era for music . . . CBC said, "You can't leave here. We've got a big career for you; you can be here for the rest of your life and you're making a big mistake . . . we're paying you so much money and you're going to go there and work for almost nothing."

Oddly enough, that was never a barrier to people wanting to work at Much or MusiquePlus. Plus was operating out of the Much studios in Toronto at first, shooting when the day was done at Much with a fresh Francophone crew. It was a temporary situation at best.

NATALIE RICHARD The VJs were staying in a hotel, going back and forth from Montreal to Toronto. That's how I became an elite member of Air Canada.

MusiquePlus opened their new Montreal studio in September of 1988, appropriately enough, on Mitsou's 18th birthday. In 1989 Natalie left

MusiquePlus and was working as a singer/actor. Based on her three years on Plus, we were very familiar with Natalie's work when Much was looking for a new VJ in the fall of 1991. I was particularly aware of Natalie because she had graciously played co-host to the Charles de Camembert nonsense on many editions of the annual year-end video cheese-o-rama, *Fromage!* She moved to Toronto to work full-time at Much; I asked her about the difference between working at Plus and Much. The vehemence of her answer surprised me.

NATALIE RICHARD It was like living in a house with one room, like a studio apartment, and moving into a mansion in Beverly Hills . . . it was like the difference between being a TV personality and being a star.

The audience took to Natalie right away, despite her uncertainty about their response.

NATALIE RICHARD At first I thought they wouldn't like me because I was French and I realized . . . it's the opposite, because when I finished MuchMusic five years later, I think I lost a bit of my accent, and they were, "Oh, too bad you don't have your French accent anymore."

She got some attention from other sources as well. At the Gemini Awards in Toronto a few months after she started on air, Mike Myers was hosting.

NATALIE RICHARD He gave the "Top 5 Reasons Why Quebec Should Stay in Canada" and the last one was, "Natalie Richard, *la renarde* [the fox] . . . schwing!" It was all over the papers the next day.

Natalie interviewed a parade of artists of all types, but her most memorable encounter was with Tony Bennett. They danced!

NATALIE RICHARD I was swept off my feet . . . he was maybe seventy at the time . . . he seems ageless to me. I remember thinking this is how I want to be when I'm older . . . you can't make a bad dance move when Tony Bennett is turning you around . . . this was the best moment of my life.

I had to ask about her *Fromage!* experience with the cheesemeister, yours truly.

NATALIE RICHARD My highlight was always doing *Fromage!* This was the show people talked the most about. Charles de Camembert was like me—a music lover and a food lover, so passionate. He was

ahead of his time because he understood the relationship between music and food, especially cheese.

Natalie hosted a daily half-hour show featuring French videos, but her role at the show was much more than on-air presenter.

NATALIE RICHARD **I went to Moses with the name for a show: *French Kiss*—the meeting of two tongues, English and French. He loved it. I was the programmer, the director, the host of the show. My television skills became complete. When I went to the French communities I would take my own camera and I became a videographer.**

As always when these two cultures meet, there is a "frisson."

NATALIE RICHARD **The French videos were always controversial— people thought they were too *osé* [daring], showed too much skin, too sensual. We'd get letters from Saskatchewan.**

Natalie and I talked about life after MuchMusic for the VJs. I had moved to the U.S. immediately after leaving Much and went from being recognized wherever I went in Canada, to being completely anonymous. Her experience was different, and not an entirely comfortable transition. Her description of that point in her life was poignant.

NATALIE RICHARD **MuchMusic was for me like *The Mickey Mouse Club*. I spent all my twenties up till I was thirty-three on TV, so the relationships I developed with people were not normal. When it was all over and I was thirty-three, I thought, "Now what?" I was totally maladapted to real life. I was in a bubble all this time. It was a beautiful time but it was also hard to land back in reality where everybody else lives. People don't treat you the same after—you remain a celebrity even if you're not doing anything. And you can't do anything that's not spectacular or you're a "hasbeen." You're still being watched all the time.**

20 The Specialty Shows—Part Two

In 1984, there were other music-video-driven shows out there. CBC had *Video Hits* hosted by Samantha Taylor, and *Good Rockin' Tonite*, hosted originally by Terry David Mulligan and later Stu Jeffries. Joel Goldberg had been working as a VJ at local Toronto outlet CFMT-TV with co-host Shirley McQueen, but had his heart set on MuchMusic well before he worked there, regularly pitching Moses on show ideas and sending tapes.

JOEL GOLDBERG MuchMusic had the resources, passionate people, the audience reach, the industry connections and the "hip" factor. If you were in the business and interested in pop culture, MuchMusic was nirvana . . . Citytv/Much was a building full of misfits . . . Personalities, skill sets and vision that would not work in the more structured broadcasters of the time.

Eventually, Joel got his first gig in the building as associate producer on *Toronto Rocks* in 1985, a show he describes as "basically radio on TV."

JOEL GOLDBERG It was a simple but effective concept. One camera on Brad Giffen [and John Majhor before him], interviewing music celebrities in a small control room/studio, and hyping local music events.

I remember subbing for John for a week and it was the smallest space I have ever worked in. It was aptly called a "shot box," and featured one locked-off camera and a fake switcher for transitioning to video. When guests came, it got very intimate!

Dave Stewart of Eurythmics and Brad Giffen

Toronto Rocks bled viewers as Much became more established so Moses and John approached Joel with a new idea.

ELECTRIC CIRCUS

"WE HAD THE FEELING THAT *EC* WAS LIKE ICE CREAM."

JOEL GOLDBERG The name was born over drinks with John Martin and Kim Clarke Champniss.

KIM CLARKE CHAMPNISS John Martin wanted to do a dance show. He had in mind something similar to the legendary U.K. music show *Ready, Steady, Go!* meets *Top of the Pops*. He called a meeting at X-Rays, and asked for name suggestions. Discos always seemed to have female names, so I suggested things like "Julianna's," and "Annabelle's," ideas which immediately fell flat. And then I remembered that the old Much/City studios at 99 Queen East was [now] the location of a well-known Toronto club called "Electric Circus." I put forward the name and suddenly the light bulb went on.

The idea was to have a dance club atmosphere in front of the windows of 299, so people on the street could watch. We would also have field reports examining club culture across the country.

Joel remembers meeting the woman who would become the first host.

JOEL GOLDBERG I first met Monika Deol when John Martin brought her to Much. She was quite the presence. Beautiful, and very well-versed in pop culture. She was also a DJ in Winnipeg, so she had a foundation in the dance club community. John introduced me, but it wasn't until a week later that I was called up to Moses's office and she was officially introduced to me as *EC*'s first host.

Monika recalls how she got the gig.

MONIKA DEOL The reason Moses asked me to host that show is not because I liked fashion, and could wear a cute outfit. It's because I was a club DJ; I was a club kid—I knew the club culture. Fashion is part of it but there's more to it. And it's not as superficial as people would like to believe.

Navigating a career in club music was not as easy a road as one might imagine. Monika had to pay a price for choices that ran counter to her Indian-Canadian family's expectation of a young woman from that culture.

MONIKA DEOL I was a bit of a rebel . . . I had a band in high school. I went to university like I was supposed to. I got a part-time

I was a club kid— I knew the club culture.

Monika Deol

job as a club DJ. My dad didn't speak to me for a year. He'd be in the same room I was in and would not acknowledge I existed.

Monika spoke passionately about what the club culture meant to her.

MONIKA DEOL I loved the fact that everybody was accepted. You could be any skin colour, you could look like anything and you could make it a look. I loved the fact that you could be free and be totally into music. I loved loud music and just dancing. When I was younger I didn't drink, I didn't smoke, I didn't do drugs—I didn't do any of those things, but I loved clubs . . . and I loved the Scorpions as much as I loved Madonna.

Although the show became a hit, there were some bumps on the way. Joel talks about building a following.

JOEL GOLDBERG The early days of the show were rough. We had to establish credibility in the club community as well as create a buzz for television viewers. I remember having to go out in the street with [production assistants] and try and recruit dancers for the early tapings! If we saw a person or couple who looked like they could dance, we'd try and convince them to come in and dance. We brought in a dance coordinator when we were having trouble getting a variety of dancers on the show. We had begun to get a good core group, but we wanted to have different faces and different styles of club dancing for every show. More variety. The idea was bring someone in from the dance community who had connections in the clubs and could recruit good dancers for the show. It took a lot of pressure off me so I could concentrate on production. Once we started to gain momentum and actually had a pool of dancers that wanted to be on the show, the dance coordinator helped make sure we had the best and most stylish dancers on each show.

Club culture began in cities like Miami and New York in the '70s and with the widespread popularity of disco, expanded into a full-fledged phenomenon in the '80s with a very broad-based international audience. Propulsive beats pumping through killer sound systems made for a visceral experience that crossed all the borders of age, sexual orientation and culture. As the "party" got bigger, bands soon figured out that doing a dance remix of their hits could only expand their popularity. Monika recalls how the show found an audience, even if it wasn't the one they thought it would find.

MONIKA DEOL *Electric Circus* was completely live, dangerously live, considering the kind of show it was. It was like a United Nations in a small place. We had somebody from every culture in

that room. No security people. We had the feeling that *EC* was like ice cream. People didn't want to admit that they stayed home Friday night and ate the entire gallon of ice cream. But in fact—yes they did. The way I could tell is because people would say, "I love your show," and I'd think, "You're a sixty-year-old business person, you're an accountant, you're a flight attendant, you're a taxi driver." How could all these people be watching this show? But you'd look at them and say, "Oh, I didn't think you were the kind of person who watched *EC*." And they'd say, "Oh, I don't really watch it."

Michael Williams was the original co-host of this guilty pleasure, but soon other personalities emerged as they often did in the Much family. Joel explains.

JOEL GOLDBERG **Moses also wanted to show production "process" which is why George Lagogianes, who was a videographer on the show eventually became the co-host. George was a great camera operator as well as a very good-looking guy! We would take shots of George taking shots of dancers, then cut to George's shot. And this is also where Craig Halkett became popular on-air. Only on MuchMusic could a floor director become an on-air personality. Craig . . . endeared himself to the dancers and viewers, and became a very popular and important part of the show. But George and Craig never stopped doing their jobs: camera-op/floor director.**

EC grew into one of the most popular specialty shows we ever had. Joel talks about the growth of the show.

JOEL GOLDBERG **It was Sharon Kavanaugh, then my associate producer, who brought *EC* to much higher levels. One of the first things she did was to convince Moses to do the show live on Friday nights rather than taped in the afternoon. She also brought in art direction and more attention to lighting.**

The specialty shows couldn't all be winners, so rather then sweep the unfortunate, not-so-successful efforts under the video carpet, Steven Kerzner, creator of "Ed the Sock," talks about his Much debut.

STEVE KERZNER **I did a show called *Ed's Smash or Trash* which was based on a show from Moses's youth called *Is It a Hit?*—it was a panel show . . . we'd run a music video and have people from the music industry [comment and rate it]. It was Ed co-hosting with Steve Anthony—Steve was supposed to be the control mechanism. You can understand how chaotic this was going to be. We'd play the video for three or four minutes and then talk about the video for seven minutes and it was the most dull, pedantic . . . you know**

THERE'S A LINE FROM *STAR WARS.* "A GREATER COLLECTION OF SCUM AND VILLAINY YOU WILL NEVER FIND IN ONE PLACE."

when your dad comes down to the kids' parties and says, "What are you kids listening to on the hi-fi?" It was taking everything that was cool about the video and about pop culture and making it dull and boring and there was no way to save that program . . . it was just inadvisable.

In spite of this, Ed the Sock became a beloved character on Much.

OUTLAWS AND HEROES

The week he graduated from Seneca College's radio-and-TV broadcast course, Bill Welychka got hired as an editor at Much. He was a big country music fan when the so-called "new traditionalists" were emerging—Randy Travis, Dwight Yoakam and Steve Earle. Bill pitched John on an idea for a show but John was already on it. *Outlaws and Heroes* was Canada's first country music video show, and Bill became the editor. Soon, he was helping program it and in a classic Much move, stepped in as host for Denise Donlon, who was on maternity leave. Years later, when the specialty channel Country Music Television had taken over that territory, and the show was cancelled, Bill moved to full-time hosting on Much.

BILL WELYCHKA During this entire time, I continued to edit and loved the entire production of television . . . I could travel, interview someone, come back to the station, edit and produce and post-produce an hour special!

If Bill was looking for feedback from management regarding his on-air skills, John provided some.

BILL WELYCHKA After my first taped show with *Outlaws and Heroes*, I was at work in an edit bay. The crew had just aired my very first [taped] throw. There was some kind applause from the crew on the floor. John Martin came over to the edit bay and said to me . . . "Were you citing the Declaration of Independence? Keep it short!"

Bill Welychka and Bob Seger

ZIGGY AND MUSHMUSIC

"JOHN MARTIN TOLD ME I WAS THE WORST INTERVIEWER HE'D EVER SEEN."

"Let there be Mush" was one of those dictums that could only have come from Moses. John likely held his nose at the thought of Ziggy Lorenc on the leopard print couch breathily introducing Yanni and Michael Bolton videos on a show called MushMusic. But who knows? Maybe John's rock 'n' roll heart would have enjoyed the campiness of it all.

Before *Mush* came to 299 Queen West, Ziggy had made her way through the ranks at Citytv, starting as a receptionist, or Switchette, as they were known, and then working in publicity. Eventually, her naturally theatrical and engaging personality led her to be on air.

ZIGGY LORENC I'd been working on *Toronto Rocks* doing community reports from high schools, so I had a following of teenagers. Joel Goldberg approached me with an idea for a program with romantic music videos and asked if I wanted to host it. It was live five days a week on Citytv at noon; it was called *MushMusic*.

With her "straight from my diary"–type confessions, Ziggy was ahead of her time.

ZIGGY LORENC What I would do is cull from my life and tell people what I'd done the night before, what dates I'd been on, what shoes I wore and what happened in the shoes while I was wearing them. It was kind of *Sex and the City*.

And like other women on-air, Ziggy had to deal with public reaction that could go from rapturous to venomous.

ZIGGY LORENC When I walked down the street a lot of people would yell out "slut!" It was pretty tame. I had a big drag queen following. MushMusic was campy and I'd been a disco bunny prior to this, so it made sense.

Once Moses moved the show to Much, Ziggy was under another kind of scrutiny.

ZIGGY LORENC John Martin told me I was the worst interviewer he'd ever seen. I tried to work on it.

> I go to the library. I come here. I go shopping. That's it.
> Ziggy Lorenc

She recalls that first day at Much live.

Rick Astley and Ziggy Lorenc

ZIGGY LORENC My dad was in hospital; he had come out of surgery. I was such a mess; I couldn't breathe through the entire show. At the end of it, all my friends in the building were there cheering. They had flowers. My dad was watching . . . Rick Astley was my first interview. He was great.

It's one thing to ask Ziggy to interview Rick Astley, but Henry Rollins, the fire-breathing spoken-word artist and lead singer of Black Flag, who once called himself "a scream looking for a mouth"? This sounded like human sacrifice. But Ziggy held her own.

ZIGGY LORENC It shouldn't have worked but it did. He was kind to me. My campiness [paired] with his brain power seemed to work.

It worked because Ziggy, despite the ditzy delivery and the pure kitsch of her show, is well-read and articulate, and Henry respected that. I asked Ziggy about her inspiration in life.

ZIGGY LORENC My mother was in the gulag in Russia and one of the few people to come out alive. She made a trek through Soviet Central Asia to Tehran and then joined the British Navy. She was a big supporter of mine. My mother had a beautiful voice and had wanted to be a singer; if I wanted to do something, she'd say, "Do it!"

There is a legendary Ziggy quotation worth recalling.

ZIGGY LORENC I was fixing my DK tights with duct tape and they were shooting it. It was live on MuchMusic. [I said], "Sometimes I hate my hips more than I hate nuclear war."

She offered a wistful coda to her time on air.

ZIGGY LORENC I wish my shelf life had been longer. When grunge came in, I felt out of my element. They tend to dispose of women at a certain age.

I REMEMBER THINKING, THE RECORD COMPANY WILL NOT BE PLEASED

21 Mecca in Memphis & Black Velvet

I met Alannah Myles in 1979 when she was still Alannah Byles and living at her parents' home, and on our first date, she invited me in . . . to play me songs that she had written! I was smitten and a grand partnership began as we became a couple and musical collaborators. Alannah was as single-minded and focused then as she was when she broke nearly ten years later. She'd been schooled in show business by her father, Bill Byles, who had worked in the beginnings of Canadian radio and television on *The Happy Gang*, *Juliette* and *Wayne and Shuster* shows.

In those days in the early '80s, Alannah was singing solo with acoustic guitar in fern bars, covering Linda Ronstadt songs with a powerful and very pure voice. But she really wanted to be a rock 'n' roller. We started writing songs with that goal in mind and right from our first demos the template was set. We moved in together and I played her Mavis Staples, Aretha and Bonnie Raitt and she absorbed everything. One magic day, she found that voice you know, the one with the Tina Turner-esque rasp, by trapping

phlegm at the back of her throat when she sang. As bizarre as this sounds, she created it by drinking milk before she sang, any vocal coach's nightmare. Eventually, she didn't need the dairy products; the rasp became second nature and Alannah Myles was born.

We wrote songs, made demos and Alannah formed band after band. We were a DIY set-up—writing, record-ing and rehearsing in the living room of our apartment in the Beach area of Toronto. I took her first promo shot in

First promotional shot of Alannah Myles

the bedroom with one of those fold-up emergency blankets used as a backdrop.

I got hired by MuchMusic, which meant that there was a little more money for recording. Having been turned down multiple times by every label, we decided to make a record on our own and secured a small FACTOR grant (the Fund to Assist Canadian Talent on Record, created in 1982 with contributions from Canadian broadcasters). Around this time, we met David Tyson, a brilliant young piano player, songwriter and producer. Dave was the missing piece, creatively, and we started writing and recording together. Alannah, as always, was thinking big, so we decided that the way to get the attention of U.S. labels, who we knew weren't going to fly to Toronto to see her, was to make a video demo to send to them.

I knew how telegenic Alannah was and had learned the power of a good video on a daily basis at Much. We rented the Diamond Club (Toronto's premiere dance and concert club from 1984 to 1991), got Alannah's friend, fashion photographer Deborah Samuel to direct and chose a song, "Just One Kiss," that later made it onto her first album. Deborah talked about their creative relationship.

"A new religion that will bring you to your knees"

DEBORAH SAMUEL Brainstorming was a joy with Alannah as she had a great sense of wardrobe, of the dramatic.

I'd been visiting the broadcast class at Centennial College for the last couple of years to talk about working in TV and I convinced them to further their education by being extras in the video shoot. We ended up doing the old trick of moving them around the room as a group and shooting from different angles so it looked like there was a crowd.

Bob Roper, A&R at Warner Canada, saw the demo video, heard the songs and liked Alannah, but felt that he couldn't sign her. He graciously agreed to send the package on to his counterparts in the U.S. I was in a Vancouver hotel room on a MuchMusic promo trip when I got the call that changed it all. "Christopher," said a man with a heavy Turkish accent, "this is Tunç Erim, Atlantic Records in New York. Your artist, Alannah Myles, is a star and I want her on my label. Who is your lawyer?"

No foreplay, no pussyfooting, no nonsense. It tuned out Tunç was head of A&R for the label and was an old crony of label chairman Ahmet Ertegun. If he wanted to sign something, it got signed. No committees required.

Once Alannah was signed to Atlantic, she, Dave Tyson and I started writing songs in earnest to add to what we already had. One day, Dave suggested that we could use a song with the classic "shuffle" beat, one that appears in songs from Chuck Berry's "Reelin' and Rockin'" to Tears For Fears' "Everybody Wants to Rule the World." I had recently been sent to Memphis on a MuchMusic trip and had been working on a song in a bluesy shuffle feel since that trip, so I played them what I had written. The opening line was, "Mississippi in the middle of a dry spell," and the song was loosely to do with Elvis. Alannah loved it and Dave asked if I had a bridge for the song since the chorus and verses were already done. When I said no, he asked if he could take a stab at writing one.

Backtracking a bit, I'd been sent on a Much trip to Memphis in August of '87 with a cameraman and forty Elvis fanatics on a Greyhound bus. With time on my hands, I'd been reading about Elvis's life, in particular a book called *Elvis and Gladys* about his relationship with his mother. The author, Elaine Dundy, spoke of visiting the church in Tupelo, Mississippi, where the Presley family had lived and seeing the preacher exhorting the congregation and falling on one knee. She made the connection to Elvis's stage moves. In my ever-present notebook I wrote the phrase "a new religion that will bring you to your knees," thinking of rock 'n' roll as the "new religion." As someone who liked Elvis, but wasn't a devoted fan, I'd been talking with the people on the bus, absorbing their deep connection to the late singer, and how it at times bordered on a religious dedication. We later called the show that came from this trip *Mecca in Memphis*, and included interviews with Vince Gill, Reba McEntire and Mae Axton, who had co-written Elvis's first hit "Heartbreak Hotel." By the time I was back in Toronto I had the ideas I needed for the lyric and typical of many songwriters, I played the shuffle groove that the

ELVIS WARD

Thank you Thank you very much

song is built on a few million times into the wee hours, until the phrases started to fall in place.

Dave did write the melody for the bridge, and I finished the rest of the lyric. Alannah wrapped her voice around it with ease, given her affection for bluesy melodies. We got great reactions to the song; interestingly, even though the label in Canada loved it, they went with a different song to lead off the album.

Alannah and I separated as a couple while making the record, but our friendship and faith in one another was intact. When Alannah's self-titled first album came out, it was ignored in the U.S., but took off immediately in Canada, thanks largely to the faith in her that Warner Canada had. She didn't have a manger, so along with my regular shifts on Much and filling in for Laurie Brown on maternity leave from *The NewMusic*, I did the job as best I could. It soon became too much.

Someone asked me, "How did you know you had a legitimate hit record, one that gave you the confidence to quit your job and move to L.A.?" That moment actually occurred before "Black Velvet" became a hit.

I was working late on a story in an editing bay at Much and hit the street as the bars were getting out. There was a guy, obviously drunk, rolling down the sidewalk, singing at the top of his lungs and I realized, as he got closer that it was the chorus to "Love Is," Alannah's first single. It stopped me cold. I watched him walk past me on Queen Street, bellowing, "Love is what you want it to be/ Love is heaven to the lonely," words that I'd written not that long ago and I thought, "That's it. We struck a vein."

I'd been working with Alannah for so many years and we'd gotten used to being turned down by everyone—agents, managers, every label in the country—multiple times. Even friends, normally my last stalwarts, were beginning to question my dedication to this cause that Alannah represented. And in that moment, I realized that we'd done it, we'd gotten into people's heads and their hearts and made that powerful connection that pop music can make.

Kim Cooke, who was head of promo at Warner at the time, recalled a conversation with Alannah in which he complimented her work and said, "You know, I think you could have a platinum record here [representing 100,000 units sold in Canada]." Her retort was, "Platinum? I'm going to sell a million!" The album did become the first by a female artist to go diamond, the mark of a million records sold, and went on to sell 1.2 million in Canada.

I remember Kim Clarke Champniss interviewing me a few months after I left and that day "Black Velvet" had gone #1 on *Billboard*, which was a lifelong dream to me. I recall telling him that the coolest thing about it was that I would get a page in the *Billboard Book of #1 Hits* by Fred Bronson, a book that I loved and had frequently used for research during my on-air days. That did happen, and yes, it was cool. I'd followed the charts since I was a little kid.

My friends and I would go down to Sam the Record Man in Toronto on Saturday mornings to ogle the new singles on the wall for sixty-six cents and to get the latest CHUM chart. When my family would go up north for summer holidays, I used to bug my dad until he'd let me sit in the car in the drive outside our latest rented cottage at night, when you could hear the big U.S. radio stations, listening to WOWO West Virginia and WBZ Boston and WABC New York with Cousin Brucie. I'd make notes on all the new songs I heard and make my own charts until I could get back to the city.

When J.D. Roberts left Much, there was a big on-air goodbye and a pie in the face, but I didn't want that, especially not the shaving cream. I sensed that my life was about to change; I was drained from the demands of the two gigs at Much and managing Alannah, something I never aspired to, but wasn't willing to let someone else do badly. And she trusted me like no one else. I'd gone on holiday over New Year's with my then-girlfriend to St. Barths. The first night there, I walked into a sliding-glass door, sober, holding a glass that shattered in my hand. It was late at night; we didn't have a phone and my girlfriend didn't speak French.

I was in the midst of a Peckinpah moment in the bathroom with my hand spurting blood, and I was holding my arm up in the air, trying not to faint. There was no ambulance service but she knocked on doors until a neighbour got the fire department to pick me up and take me to a small local hospital. Much joking around took place, in French, with the fire department guys but the doctor who'd been awoken to treat me was not amused. He kept saying "merde, merde" as he brusquely stitched me up. When the feeling hadn't returned in my hand a few days later, I figured that there was probably nerve damage. I returned home at the end of the holiday and headed straight to surgery to reattach the nerve. It's never been the same.

There's a "best-of-times worst-of-times" moment here because during my recovery, "Black Velvet" was starting to show signs of life in the U.S. and Alannah's new U.S. manager, Danny Goldberg, told me that Doug Morris, the president at Atlantic, was getting amazing reports from two small markets that they considered bellwethers for cross-border records—Harrisburg, Pennsylvania, and Missoula, Montana. Amazingly enough, he was going to do what only the major labels can do—put all their considerable muscle behind making it a hit record. Push the big button!

I asked John Martin and Nancy Oliver if they'd meet me at X-Rays, a bar down the street from Much and one of John's regular spots. Over lunch, I suggested that they stop paying me and that was the end of my time at Much. No on-air party, no goodbyes, no "last" show. And that was how I wanted it.

Video was an essential element in Alannah's success and she continued to collaborate with director Deborah Samuel. Deborah recalls the shoot for the first single, "Love Is."

DEBORAH SAMUEL We had fun as there was nothing stopping us from doing what we wanted to do. The camera was strapped to Alannah in the introduction segment in order to film her walking in her infamous red shoes. The performance segment was shot in a very small bar in Toronto [The Spadina Hotel] which led to an intimate performance as there was no room to move.

Although the label went with another director for "Black Velvet," the second single, Alannah continued, whenever possible, to work with Deborah, who did the album cover photography. I think their finest hour was the video for "Lover of Mine," the third single from the record, shot in County Clare in Ireland, tapping into both women's family origins. Deborah recalls that day.

DEBORAH SAMUEL There had been a hurricane on our arrival in Ireland where "Lover of Mine" was shot. We were unable to shoot until the tail end of the hurricane. The record company was uneasy to proceed because of insurance issues concerning the inherent

Shooting the video for "Black Velvet" in Buckhorn, Ontario

dangers of the weather. The weather actually added to the feeling of this song as it was extremely windy with so much rain and fog that it created a loneliness to the imagery. In the last scene, Alannah is seen running up a cliff face of rock with a wind that could easily have knocked her into the very angry ocean below. I remember thinking, "The record company will not be pleased."

And if that wasn't enough to deal with, Deborah had an idea for an effect that worked beautifully in the final product.

DEBORAH SAMUEL We double-sped the track which meant that the music playback was doubled in speed. Alannah had to sing to playback that . . . sounded like a chipmunk singing the track. We shot the visuals in slow motion so when coupled with the slowed down track to normal speed it would sync between the slow motion footage and the double-sped track.

Got that? If you watch the video, you'll know what she means.

Atlantic Records insisted on using hot director-of-the-moment Doug Freel who had done work for Roxette and Def Leppard, to direct the video for "Black Velvet." There were two shoots—one in a Kingston club at the end of a gig for the live-band parts and the other in front of a log cabin that was on Alannah's family property near Buckhorn, Ontario. Here's Alannah's recollection of the planning session.

ALANNAH MYLES The director envisioned a dark, dungeon-like, rain-on-the-roof atmosphere. The night before the shoot, I argued with him, sitting around the dining-room table at the cottage, till I convinced him to shoot in the light of midday sun, like the heat of Memphis, Tennessee, not Darth Vader in the British Isles.

The day of the shoot, we pointed out the antique Victrola, which was in the cabin, to the director. He ended up using it as the opening shot, tying in nicely with the lyric, "Jimmie Rogers on the Victrola up high." The image of Alannah in the cabin doorway was the first that most people saw of her in a video seen around the world. Her impression of that day will differ from theirs—oh the glamour of the video shoot.

ALANNAH MYLES I'd lost my voice, sick with strep throat and felt about the furthest thing from "sexy," as some folks have attributed. The fact that I'm sexy is because [it felt like] somebody whacked me with a two-by-four and I'm not doing a lot of movement.

22 The New School

MTV in the U.S. waited a long time to embrace hip hop, and in the meantime had to face charges of racism in its programming. The lore goes that CBS Records president Walter Yetnikoff threatened to pull all of the label's videos until the network aired Michael Jackson's "Billie Jean." MTV offered the defence that they were essentially a rock network and that the black music videos of the day didn't fit with their programming style.

The NewMusic had long given exposure to black artists and featured early rappers like Grandmaster Flash, Eric B. & Rakim, and A Tribe Called Quest. In a matter of a few months, I had LL Cool J, Run-DMC and New Edition on my show on Much. It was the Canadian hip-hop artists who were in danger of being left behind, and it took a long time before acts like the Dream Warriors, Devon and Michie Mee received any exposure. The major labels largely shied away from rap until one artist came along and made a difference. Michele Geister, who produced Soul in the City and RapCity, explains.

MICHELE GEITSER Until Maestro Fresh-Wes busted out, I don't think the powers-that-be even realized this was music for youth of any skin colour, that kids in the Prairies were rocking Public Enemy T-shirts. Wes's career was the tipping point for the labels to take the music seriously and get some streetwise support.

MAESTRO FRESH-WES

I asked Wes where he had looked for inspiration while he was coming up.

MAESTRO FRESH-WES Public Enemy, Big Daddy Kane, Eric B. & Rakim, KRS-One, Kool Moe Dee and Ice-T. [Ice-T] wasn't from New York and he was dope, and he sounded different, so if he could do it, maybe I could do it, too.

In "Conducting Things," Wes's lyric says, "Just because I'm from Canada doesn't make me an amateur."

MAESTRO FRESH-WES There was always the underdog mentality up here because there was no point of reference . . . "Let Your

Backbone Slide" was like Canada's version of "Rapper's Delight" [the Sugarhill Gang song that was the first rap record to chart in 1979] ten years later. From an industry perspective, we were ten years behind.

Wes often refers to Canada and specifically Toronto in his songs and has incorporated samples from the Guess Who (using the vocal hook and the signature electric piano riff from "These Eyes" in "Stick to Your Vision") and Gowan's "Criminal Mind." Wes explained where that instinct for hometown loyalty came from.

MAESTRO FRESH-WES The artists that I listened to always referenced where they were from. The golden era hip-hop artists laid out a template for how things should be conducted—[and for] the importance of documenting history and documenting where you're from . . . I was the local cat that came with the beats, that came with the rhymes, with the energy, straight outta Scarborough with style.

It was during a visit to *Electric Circus* that Wes made a career-changing contact.

MAESTRO FRESH-WES I performed [at *EC*] and a label from NYC just happened to be visiting Toronto . . . while I was performing "Let Your Backbone Slide" for the very first time.

E.C. producer Joel Goldberg tells the story.

JOEL GOLDBERG I met Wes Williams [Maestro] and Farley Flex, his manager, on the set of *Electric Circus*. I had booked Wes on the merits of a cassette tape he sent me with some of his early raps. He was great, so I booked him for a second show. The R&B artist Stevie B. was also booked on that *EC* episode and he was so impressed with Wes, that he called his New York–based record company, LMR records, and recommended they sign him, which they did! In appreciation of me booking Wes and giving him the opportunity, Farley pitched me to LMR to produce and direct the "Let Your Backbone Slide" video, and the rest is history . . . "Let Your Backbone Slide" had a huge impact on Canadian pop culture. Based on that video, a hip-hop scene emerged for the first time in Canada and acts like Michie Mee and the Dream Warriors, among others, came to the forefront.

The relationship with Joel led to the two of them working together on a series of videos, including "Let Your Backbone Slide" and "Drop the Needle," which won the Juno for Best Video in 1991. Wes also won the first-ever Juno for rap. He puts these victories into perspective.

Erica Ehm and Maestro Fresh-Wes

MAESTRO FRESH-WES When I got those two awards I felt really good about myself, but then Leonard Cohen was getting a lifetime achievement award. His award was about the size of a grand piano. So I looked at my two Juno awards which were each about the size of a water bottle then I looked at Leonard Cohen's lifetime achievement award. That really inspired me to continue making more music.

I raised Michele Geister's point that Maestro's career was a tipping point for hip hop in Canada.

MAESTRO FRESH-WES I'd like to think so because I got a record deal and that was a great opportunity for me and a great opportunity for not only hip-hop artists, but black music in Canada—reggae, R&B—that was an opportunity for us to do something that we never did before.

Wes has continued to inspire the rappers that followed him like k-os, Kardinal Offishall and Drake.

MAESTRO FRESH-WES I'm sure I inspired them in some capacity, but they all inspired me and continue to inspire me. I never had older guys to look up to [when I was] coming up. I learned from a young age, career-wise, that it's okay to ask questions and learn from cats younger than you.

MuchMusic and the MuchMusic building and all you guys were very instrumental in my life. Every time I drive down Queen Street West I think of Toronto back then and what we had, not what we didn't have, but what we had—the climate and the energy. Stepping into that MuchMusic building, you guys were so accommodating to me. Having my videos played gave me exposure across the country that I could never have imagined. I didn't know there were fans in Vancouver. I'm in Calgary and I'm getting love! Calgary? You got to be kidding me!

THE CRASH TEST DUMMIES

BRAD ROBERTS, singer I would say the old theory that either you play hockey or you make a basement band when you live on the Prairies is quite true . . . everything was more isolated then because there was no internet.

The prohibitive distances between towns and cities for young bands to travel to play can often have the effect of turning a band's hometown scene into an important incubator for talent. Spurred by radio station homegrown competitions and support from local college radio together with an active club scene, a band had a chance to build a loyal following at home while they developed their stage skills and songwriting. Getting out was often the best option. Brad Roberts of the Crash Test Dummies remembers his beginnings in his native Winnipeg, a city always known for its vibrant local music scene.

BRAD ROBERTS In the late '80s I worked first at the Blue Note Café and later at the Spectrum Cabaret. I had a feeling of camaraderie with the band Bob's Your Uncle from Vancouver and Sook-Yin Lee, who was with Much for so long, fronted that band. I was the bartender at the Spectrum and I used to play with them for some blues number at the end of their set.

So I make a demo tape back in '88 or '89 and I send it off to a bunch of festivals hoping to get booked. Nobody was interested in booking me but one agent calls me back, Richard Flohil.

All the A&R people, including Richard Flohil, got on a plane to come to Winnipeg for this conference, and it was a showcase for Winnipeg talent . . . Richard chatted these guys up on the plane and said, "You gotta check out Crash Test Dummies above and beyond all these bands." We didn't play in bars; the only place we played was the Blue Note because the drummer was the owner . . . They put us in a separate room and if it wasn't for Richard, no one would have known we played the showcase. There was a bidding war [for us], won by BMG and David Bendeth, who was the only A&R guy who wasn't there.

An unconventional start for a young recording act, but then the Dummies were iconoclasts from the get-go. Brad had reservations about making music videos, but it wasn't an optional thing, a video was essential.

BRAD ROBERTS I was very suspicious of the whole idea of videos. I hadn't grown up with them and I didn't like them. I thought they were an unnecessary appendage to the song. They seemed to be important as a marketing tool. Of course I was so naive . . . because indeed it was MuchMusic that drove our sales like fuckin' crazy. They had a huge influence on the market.

Ok, so with this reluctance, how did the first one go?

BRAD ROBERTS "Superman Song" was the first video. Dale Heslip did the video . . . The video was tasteful and interesting . . . I had expected to come out looking like a jackass.

So far so good, except for one small thing.

Erica Ehm with Ellen Reid, Brad Roberts and Dan Roberts of the Crash Test Dummies

BRAD ROBERTS The guy who had just become president of BMG saw the "Superman" video and he thought it was a little too melancholy, so at the very end he had me fly to Toronto—we all lived in Winnipeg—and do one final extra scene that became the ending and it was me in a phone booth; and I wink at the camera. It gives the ending a levity. Dale was not happy; he thought it was a sell-out.

Something worked because "Superman Song" became an unlikely hit.

BRAD ROBERTS [The song] wasn't doing much but suddenly people kept calling in [to radio stations] about my voice—"Who's the guy with the low voice?"—which was something I hadn't even thought about. I thought my voice was a handicap because it was too low; I just couldn't find anybody to sing the song in a way that I felt represented what I wanted to hear.

Fortunately, keyboard player and vocalist Ellen Reid was very interested in how the band's videos turned out.

BRAD ROBERTS [Almost] every single video we have ever done has been the brainchild of Ellen Reid. She never got credit on any of them and she was never paid a cent.

Brad talked about what Ellen brought to the band's videos.

BRAD ROBERTS Ellen did theatre in high school as did I. The theatricality is built right into the narrative for the "Mmm Mmm Mmm Mmm" video which has a stage in it . . . there is a theatre motif . . . the puppet in "God Shuffled His Feet."

Unlike the artists that preceded them by a few years, reluctance where video was concerned was a common thread among the acts emerging in the late '80s and early '90s. A desire for authenticity trumped glamour and that's arguably more difficult to portray on a screen in a way that focuses attention on the artist and the song. In Canada a small handful of directors and artists solved this in innovative ways. Trust was at the core of these successful collaborations.

JANN ARDEN

JANN ARDEN I did ten videos with Jeth Weinrich . . . The first video that I shot was for "Will You Remember Me" off my first record. It took a month to do it. We shot it all in 35mm film and we didn't know what we were doing so we shot and shot and shot . . . We never had any stylists. I was lucky if I had a makeup artist. It was a really stripped-down crew . . . All the money went into film. Every dollar. If we had $30,000, it went into film. He never put a buck in his pocket.
    Location was everything for him . . . Even when I look at the videos now they're really timeless; they stand up really well . . . He had such a good eye. We didn't do anything where we look back and go "my hair was so '90s" . . . I just had on a pair of jeans and a coat. . . . They were very organic; they were very much about people's faces, their hands, their feet, walking.

Like Margo from the Cowboy Junkies and Brad from the Crash Test Dummies, Jann is candid about how she felt.

JANN ARDEN I was never comfortable doing videos. I knew that they were something that I needed to do in order to be in the business of music but if I'd had a choice I would never have done it. I would never have gone, "Yay! We're doing a video today." I was mortified.

From the early days of music video in Canada, artists who embraced the medium like Corey Hart and Platinum Blonde had to learn quickly how to adapt to the instant success that they'd been seeking and the sudden unforeseen changes it brought to their lives. Ten years on, an artist had to know the possible outcome of that camera that captured them performing their next single. Even knowing this, Jann had to adjust quickly to the influence of music video on her career and her life.

JANN ARDEN I went from complete obscurity to being constantly stopped on the street two weeks after the [1993] "I Would Die for You" video came out. My life was one way, and two weeks later it was another way, and it hasn't changed since.

I wondered which artists had inspired Jann before her breakout success.

JANN ARDEN I loved Jane Siberry—everything she did, I was so enchanted by it . . . "Mimi on the Beach," the whole *Speckless Sky* album. I must have seen her live fifteen times . . . I wrote her a note not so long ago; I said I'll sing anytime you want me to; I'll do anything for you. . . . I lived in this little tiny basement apartment and I had a cassette of hers; I literally broke it and I got Scotch tape and fixed it. Thank god I was only missing a few seconds of a song; I just wore [the tape] out.

Despite her misgivings about the medium, Jann voiced respect for an artist who used it to create a memorable and breathtaking performance.

JANN ARDEN Sinéad O'Connor—that iconic "Nothing Compares 2 U." I think for me she was the first superstar launched from a video format. You saw her face, the black background, her shaved head, the tear coming down at a very strategic time in the song, those eyes that were as big as the ocean; and it didn't matter who you were, you couldn't help but be ripped apart by the steady one-shot look of it. There were no bells and whistles. Her life changed forever; it was never ever the same and it was because of that video.

Jeth Weinrich won the Juno for Video of the Year in 1994 for Jann's "I Would Die for You" and again two years later for his exquisite treatment of "Good Mother."

JANN ARDEN He chose a really simple story, he chose to represent someone yearning for home which is so universal, somebody getting lost . . . letting me narrate the story . . . the woman that played the mother and the kids with the cardboard masks . . . the way that he shot them—it's haunting, really, because you get a sense of what family is and how fragmented it is and how fragile it is.

Despite the lack of pyrotechnics and video chicanery for her music, Jann did have one good disaster story to tell from the shoot for her biggest hit, the song that broke her career internationally in 1994, "Insensitive." Here's the behind-the-scenes look at a seemingly innocent moment in the video.

JANN ARDEN Near the end of the video there are these big white banners that drop from the top of the apartment building in Calgary. My mom sewed all those banners; she was up to her ass in fabric. She sewed hundreds of feet of this white sheet cotton that we bought at Fanny's Fabrics in Calgary. We were trying to figure out how to have them unroll as they went down in super slow motion. We were so unsuccessful; they kept folding in on themselves and twisting and we couldn't see what was written on them and so Jeth thought we should put something heavier and my dad, who was a concrete guy, suggested rebar [reinforcing steel bar]. Well you can imagine the disaster that was about to happen. We stitched the rebar in and strung it through there and the first time they hurled that first banner off, Jeth was down below filming. Well it fucking came swinging down at about 180 miles an hour and when it came to the end of its tether, smashed through some poor person's apartment windows at the very bottom of its length. So we thought, "That's not gonna work." I think we finally ended up using two-inch pieces of broom handle that we cut up from a broom and put in to give it some weight. But it was hundreds of tosses; he was so frustrated trying to get them to open so he could see the things that he'd written. The rebar was not a great idea.

Jann Arden and Natalie Richard

Jann spoke with her customary candour about her discomfort when she visited MuchMusic.

JANN ARDEN I wasn't cool. I was from the Prairies; I wasn't particularly beautiful or anything like that. We didn't integrate that well in Toronto . . . I wasn't from there; I didn't move there; I still live five miles from where I grew up. I wasn't part of that scene and when I came in to do it, it was almost like I was coming from another country, and I was doing adult contemporary music and

I was funny. I didn't take myself seriously like (she says in a low, dramatic tone), "I did this because it was very cathartic." That was never me; it was like, "Yeah, I made this song up about this." I didn't have an entourage; I didn't have anybody. We just showed up and played songs and left.

She hastened to give Much credit for its programming approach.

JANN ARDEN When you guys added a song, it was because you sat there and said, "This looks great. I don't know what it's doing in the rest of the world. . . . I don't know what the numbers are or who else is playing it." But that's what radio does. We had limited radio support; it kind of came on after Much. . . . The video would be flying up the charts and the programmers at radio stations would be going, "Fuck, I guess we need to add this," because people were phoning the station. [Video] just changed the game so much.

Jann expressed gratitude for the incredible career she's had.

JANN ARDEN I'm still touring all the time and I'm always blown away that people show up, that they come to hear those songs . . . I'm so happy that I was a product of the '90s; I worked in the bars all through the '80s, earning my stripes. . . . I just remember thinking, "I'm the luckiest person on the planet to do this."

SLOAN

Halifax has always had a strong local music scene and, like Winnipeg, it was at least in part due to geography. Jay Ferguson of Sloan recalls what it was like for his band in the early days.

JAY FERGUSON We came from more of an underground music scene. Chris [Murphy] and I played in a band called Kearney Lake Road from 1987 to '90. We would play benefits for college radio, or in a church or in someone's living room. It was like thriving in obscurity; it was like REM's early scene in Athens, Georgia, or Minneapolis or Seattle. There weren't a lot of places to play so you had to invent them.

I asked Jay if he thought this was creatively healthy for a developing act.

JAY FERGUSON I think it is. I feel bad for bands you'd read about in the [British music magazine] *New Musical Express* who are starting in London and having their second or third show reviewed in the *NME*. [The media is] blowing them up and they're probably not ready for prime time. By the time their debut album comes out they're already getting thrashed by the music press.

Jay touted an approach that has worked for bands from Canada for a long time: "It's the Malcolm Gladwell 'put in your ten thousand hours' and you're ready."

When Sloan got their major label deal, they faced the same challenges that other acts did in figuring out how to do videos without giving in to a label's misguided notions of image making.

JAY FERGUSON When we were on Geffen we were being given treatments; there was no way we were going to do that stuff like—"there's an old man, a businessman spread out on a table with business files blowing around him, hearkening back to his childhood."

With few exceptions the band built their video look on live performances with added stylistic touches like the ones in the video for "Money City Maniacs."

JAY FERGUSON It was a basic performance video, but a lot of the graphic stuff was inspired by a graphic designer named Saul Bass, and he did a lot of the really great film intros to Alfred Hitchcock movies [he provided the title sequences for *Psycho*, *Vertigo*, *West Side Story*, *Goodfellas* and many others]. They were really simple images with moving graphics and lines.

The band members were well-versed in pop culture and wanted to make references to specific sources while still maintaining a live performance feel.

JAY FERGUSON The video for "The Lines You Amend" was shot in black and white and it's very much an homage to a Rolling Stones '60s-type appearance. We shot it at York University in a lecture hall where we performed the song with the audience behind us and then we turned all the gear around and faced them so when it's edited it makes it look like it's on a 360 [degree stage].

The one exception to this approach was the video for "The Good in Everyone," which features a long tribute to the Peter Fonda film *Easy Rider* at the beginning.

JAY FERGUSON I'm embarrassed—I don't think I've even seen *Easy Rider* all the way through, but the night before we were filming the intro to that video I basically watched those thirty seconds of *Easy Rider* over and over to get all my "acting" down

pat . . . We went out to Pearson [International Airport in Toronto] to find a good little spot where we could film it that looks like the scene in *Easy Rider*. We thought, "Wouldn't it be funny to film the whole minute of acting leading up to that?" It's kind of absurd because we did the *Easy Rider* scene and then we all stop what we're doing and go and play the song for no real reason.

Ah, the things you can get away with in a successful rock band. Usually, but not always.

I use MuchMusic mostly to see how old I've gotten.

Chris Murphy, Sloan

JAY FERGUSON There was a video for "Coax Me" that we took into MuchMusic and Simon Evans basically tore it apart . . . He showed the video and said, "What were you guys thinking?"

Fortunately, Jay has better memories of an earlier performance.

JAY FERGUSON The first time we played on MuchMusic was May of 1992 and we didn't even have a record out. We had toured out to the Music West conference in Vancouver. We'd made a record on our own in Halifax; we sent some tapes around and it got the ear of Geffen in L.A. A guy from Geffen said, "I'm going to Music West. If you guys make it there, I'll come and see you play." We were determined to get from Halifax to Vancouver and I think we played four shows on the way, Moncton and Winnipeg, maybe Calgary and then Vancouver. Word got out, "Who's this band from Halifax that Geffen is interested in?" On the way back, we'd been invited to play at Much [Toronto]. We set up in the Much space and my mom taped it at home so I still have a VHS of the performance. We played our song "Underwhelmed" and we got a little interview and that was pretty thrilling.

BARENAKED LADIES

Barenaked Ladies arrived in the early '90s, when the power of music video was undeniable. They grew up watching MuchMusic, as band member Ed Robertson recalls.

ED ROBERTSON I remember huddling in my friend's basement to watch Much go live on the air. I remember how excited I was for that moment . . . At the dawn of the video age . . . I was super into Rush and other rock bands. All of a sudden I was being inundated with videos from all kinds of genres of music and it exposed you to things that you probably wouldn't go and seek out on your own. A great video and a catchy song would suddenly turn you into a Talk Talk fan, a Eurythmics fan and a Police fan.

Of all the bands that made the most of the opportunity Much provided to connect with their fans, I think of Crowded House, in the very early years of the station, and later, Barenaked Ladies.

ED ROBERTSON They were a huge inspiration for us early on. I saw them at Roy Thomson Hall and I felt like I was in [Crowded House leader] Neil Finn's living room. We always used to say, "We're not a garage band; we're a living-room band."

The Ladies' introduction to the living rooms of the nation came courtesy of Speaker's Corner, a photo booth at the corner of Queen and John streets, with a camera and a slot for depositing a loonie for two minutes of time to record whatever you wanted. The band made brilliant use of those two minutes.

ED ROBERTSON We were the guys that crammed into Speaker's Corner, popped in a dollar and essentially made a music video. We went in there and promoted upcoming shows. We saw it as this excellent tool; I just thought it was the greatest idea ever . . . at the time you couldn't record a video on your phone and upload it to YouTube and send out an email blast about it. It was the rudimentary version of that technology and I remember when we first did that, [Much director] Dennis Saunders contacted us . . . and he said, "I love it. You guys are the first to use Speaker's Corner as a blatant promotional device." It kind of hadn't occurred to anyone yet. It was all people bitching about parallel parking on the street and cyclists, community voices and people going in to make out. We were put into high rotation on Much; so for one dollar we were competing with million-dollar videos.

Barenaked Ladies' *Intimate and Interactive* concert

And behind the wackiness lay a clever strategy.

ED ROBERTSON "Be My Yoko Ono" was the first thing we did at Speaker's Corner and then we went in to promote the biggest show we'd done to date in Toronto at the Bathurst Street Theatre . . . We sang this minute-and-a-half-long song that described what time the show was and where it was and how to get there. There was a line in it that said, "And you won't have to lineup because lineups make Dad mad!" The show ended up selling out.

Despite this adventurous approach and the band's engaging personalities, Ed says they struggled with videos at the outset.

ED ROBERTSON We never had that cool French stop motion artist who was a massive fan of our work approaching us and saying, "Oh, can I make this video for you; I did it as my art school project." It was us trying to pursue hot directors, then pay exorbitant amounts of money to make videos, when, in the end, it was hard for us to be cool. We were goofy-looking guys; we were averse to being styled in any way, to our own detriment. We could have helped ourselves a little bit by laying off the denim shorts and Früvests [the colourful vests Moxy Früvous sold as merchandise at the time].

Once BNL broke in the U.S., the stakes and the budgets grew and the celebrity endorsements followed. Sort of.

ED ROBERTSON [Brian Wilson] came to the studio to play us his recording of that song ["Brian Wilson"] and it was the most bizarre thing. Afterwards there was this silence in the room and Brian looked up and said, "Is it cool?" I'm thinking, "Is it cool? It's one of the fucking coolest things I've ever heard." Then he left the studio and said, "Okay guys, don't eat too much." Words of wisdom from one of the great musicians of all time.

Ed talked about the video for their U.S. breakthrough, "One Week."

ED ROBERTSON McG was a hot new L.A. director and he really got the band and was excited to be working with us. I remember going to a pitch meeting for the video and he was fucking electric . . . bounding around the room, framing shots with his hands . . . at one point he actually jumped up on the conference table to illustrate a pan that was going across the band. We showed up that day and they had replicas of the *Starsky & Hutch* car and there was a motorcycle jump planned. The girls from our video ended up becoming the Pussycat Dolls. It was very L.A., big budget.

Every band has their disaster story and Barenaked Ladies are no exception. Ed has this recollection about the video for "Shoebox."

ED ROBERTSON It was a really big budget video and it was on the *Friends* soundtrack. We hired this hot new director who had success with *The Basketball Diaries* [Scott Kalvert]. The video was to be a funny relationship story featuring Lisa Kudrow and Matt LeBlanc. On the day of the shoot, neither of them showed up. So here we are paying a half a million dollars for a video without the star power—it didn't make any sense whatsoever.

There's a part of the lore that had to be revisited when Ed and I spoke—the story that the band recorded one song per album, naked.

ED ROBERTSON We did that up until maybe *Maroon* because it's really funny and it provided this ridiculous jolt of energy. We did it on a song where things weren't working and we needed a bit of extra, unseen energy to take the track into a different place. But after doing it for twelve years, we were just so used to each other's naked bodies that it literally did not change the energy of the song whatsoever. It was like, "Oh, we've got to do another take. Yeah, that's Tyler's dong; I'm very familiar with it. What's the big deal?"

Steve Anthony with Barenaked Ladies

The Ladies' playful approach to their work was a perfect match for the prevailing attitude at Much. And the connection held from their Speaker's Corner moments through an early *Intimate and Interactive* concert.

ED ROBERTSON It was a formative time for the band and there was a national network that was willing to play along with us and do stuff that was fun. It just seemed that we were on the same wavelength, from the VJs to the floor directors to camera people. And it wasn't about, "Will you promote this thing we're doing?" It was, "That's a place we can go and do cool things."

MY
ROCK
TASTES
RUN
FROM
THE SIMPL
TO THE
IDIOTIC

23 Favourite Interviews

The most extraordinary seventy-two hours I spent while employed by MuchMusic were spent 5,700 kilometres to the east, followed by 3,500 kilometres to the west of the Toronto studio.

In the spring of 1989, Paul McCartney announced his first North American tour in almost fifteen years, named Flowers in the Dirt after his latest release. John Martin chose me to go to London, where McCartney and his band were rehearsing, to do the interview. Cameraman Dave Hurlbut and I were booked on very short notice to fly to London and do the shoot the following day at a rehearsal facility outside of the city.

This was a seriously phenomenal assignment, a once-in-a-lifetime opportunity and I was pumped. Until I noticed that my passport had expired and that there wasn't enough time to get it renewed. I went to John's office to confess and was met with classic Martin indifference.

"Oh, don't worry, Christopher, it'll be fine."

Dave and I got to the airport and I sized up the airline agents, knowing they'd be looking at my passport. I chose the youngest one, the one most likely to be a Much viewer. She was—so I chatted her up big time, telling her all about the trip we were going on and who we were going to interview and . . . she waved us through. I'd forgotten that there might be some customs agents at Heathrow who might be less charmable and who would also be checking my ID. Three did, and all of them waved us through. Whew!

The following morning we travelled to an airplane-hangar-sized rehearsal facility known as the BBC Elstree Studios. We hadn't been there long when Paul walked in on his own and came over to greet us. I was wearing a sports jacket that for some reason had asymmetrical lapels so the first thing Paul did was grab the lapels and roughly begin to straighten them in full clown mode. This was a man who knew how to put people at ease. We were with Nicholas Jennings, a journalist who wrote for *Macleans* magazine, who showed Paul some of his work, including a story about the isolation of John and Yoko, post-Beatles. McCartney became very serious and said that he had been very concerned during this time period about their alleged heroin use and told us how he had tried unsuccessfully to get through to John at the time. This was my first of a few "Am I really having this experience?" moments during this assignment.

The interview with McCartney was brilliant; I got all I could ask for and more. He talked about the tour and how he chose the songs; how he was performing Beatles songs that had never been played on a stage before. He spoke about his recent collaboration with Elvis Costello. I was gathering bits for a songwriting special so asked specifically about the origins of some of my favourite Beatles songs. He talked about his approach and the source of songs like "Hey Jude," "Let it Be," "Eleanor Rigby" and "Eight Days a Week." Cue the "Am I really having this experience?" moment number two.

PAUL MCCARTNEY Usually it'll be somebody says something, like Ringo, "Ah, that was a hard day's night." Or a chauffeur once, I was driving out to John's for a writing session. He used to live a couple of hours outside London in a place called Weybridge, [in posh accent] a very golfy area. I had this man driving me out and he was talking away and I asked him, "How's tricks?" and he replied (in Cockney accent) "Oh, you know Paul, I'm working eight days a week." (Paul mimes making notes). I got to John's place. "Hey, I've got a great idea." Like that—it just arrives on your doorstep, and you think, "I've never heard of a song called that."

They rolled a couch out into the centre of the floor in the cavernous rehearsal space and Dave, Nick and I sat down as the only audience members for what turned out to be a full production rehearsal for the tour. The band consisted of Paul; his wife Linda on background vocals, keyboards and percussion; Hamish Stuart, formerly of the Average White Band, on bass and vocals; Robbie McIntosh, a long-time McCartney band member, on guitars; 'Wix' Wickens on keyboards; and Chris Whitten on drums. They played songs like "You Never Give Me Your Money," "I've Just Seen a Face," and "Fool on the Hill" which had never been performed on stage, the latter featuring a rotating pedestal that kicked into action on the "round and round and round" refrain of the song. Full lights, full sound, every song in tour sequence; Paul did the jokes and we drank in every note. Cue moment three.

Nick, Dave and I went out that night for Indian food and beers in London, high on the day's experience. When I got back to my hotel room around 2:00 a.m. there was a message from Much producer Michael Heydon, asking that I call him when I got in. Assuming it was to get a recap of the day, I phoned Michael, who informed me that I was not going to be coming home quite yet. I'd be stopping in Toronto long enough to change planes and pick up a fresh cameraman, Basil Young, then heading to Los Angeles to interview Neil Young. Okay. Great. Anything else? Yes, it was for his upcoming release *Freedom*, one that I hadn't heard. "Oh, don't worry," said Michael (a now familiar refrain), "we'll have a copy waiting for you at your hotel and you'll do the interview the next morning." I didn't even think about my passport.

When Basil and I got to Neil's manager, Elliot Roberts' office in Santa Monica the next morning, we were given a room to set up in and just as Basil was taking his lights out of the case, Neil walked in and sat down.

Now, this is not a good thing when an artist is early for an interview, because you have to talk to them, but you don't dare talk about anything you might want to touch on in the interview, because then they'll say something like, "Well, like I said before," or even if they do reiterate it, it won't be fresh.

I remembered that Neil had gone to the same school in Winnipeg, Kelvin High School, that I had gone to some years later. I mentioned this, and started asking about various teachers that we might have had in common. We hit upon one shared monstrous math teacher who terrified all in his classrooms and laughed about that while Basil got his gear up and tape rolling.

Neil was funny, serious, heartfelt, thoughtful and open, by turns, in one of my favourite interviews that I did during my time at Much. I asked about the opening song on the album, one that came to be one of his best-loved songs.

NEIL YOUNG I know I wrote it while I was travelling down the road in my bus. I've been touring all year off and on; it's all kind of a blur now. I got really confused trying to remember when I was on the road and when I was at home so it must be time to stop for a while . . . I thought of the first line, "Keep on rockin' in the free world" . . . I thought that really says something but it's such a cliché . . . such an obvious thing, then I knew I had to use it. (Grins) . . . The words to the verses—who knows where they came from? I can't even remember writing them . . . Freedom to me is a more personal thing . . . it's based on the stories of people on the street, homeless people, rich people with problems. Freedom is an abstract . . . how can you describe freedom? I tried and I failed.

It may be a classic interviewer's dilemma, and admittedly a good problem to have, when you have to set aside your personal admiration for an artist's work while you do your job. All those times I had spent listening to Buffalo Springfield, Crosby, Stills, Nash & Young and Neil, solo, informed the interview as subtext, but I didn't dwell on that while we conversed. It worked.

My time at Much gave me the opportunity to encounter some extraordinary people at fascinating points in their careers. I spoke with Whitney Houston on her first press tour in 1985, when she did a brief show singing to pre-recorded tracks in a local Toronto club. She was sweet, shy and yet very composed. By the fall of that

Leonard Cohen and Christopher Ward

Whitney Houston and Christopher Ward

(Above) Christopher Ward and Tina Turner
(Left) Alice Cooper and Michael Williams

year "Saving All My Love for You" was a
Billboard #1 song and she was headlining
Carnegie Hall in New York.

Leonard Cohen came to Much and
I was as intimidated as I was at any time
that I did my job. I'd grown up reading
Cohen's poetry and novels as a teenager and this was a literary hero of
mine. He was gracious and generous and I survived.

Another major inspiration from my teenage years, Pete Townsend,
recorded a musical version of the Ted Hughes children's novel, *The Iron
Giant*. He was in town for the Who's twenty-fifth anniversary tour and the
good news was that I had an hour for my interview. The bad news—I was
only permitted to ask about *The Iron Giant*! As soon as the words "The
Who" were mentioned by Pete, I took it as my cue to start talking about
the band, which Townsend was happy to do.

Of all the artists that came to Much for a live interview during my time,
the person that for me most carried the aura of a star was Tina Turner. Not
a star in the self-important, look-at-me way that some affected, but
someone who was genuinely radiant and all-embracing in the way that she
treated everyone that she came into contact with. After the interview, in a
rare moment, the crew asked to have a photo taken with her, a request she
graciously accommodated. That photo, framed, was on the wall in the
studio for years.

I asked my fellow VJs about their favourite interviews, many of which have already been excerpted in earlier chapters, but here are a few "best of" moments from the point of view of the interviewers.

J.D. Roberts surprised me with one of his choices.

J.D. ROBERTS Besides Robert Plant, my favourite interview was with Alice Cooper. Though I had listened to some of his music growing up—"School's Out" and "Billion Dollar Babies," you couldn't really count me as a fan. But he was just such a compelling character and extremely articulate.

J.D. ROBERTS You've had a longstanding relationship with reptilian creatures.

ALICE COOPER You'd be surprised, you bring a boa constrictor on stage, the reactions you get. This person will think it's funny; this person will be horrified; that person will think it's sexy. If you bring twenty images like that during a rock concert on stage, what you're really doing is attacking everybody's imagination and you make them [confront] their own phobias; you make them invent their own stories. At the end of the show, you ask ten people what they saw, they'll tell you ten different things.

Denise Donlon spoke about the difficulty in getting Don Henley to open up during their interview. And then, maybe he opened up a little too much.

DON HENLEY I have the good fortune to be able to travel all over the world. I see a lot of people and I see how things are. I get a pretty good overview of the way things are politically, spiritually, artistically and ecologically and that gives me pause sometimes and I write about it.

Michael Williams had an interview with Run-DMC early in their career.

RUN, RUN-DMC I find kids do a lot of the things I say; they're like followers of the lyrics I say. "The things I do make me a star and you can be, too, if you know who you are." So it's just like a pep talk to the kids, a lot of rap.

The myth was that Erica Ehm was over her head during her early years at Much, but watching her go toe-to-toe with one of the toughest in the business puts the lie to that notion. You have to ask the right questions to get answers like these.

YOU WOULD
NOT BELIEVE
THE CHAOS.
THERE'S
FIFTY PEOPLE
DRINKING TEA
AND MAKING
LOVE ON THE
CARPET.

(Top) Laurie Brown, Chrissie Hynde with Erica Ehm
(Bottom) Noel Gallagher of Oasis, live on Queen Street

CHRISSIE HYNDE I can't rely on my juvenile habits and my immaturity much longer. You can't act like you're fifteen when you've gone grey.

It's hard for me to send my kids out to school where most of the people in the world are still eating meat, which I should think will be a practice that will be considered very much akin to slavery and cockfighting in the next ten years . . . if we have ten years.

It required all of Simon Evans's toughness to get anything from Liam Gallagher of Oasis, who had just had a brawl with his brother prior to the interview.

LIAM GALLAGHER The music that comes out of this place, America, is dreadful. That's just the way it is. I'm not being "Oh, hurrah, dear old Blighty." That is just a fact that the best bands with the right songs come from England and I'd like it for other bands to come from America, Japan and all [those places] with a good song because that would change the whole thing in music. But they don't; they just come out with grunge noise and that's it.

During the course of the infamous Ramones interview in which Joey threatened to slit Steve Anthony's throat, there was a shining example of rock 'n' roll hubris.

JOEY RAMONE We changed the course of rock history in '76. I think we brought a whole new attitude and a whole new sound, new spirit, new excitement and fun to music that was no longer there and in a sense, revolutionized rock 'n' roll and affected everybody to this day.

J.D. interviewed Sting on the road in England.

STING I don't try and write on the road. It's madness. You end up with garbage about how miserable travelling is.

I love when famous people say completely obvious things with a posh accent.

STING The challenge and the struggle with any writer is to find something new to write about.

Joe Elliott and Rick Allen of Def Leppard were incredibly open during an interview with Michael Williams that touched on the accident that led to drummer Allen's arm being amputated.

JOE ELLIOT We had drum tracks down on tape, things to do, so we made a decision the day after we heard the news [of Rick's accident] that we were going straight back in the studio and get on with it. There was no point in us hanging around in the waiting room of some hospital . . . we got on with it and waited for the phone to ring.

RICK ALLEN When I first went to the hospital they said, "You'll be in here at least six months. Forget about the band." I was out in three-and-a-half weeks; two weeks after that I was back in Holland working with the band again. I never let myself get down or depressed.

MICHAEL WILLIAMS You weren't worried that you'd never come back?

RICK ALLEN It wasn't like that. The band wouldn't really let me leave.

I loved the challenge of doing interviews, where you have to bring the right combination of preparation and curiosity and the ability to stay in the moment so that you take what the interview subject is giving you and roll with it. What you get can be predictable, outrageous, surprising, and revealing by turns.

Geddy Lee of Rush is a very bright and thoughtful artist, one who really considers what he says in an interview. I could almost see him working through a conflicted point of view about music video.

GEDDY LEE Videos are a very difficult subject for us. It's obviously not a very pleasurable experience to do videos. Surprisingly, we've kept an open mind and we've worked with a lot of different

directors . . . we keep hoping for that masterpiece. The making of the video for "Time Stand Still" was such a long, involved process—those things are hard to justify, looking at it from a musician's point of view. Neil [Peart], especially. He just wants to play; he doesn't want to be an actor; he doesn't want to be a model. He wants the guy to film us playing; that's a severe limitation to put on a video director. They're going, "I have all these ideas for you guys to be running here and doing this."

Geddy and I share a love of baseball that opened up an interesting avenue of conversation.

GEDDY LEE I've met a lot of athletes in the last few years, [because of] my attraction to baseball, their attraction to music. Very similar lives we lead, the kind of concentration, the kind of "live and die" in front of the public, the kind of itinerant lifestyle . . . the being yanked out of your home life and thrown into a professional life that's separate but not separate. An athlete can't hide his mistakes as well as a musician can—I think it's a more humbling profession.

Sometimes, your own work can be humbling to have to reconsider.

GEDDY LEE [The] "Subdivisions" [video] is not so bad, but the other night I was sitting in front of the tube watching Much and [the] "Vital Signs" [video] came on and it was like, "Oh my god," it was like looking at a picture of yourself from high school. It's very difficult to take some of those earlier videos.

When Janet Jackson visited Much in 1986, she had recently gone through personal and professional changes, having broken off business relations with her family and recording her new album with Jimmy Jam and Terry Lewis from the Prince camp. *Control* was a statement album featuring themes of self-empowerment and it broke her career wide open. I asked Janet about the reaction from her family when she got back from Minneapolis and played them *Control* for the first time.

JANET JACKSON They were so excited. They were really proud of me; they knew it was going to be a hit. My mother really enjoyed the album except for the moaning. She said she doesn't like to hear her baby do things like that.

I asked if she ever disguised herself so she could go out due to her increased fame, post-*Control*.

JANET JACKSON I went to Venice Beach and I had on a hat and a moustache. Michael coloured my eyebrows and made them this

Stephen King and Christopher Ward

thick (gestures indicating two inches) and [I wore] sideburns. I was walking my dog and people were looking at me and this girl came up to me, she says, "You really don't look like a man." It was a lot of fun.

Stephen King visited to promote the film *Maximum Overdrive*, his first and last experience as a director. I was curious about his writing methods.

STEPHEN KING [Listening to] rock 'n' roll is the way I work. I poison the air around me and then nobody dares to come close. It's caused a certain amount of ear damage over the years. My rock tastes run from the simple to the idiotic.

Annie Lennox talked about lyric writing.

ANNIE LENNOX "Missionary Man" was probably one of the few songs where the lyrics were written beforehand as a complete whole and I had actually written them with Bob Dylan in mind. I had shown him the lyrics and asked him whether he liked them or not, of course rather hesitantly. He liked them and encouraged me, and then Dave [Stewart] said he didn't like them so I left it. And then a few months later, he said, "You know the words for the song 'Missionary Man' are really good," and I said, "What? You told me you didn't like them." He said, "No, I didn't say that; I think they're really great and we have to use them for us, not for Bob."

And then there is the wonderfully unpredictable Nina Hagen for whom you just have to switch her mic on and let her talk.

NINA HAGEN I'm getting married to my seventeen-year-old boyfriend whose name is Iroquois. He grew up on a Spanish island in the wilderness. He can climb trees. He can play bass and he has a big huge Mohican [haircut] with leopard patterns on the sides . . .

About three in the morning I got a call his voice like out of *The Shining* going, 'Nicky, is that you/ I thought your hair was brown not blue.' And he went off on this tangent. He's a good lyricist.

Dave Stewart (on co-writing with Jack Nicholson)

this is a spiritual marriage between the punk rock movement and the New Age movement, which I belong to. See—I'm wearing crystals and I believe in God and flying saucers.

Alison Moyet had this to say about women and body image.

ALISON MOYET I think a lot of women can relate to me because I'm not something they can't be. A lot of women open magazines and see real goddess-y women spread across the pages and they think, "Damn. I'm not a real woman because I don't look like this and I feel like a lesser being." So, of course, when they see some great lump trundling around the stage they think, "Well, this is all right, isn't it? I can make something with my own talents. I don't have to be this archetypal woman to achieve something."

Nina Hagen

A freedom that I cherished was the opportunity to step outside the usual run of interview subjects. If someone interesting was in town to promote a film, a book, or making any kind of public appearance and we caught wind of it, we set our sights on getting them into the studio. Hence, we had encounters with André the Giant (which took place in a pseudo–wrestling ring with a PA in a referee sweater introducing us with a description of our relative weight, height, etc.),

Christopher Ward with a hamadryas baboon

Phyllis Diller, who was hilarious and charming, and this distant relative (see left).

One of the most entertaining interviews I ever did during my time at Much was with film director John Waters (*Pink Flamingos*, *Polyester*, *Hairspray*).

JOHN WATERS The nuns in Catholic school used to read us the list of movies we'd go to hell if we saw and I ran out and saw every one of them. It was really divine intervention. I feel like God told me to make these movies.

Waters weighed in on the shortage of good publicity gimmicks.

JOHN WATERS With *Gandhi*, you could close the concession stand and let the audience starve to death to get into the spirit of the whole thing.

And regarding Graceland, "It's a hymn to necrophilism. You go there and you wish you were dead yourself."

While he was on the Amnesty International Human Rights Now tour, I interviewed Peter Gabriel. He spoke with quiet intensity about philanthropy in the artistic community.

Christopher Ward and John Waters

PETER GABRIEL In the sixties it was great for image, style and rebellion, but actually achieved very little, and if the eighties has done one thing, it has shown that real, direct and practical action makes direct differences to people's lives and maybe that's a more adult and boring and realistic viewpoint or world view but I'd rather live in a society where people are making some attempts to improve the world.

My favourite moment at MuchMusic was getting to dance with the Temptations. David Ruffin and Eddie Kendrick, the two lead singers from the original band, had been experiencing a bit of a revival courtesy of Hall & Oates and a live video from the Apollo Theater of the four of them performing together. The Temptations' promo rep took me aside when they arrived. "Don't expect much," he said, "they're in a really bad mood; the interviews have not gone well; people have mixed them up with the Four Tops and don't know their music." So for the first half of the interview, I let them know how respected they were and made sure they knew that I was very aware of their music. When we went to video, I told them that my lifetime dream had been to dance with the Temptations and they seemed amused. I asked if they would indulge me and they said "sure." The crew was ready and out came the microphones and a space was cleared in the studio. We sang "The Way You Do the Things You Do" and I was as ready as a Canadian Motown nerd could ever be. I danced with the Temptations . . . and sang with them, too . . . and they complimented my singing. As of that moment I could die a happy man.

(Top) Peter Gabriel and Christopher Ward
(Bottom) Christopher Ward with Eddie Kendrick and David Ruffin of the Temptations

Much Toronto staff in 1985

This is the most excitement I've seen in twenty-five years. To see this many young guys and young girls who have work.

Phyllis Diller

Door at Much studio autographed by Phyllis Diller, the Supremes, Iggy Pop, Tony Bennett and Phil Collins, among others

Conclusion

Unruly and whimsical as it was, MuchMusic was a part of the lives of millions of Canadians in the '80s and '90s. They came home from work or school, turned Much on and ate dinner, did homework, and stayed up late watching, as they hung out with television's new kid in town. Because the shows were live and improvised, the viewers and VJs shared the experience as it happened; we and our viewers grew up together, excited by the new music and the parade of images that came with it.

In the absence of an internet to shrink the great distances between Canadian communities, Much truly engaged and connected music fans in every corner of the country, in an unprecedented way. The big, shiny era of the music video unfolded at a breakneck pace. Viewers saw into the world of the artists they loved as never before, and artists quickly adapted to the newfound visibility, presaging the full-exposure era of YouTube, Facebook and 24/7 paparazzi.

After launching in 1984 Much rolled along, winning viewers, gaining confidence and getting recognition as a player in the Canadian music world. The summer of 1985 brought events that signalled Much had arrived as a major influence. Duran Duran landed at Much, creating mayhem in the street; we covered Live Aid in London and the legendary Robert Plant showed up to be interviewed on the rooftop at 299 Queen Street West. The same roof that we threw a Christmas tree from! We went big but stayed humble.

When I returned to the archives at 299 Queen Street, I found that there was no shortage of memories from this brilliant time in music and television. Many of them found their way into these pages. I'm so grateful I was a witness to this time, and I'm happy you were watching.

There are some guys whose achievements and inventions and innovations are so simple and brilliant that they pass right into the culture and lose the name of the inventor, like Kleenex, like Aspirin. What Moses has done is something so simple and brilliant that it's caught on all over the world and it doesn't even have his name attached to it. But wherever you find people with their noses against the glass like you find over there, wherever you find that certain ambience and tone in a television studio, that's this guy's invention and a lot of people don't know that. This didn't just happen. This was not inherited. This was dreamed up.

Leonard Cohen

Acknowledgements

Power chords of gratitude to my agent, Sam Hiyate, who made my idea for this book into a reality through his belief, wisdom and tireless hard work.

Marshall stacks of appreciation for my brilliant editor Deirdre Molina for her insight, patience and faith in the book.

Thank-you to Moses Znaimer—for a brilliant opportunity and a high rotation of freedom.

Much thanks to all my former colleagues—VJs, producers, audio and camera people, VTR operators, directors et al—many of whom chased down memories to help me.

In particular, I want to thank my friend and fellow Limitoid, Simon Evans, who went the distance on this project from "Hey, what do you think of this idea?" to this acknowledgment and beyond, and who helped me immeasurably every step of the way. Next time I call, Simon, just say "I'm in the library."

Big thanks to David Kines, whose Rolodex has another 100,000 miles on it thanks to this book. You're the "King of Connection," sir. And really, really boss!

Sarah Crawford—for your kindness and prodigious memory!

Thanks to Doug McClement, Dana Lee, Bill Bobeck, Steve Kerzner, Rick Alexander, Corey Hart, Peter Diemer, and Kristine Lukanchoff for treasures from their personal archives.

Thanks to Bell Media for their enthusiasm for this project, welcoming me back into 299 and opening the archives. In particular Justin Stockman, Erin Eizenman, Nicola Krishna, Amanda Rinaldo, Amy Doary, Adam Slinn, Brendan Frasier, and Christian Llano.

And serious gratitude to the angels of the archives for their resourcefulness, camaraderie and kindness during my days down below.

Christopher Ward with the Much librarians Liz Houlihan, Ashley Hatton, Heather Middleton and Jodie Epstein

Thanks to all at Penguin Random House Canada, including Anne Collins. Scott Richardson, Colin Jaworski, Erin Cooper, Matthew Sibiga, Marion Garner, Lindsey Reeder, Erin Kelly, Randy Chan, Carla Kean, Angelika Glover, Michelle MacAleese and Amanda Betts.

Thanks to Mike Myers for the kindest of forewords.

As always, thanks to Stephen Stohn for friendship and wisdom and to Stephen and Linda Schuyler for letting me play in "The Birdhouse."

To the artists and all who I interviewed, boomboxes of gratitude for sharing your MuchMemories.

And for a playlist of reasons, thanks to Alannah Myles, Erica Ehm, Morgen Flury, James Woods, Sherry Greengrass, Terri Walsh, Dana Lee, Mike Campbell, Dennis Saunders, Jim Shutsa, Joel Goldberg, Kim Clarke Champniss, Gord McWatters, David Kirkwood, John Roberts, Steve Anthony, Anne Howard, Paul Muntz, Connie Meyer, Dave Russell, Dave Hurlbut, Scott Burgess, Richard Oulton, Basil Young, Malcolm Brown, Terry David and Meg Mulligan (see you Friday), Rob Bowman, Devi Ekanand and all at Coalition Entertainment, Sean Kelly, Deborah Samuel, Eddie Schwartz, Sara Ramsay, Saffron Henderson, Jaymes Foster, Kathy Tempesta, Susan de Cartier, Shari Ulrich, Jo Faloona, Michelle Findlay, Victoria Levy, Mia Rankin, Dara Conrod, Marlene Palmer, Bernie Breen, Jenn Pressey, Mike Nelson, Catherine Kurtz, Deborah Theaker, Bruce Pirrie, Klaus Schuller, Karen Gordon, Jim Campbell, Gerry Young, Kevin Shea, Graham Henderson, Jennifer Hardy, Marc Aflalo, Gail Goldman, Colin James, Marc Jordan, Michael Perlmutter, Liz Baird, Nuala Byles, Jessica Pangallozzi, Tim Tickner, Rob Wells, Jeff Rogers, Lorraine Samuel, Karen Hendrick, Lesley Livingston, Jonathan Llyr, Rick Brace, Phil King, Cat Pottage who ran from the Black Frog in Gastown to return my iPad, Sarah Ward, Jeff Macks, Robin Ward, and Mister Leo for riding shotgun from T.O. to L.A. to Van.

Credits and Sources

Thanks to MUCH, a division of Bell Media Inc., for their support in the creation of this book.

The following images are courtesy of:

p. i: Laminate collage (Doug McClement)

p. 9: CW and Alannah Myles (CW personal)

p. 23: 1985 studio set (courtesy Dana M. Lee)

p. 29: John Martin (Kristine Lukanchoff)

p. 33: John and Moses Znaimer (Kristine Lukanchoff)

p. 68: Corey Hart photos (Corey Hart)

p. 169: CW and Bill Wyman (CW)

p. 170: Live Aid crowd, U2 (CW)

p. 178: Mike Myers (Rick Alexander)

p. 179: Bee suit (Peter Diemer)

p. 233: Ed the Sock (Steve Kerzner)

p. 249: Hotel room/studio (Doug McClement)

p. 280: "Elvis" Ward (unknown viewer)

p. 284: "Black Velvet" video shoot (CW)

p. 321: Autographed door (CW)

p. 323: CW and Much archive librarians (CW)

Index